National Resource Center for The First-Year Experience™ & Students in Transition

Monograph Series
Number 29
1999

Solid Foundations

Building Success for First-Year Seminars through Instructor Training and Development

Editors
Mary Stuart Hunter, Editor-in-Chief
Tracy L. Skipper

With major contributions from
Joseph B. Cuseo

Cite as:

Hunter, M. S., & Skipper, T. L. (Eds.). (1999). *Solid foundations: Building success for first-year seminars through instructor training and development* (Monograph No. 29). Columbia, SC: University of South Carolina, National Resource Center for The First-Year Experience and Students in Transition.

Sample chapter citation:

Upcraft, M. L., & Stephens, P. S. (1999). Teaching and today's changing first-year students. In M. S. Hunter & T. L. Skipper (Eds.), *Solid foundations: Building success for first-year seminars through instructor training and development* (Monograph No. 29) (pp. 13-23). Columbia, SC: University of South Carolina, National Resource Center for The First-Year Experience and Students in Transition.

Additional copies of this monograph may be ordered at $30 each from the National Resource Center for The First-Year Experience and Students in Transition, University of South Carolina, 1629 Pendleton Street, Columbia, SC 29208. Telephone (803) 777-6029. Telefax (803) 777-4699.

Special gratitude is expressed to Blair Symes, Assistant Editor; to Dr. Betsy O. Barefoot, Co-Director for Publications and Research; and to Dr. Jean Henscheid, Associate Director for their editorial assistance in the production of this book.

ISBN Number: 1-889271-30-6

Table of Contents

FOREWORD

John N. Gardner

I have looked forward to the publication of this monograph, *Solid Foundations: Building Success for First-Year Seminars through Instructor Training and Development*, for many reasons. First, I am very excited each time we add a new title to our monograph series; each is designed to address some unique facet of the student transition experience. Our overall objective in producing this series is to put one more good informational and/or pedagogical tool in the hands of higher educators who wish to enhance teaching and learning inside and outside the classroom so as to increase student learning, satisfaction, and retention. Second, I can remember back 20 years ago when there was virtually no literature base available at all in this field for educators such as myself who were attempting to refine programs to enhance the first-year experience. It is extremely exciting to know that the National Resource Center for The First-Year Experience and Students in Transition is helping to fill that void. Third, the pleasure in introducing this monograph is also personal; the editor-in-chief, Mary Stuart Hunter, is a long time colleague and friend whom I have known since 1978.

Stuart and I have been partners in hosting and organizing The First-Year Experience Conference series since she joined the Center staff in 1983. Before that she had worked in the Admissions Office at the University of South Carolina and as an academic advisor for undecided students. In that latter role, she had her first experience of developing and implementing an instructor training model for a special version of a first-year seminar section for undecided students. Stuart joined the staff of the Center and assumed primary leadership for The First-Year Experience Conferences. She also worked with a team of faculty and professional staff here at USC responsible for the facilitation of University 101's semiannual "Teaching Experience Workshop." The editorial leadership for this monograph is based on her approximately 20-year experience designing and implementing first-year seminar workshops. I could think of no more appropriate professional to guide this much needed and potentially useful monograph than Stuart Hunter.

As you may or may not be aware, the first-year seminar in American higher education dates back to the 1880s. The University of South Carolina has had its current first-year seminar, University 101, since 1972, and we were the first institution to mandate an extensive instructor training program as a prerequisite for any University employee who wanted to teach this course. Our first training workshop was three weeks long, five afternoons a week. It was designed on a classic T-group model first developed by the National Training Laboratory for Applied Behavioral Sciences in Bethel, Maine. We felt that this kind of encounter/sensitivity training was appropriate in 1972 in order to help University employees create a more humane environment for entering first-year students. Our approach to this initial training was in the aftermath of a tumultuous student riot that had shaken the campus of the University of South Carolina in May of 1970. That initial model, while having some long-term influence on what we do in the present, is not the foundation for the training scheme set forth in this monograph.

It has been apparent to me for some time that the Center's monograph series needed a publication on the concept of faculty training. Since 1972, we have received thousands of requests for information about our faculty training program, and many guests from other institutions have attended this training. They then returned to their own institutions and adapted what worked to faculty training for their own first-year seminar courses. We have offered our University 101 instructor training workshops in an abbreviated, one-day format in association with The First-Year Experience Conference series since 1982, and since the 1991-92 year, we have offered condensed training workshops in 59 cities in the United States, Canada, and Puerto Rico. All this has been in response to a demand for more information on how to do more effective teaching of the first-year seminar.

We are not trying to suggest in this monograph that you should adopt the "University of South Carolina way" for instructor training. There is no one *right* way. Instead, I think each institution has to find its *own* way, and we hope this monograph will be a catalyst for that effort.

Thus, it is with great optimism that I introduce this monograph. I trust that this publication will be put to good use to prepare effective teachers of the first-year seminar course. The ultimate beneficiaries, of course, will be instructors, their institutions, and especially their first-year students. Please do not hesitate to offer suggestions to our editor-in-chief, Mary Stuart Hunter, for subsequent revisions of this monograph based on your use of it; we look forward to using your ideas in order to be even more helpful to our colleagues in the future.

As always, let me take this opportunity to thank you for your support of our publication series and of our efforts to enhance the first-year experience in American higher education.

John N. Gardner
Senior Fellow and Distinguished Professor Emeritus

Notes from the Editor-in-Chief

INTRODUCTION

Mary Stuart Hunter

In 1982, three colleagues and I developed the curriculum for a special section of the first-year seminar at the University of South Carolina for students undecided about their academic major. The success of those special sections led the program director, John Gardner, to ask us to develop a special, "advanced" University 101 training to further sensitize instructors to issues of academic advising and career development. This workshop had a dual purpose in providing an additional training opportunity for interested instructors and in generating additional instructors for special sections of University 101 for undeclared first-year students, who at the time made up more than 50% of the first-year class. The process of developing this "advanced" training was a labor of love. Four individuals with distinctly different skills, abilities, and personalities worked together over a hot South Carolina summer to develop a week-long training program with the central goal of better serving a distinct subpopulation of first-year students.

Although at the time, I had already been teaching University 101 for several years, this undertaking challenged and inspired me to consider even more seriously the importance of comprehensive instructor preparation. It also initiated my many years of involvement with faculty development. I quickly came to believe that effective instructor training is the fundamental foundation for a successful seminar program. Well-prepared instructors are much more likely to be effective teachers in the classroom than are those who are thrown into teaching a new and different course without adequate preparation and training.

We at the National Resource Center for The First-Year Experience and Students in Transition have long known that there is a desperate need for support and information on effective instructor training. This monograph is, therefore, an attempt to provide a degree of support and, at the very least, a document that will lead educators involved with new-student seminars to focus on the critical importance of effective instructor training.

The monograph opens with a chapter by Joseph B. Cuseo that provides a research-based rationale for including a substantial faculty development component to new student seminars. He contends that a well-designed and developed instructor training program may indeed not only support the success of a new student seminar, but that it may also create a ripple effect with the potential to generate a dialogue on teaching excellence across an institution. His chapter offers compelling arguments supporting the attention paid to improving undergraduate instruction and outlines four major topics recommended for inclusion in a comprehensive instructor training program.

Clearly, any attempt to prepare instructors to teach new-student seminars must include a realistic consideration of the target audience—the first-year students enrolled in the seminar. In the second chapter, M. Lee Upcraft and Pamela S. Stephens review the significant changes in student characteristics and demographics over recent decades that make the students of today in many ways quite different from their predecessors. As we recall our own time as students, we quickly realize that these students are also quite different from ourselves. Upcraft and Stephens make a strong case for our acknowledgment and sincere acceptance of these changes as a catalyst for the shift to a more diverse and varied style of instruction. For many, this will herald a new role and perspective for us as teachers, one which will enable us to empower students to become engaged and enthusiastic learners.

In Chapter 3, Jennifer L. Crissman joins Upcraft to provide a view into the hearts and minds of first-year students through an examination of a substantial body of literature and the work of numerous theorists. They suggest that understanding how students learn inside the classroom alone is not enough for understanding them comprehensively. An examination of students' environments and individual development through attention to both their cognitive and psychosocial development will help us as we attempt to maximize their learning.

Diane W. Strommer reminds us in Chapter 4 that effective efforts to prepare instructors for teaching new student seminars must include attention to the anxiety that all instructors, even the most seasoned faculty, bring with them as they prepare to teach "something new" outside their discipline. She shares a wealth of specific and concrete ideas illustrating 10 important principles of teaching that will enhance learning in the new-student seminar and that can be easily transported to other classroom settings. A broad consideration of her 10 tips for success will also be helpful in planning and implementing an effective agenda for instructor training programs.

In Chapter 5, Cuseo provides an argument for the use of group learning strategies by reviewing the research that supports these methodologies. Additionally, he shares specific strategies for implementing these methods in first-year seminar classes. Such methods, he argues, can provide instructors with a strategy for helping first-year students learn higher order cognitive skills. The increased communication in classes incorporating collaborative and cooperative learning methods contributes to general goals and objectives of many first-year seminars. He provides a detailed description of the characteristics of cooperative learning and specific tips to enhance group communication.

The success of training experiences depends, to a large extent, on the well thought-out design and implementation of the events. In Chapter 6, Constance Staley provides a succinct and useful description of the many characteristics of effective facilitators. She assists us by outlining the qualifications and characteristics that we should seek in facilitators, as well as providing a suggested checklist of effective communication skills that can be cultivated in workshop designers and facilitators.

In Chapter 7, Cuseo and I provide the reader with concrete suggestions for recruiting instructors and developing campus-wide partnerships through the new-student seminar instructor training. We share many specific suggestions for the planning and logistics of initial training and development as well as suggestions for long-term, continuous training efforts.

Dan Berman and I follow with a chapter that describes in detail the campus-based training program we know best—the one at the University of South Carolina. We outline the four-phase training model that has been used throughout the life of our 27 year-old first-year seminar program, a model that is adaptable to the needs of unique and evolving campus cultures.

A very well-constructed and useful primer on assessment methodology related to instructor training programs is found in Chapter 9. Cuseo's chapter outlines intended outcomes common to many instructor training efforts and potential measures for these outcomes. He discusses both qualitative and quantitative methods, describing a variety of specific techniques for both. The template provides even the most novice assessment practitioner with an easily understood rationale for the importance of quality assessment and its uses.

John Gardner and I close the monograph with a set of suggestions and recommendations to guide educators in their instructor development work.

Finally, on a personal note, since taking on the challenge of editing this monograph many months ago, I have learned once again a very valuable lesson—choose your team wisely, and success is inevitable. I have come to think of myself as a coach in this project, and I have been blessed with an incredibly able group of athletes. The team, far more talented than its coach, has been much more patient with me than I deserve. The project spanned more seasons than I originally planned, frequently placed on the sidelines while more immediate and pressing demands occupied my attention. Yet, because I drafted many good friends and colleagues for this team project, I am convinced that the final product was worth the time-outs and rain delays. My sincere thanks to each of the chapter authors for their good work and contributions. Special thanks to John Gardner for giving me the opportunity to undertake this project, to Betsy Barefoot for her editorial oversight, patience, and gentle prodding to remind me that this really is needed by so many people. And finally, special thanks and kudos to Tracy Skipper for her outstanding editorial skills, her creative layout and design talents, and her tact, kindness, and gentle nature in the final stages of this project. As you read this monograph, I hope that you will find, as I have, that it provides a wonderful opportunity to gain new insights while refining your existing knowledge.

Instructor Training: Rationale, Results, and Content Basics

Joseph B. Cuseo

CHAPTER 1

A major goal of institutions that adopt the new-student seminar is to promote student retention (Barefoot & Fidler, 1992). The important role that a well-conducted instructor training program plays in achieving this institutional objective is articulated by John Gardner (1980) in one of his first arguments for an instructor training program: "Student retention cannot be improved until faculty change their attitudes, values, and particularly their behaviors in the classroom" (p. 10). Similarly, Alexander Astin (1982) argued early in the 1980s for the retention-promoting value of instructional development for college faculty:

> The pedagogical skills of college faculty members may be one of the most underdeveloped resources in the country's institutions of higher learning. Concentrating more energy on developing teaching skills could prove to be the most productive and self-protective activity that institutions can engage in during the next 10 years. (p. 15)

Thus, adoption of an instructional development program in conjunction with the new-student seminar may not only function as a preparatory experience for seminar instructors, but also as a "lightning rod" for drawing college-wide energy toward teaching excellence. The pressing need for such an institutional stimulus is strongly supported by the following two research-based arguments.

1. *Improvements must be made in the quality of undergraduate instruction.*

During the 1980s, several national reports on the condition of American higher education sharply criticized the quality of undergraduate instruction (e.g., Association of American Colleges and Universities, 1985; Boyer, 1987; National Endowment for the Humanities, 1984). A common theme in all these blue-ribbon reports is that the quality of undergraduate education has suffered for the following reasons:

- Graduate education fails to provide adequate instructional preparation of faculty prior to their entering the professoriate. As stated in a report issued by the Association of American Colleges and Universities (1985):

  > The tradition in higher education is to award the [Ph.D.] degree and then turn the students loose to become teachers without training in teaching or, equally as ridiculous, to send the students off without degrees, with unfinished research and incomplete dissertations hanging over their heads while they wrestle with the responsibilities of learning how to teach. . . . During the long years of work toward the doctoral degree, the candidate is rarely, if ever, introduced to any of the ingredients that make up the art, the science, and the special responsibilities of teaching. Yet the major career option for

> most holders of the Ph.D. degree is full-time teaching in a college or university. (p. 35)

This conclusion is strikingly reminiscent of one reached by a study group on higher education some ten years earlier: "... it is probably not an exaggeration to say that the present disjunction between the emphasis in graduate training and the work done by most college teachers is a formula for occupational schizophrenia" (Group for Human Development in Higher Education, 1974, p. 30).

- Overly narrow specialization in graduate school is perpetuated by sharp disciplinary divisions, disciplinary isolation, and lack of interdisciplinary dialogue among faculty after they enter the professoriate. As the late Ernest Boyer (1987) reported in *College: The Undergraduate Experience in America,* "The disciplines have fragmented themselves into smaller and smaller pieces, and undergraduates find it difficult to see patterns in their courses and to relate what they learn to life" (p. 3). A similar conclusion was reached in a major report issued by the National Endowment for the Humanities (1984):

  > Undergraduate teaching has been damaged by too little attention to introductory and lower division courses and narrow specialization in the graduate schools. Unless graduate schools re-examine their priorities, much of our teaching will remain mediocre and our students indifferent. (p. 16)

- A lack of open discussion exists among faculty about the teaching process and how to improve its effectiveness. This criticism reinforces the findings of an extensive survey of 1,680 faculty at 14 institutions conducted by Gaff (1978) in which he found that 42% of those surveyed said that never during their entire teaching career had anyone talked with them in detail about their teaching. Only 25% said that such discussions took place more than once. One faculty respondent stated wryly that, on his campus, "teaching had replaced sex as a taboo topic" (p. 45). Derek Bok (1986), former president of Harvard, argues that,

  > Professors are among the most independent of all professionals and guard their autonomy closely. Such attitudes help us to understand why it would not be feasible to *prescribe* collective goals or teaching methods... [however] they do not explain why there is so little *discussion* of ways to improve the educational process. (p. 64)

- There is a lack of institutional attention to and support for faculty development. Drawing from data gathered in national surveys and on-site visits, Ernest Boyer (1987) reports,

  > We found that such an obvious and important practice as setting aside a portion of the budget for faculty development is rare. We strongly recommend that every college commit itself to the professional growth of all faculty and provide them with opportunities to stay intellectually alive. (p. 134)

  Faculty development efforts that are linked structurally with teaching the new-student seminar can become "institutionalized," acquiring the potential for redressing these recurrent criticisms of the American professoriate and enhancing the overall quality of college teaching.

2. *Empirical evidence strongly suggests that instructional development programs produce positive results.*

Qualitative research findings indicate that faculty who participate in instructional development programs report that they are effective (e.g., Hoyt & Howard, 1978). Additionally, there is a substantive body of quantitative research providing empirical documentation that supports the value of faculty development programs for promoting positive change in teaching behavior. For example, consider the following findings:

- Cohen (1981) and Menges and Brinko (1986) conducted meta-analyses of large numbers of instructional improvement efforts and found that individual faculty members who received assistance from an instructional development consultant were rated significantly higher in teaching effectiveness by students than were faculty who did not receive any consultation.

- Stevens and Aleamoni (1985) performed a longitudinal study, following up on faculty who received assistance from an instructional improvement professional, and found that the positive results of such assistance persisted up to 10 years.

- Levinson-Rose and Menges (1981) reviewed a large number of studies on the effectiveness of instructional improvement workshops and found that over 80% were effective, as evidenced by improved student ratings of instruction, improved ratings of trained in-class observers, and greater student learning—i.e., improved student performance on course examinations.

- Eble and McKeachie (1985) conducted a comprehensive review of faculty development programs and concluded,

  > When effectiveness of faculty development programs is measured by participation, instructional development activities (e.g., workshops, seminars) were most effective. Our analysis suggests that even though grants for individual scholarly programs are valued, faculty members working together to achieve common objectives may be more cost effective for the institution in terms of their impact on student learning. (p. 205)

- Lacey (1988) reviewed faculty development programs and concluded that seminars or workshops that are both popular and effective are those which,

  > Address practical needs and can result in tangible changes in the way faculty teach. . . . Some of the most valuable reported outcomes of successful workshops or seminars have to do with increased collegiality and better communication among faculty . . . and better communication comes as a by-product of working on matters of importance to us as teachers. (pp. 64-65)

When all the research findings pointing to the effectiveness of both consultation and workshops for improving teaching effectiveness are viewed in conjunction with all the national reports suggesting that the quality of undergraduate teaching is in dire need of improvement, a strong case can be made for the value of instructional development programs for college faculty. Offering such programs under the aegis of instructor training for the new-student seminar and offering it not only for seminar instructors, but for faculty in general, may serve as an effective vehicle for stimulating campus-wide improvement in college teaching.

A substantive training program that provides a highly visible teaching enhancement experience may serve to stimulate campus-wide attention to and interest in effective undergraduate instruction. Linking the training program to the new-student seminar not only serves the purpose of preparing instructors to teach the first-year seminar, but it also may have the potential for filling a void in the preparation and development of college faculty at large. Empirical support for this contention is provided by Barefoot and Fidler (1992) who report,

> Both on survey instruments and in follow-up personal communications, freshman seminar administrators reported that instructor training workshops offered for freshman seminar instructors often become an institution's first, and perhaps only, systematic focus on freshman and undergraduate instruction. Such workshops often provide a forum for a campus-wide dialogue on teaching and frequently raise faculty consciousness about the unique needs and characteristics of their first-year students. (p. 62)

At the University of South Carolina, the instructor training experience for the new-student seminar (University 101) is an intensive, four-day program (Berman, 1997). In one of his early reports on the University 101 program, John Gardner (1980) noted that the course's instructor training program enabled "faculty to generalize and expand their University 101 teaching innovations beyond the confines of the course and into their regular teaching and work at the university" (p. 7). Gardner's original observation has been corroborated by more recent institutional research studies which indicate that new-student seminar instructors (a) become more "student-centered" in teaching their regular content courses after teaching the new-student seminar (University of Wyoming, cited in Barefoot, 1993), and (b) are more likely to use new or different instructional strategies in their discipline-based courses that were initially developed for use in the new-student seminar (Central Missouri State University, cited in Barefoot, 1993; Montana State University-Bozeman, cited in Barefoot, Warnock, Dickinson, Richardson, & Roberts, 1998).

Such institution-specific research evidence suggests that instructor training for teaching the new-student seminar may not only affect how the seminar itself is taught, it may also produce a positive "ripple effect" in how faculty teach in general. Given this potential for pervasive and systemic improvement in the quality of college teaching, it is recommended that the instructor training program for the new-student seminar be extensive, both in terms of its *duration* (e.g., at least three days in length) and its *inclusiveness* (e.g., all college faculty should be invited and encouraged to participate in the program as a faculty development opportunity). Relevant to the latter point is John Gardner's (1980) early observation that many faculty at the University of South Carolina had begun participating in its University 101 training program "exclusively for the faculty training experience" (p. 6). Today, faculty across the country participate in faculty training programs, not only to prepare themselves specifically for teaching the new-student seminar, but also to enhance their general effectiveness as college instructors (Gardner & Hunter, 1994).

A substantive training program that provides a highly visible teaching enhancement experience may serve to stimulate campus-wide attention to and interest in effective undergraduate instruction.

Content of the Instructor Training Program

Four topics are recommended as major components of a comprehensive instructor training program in order to make the experience relevant for new-student seminar instructors, in particular, and for college faculty, in general: (1) understanding first-year students, (2) understanding the institution, (3) selecting and sequencing course content, and (4) teaching and learning strategies. The first of these topics will be discussed in this chapter and in Chapter 2. The second and third topics will be addressed in the remaining sections of this chapter. The fourth topic, teaching and learning strategies, will be covered in Chapters 4 and 5 of this monograph.

Understanding First-Year Students

This component of the instructor training program focuses on promoting instructors' knowledge of contemporary first-year students, both as learners and as individuals. The importance of this topic for effective teaching is underscored by William Perry (1980), pathfinding researcher on college students' stages of cognitive development, who argues that, "Faculty development begins with an understanding of student development; students are our common purpose" (quoted in Knefelkamp, p. 24). At the University of South Carolina, where its 27-year old instructor training program serves as a national model, the first step is to "start with the learner" (Gardner & Hunter, 1994). Initially focusing the program on the learner also carries the additional advantage of reducing faculty defensiveness about being "trained" to be effective teachers. Beginning the program with a focus on the learner takes the emphasis (and the onus) off the teacher and puts it on the *learner* and the *learning process*, serving to reduce the likelihood that participants will view the program as "teacher training" or "faculty development." As one veteran faculty-development specialist warns,

> At times the phrase "faculty development" has a scary ring. Too often "develop" is used in the active sense: faculty are wanting, and something will be done to perfect them, evolve them, or promote their growth. The spirit resembles that of Western colonialism. Let us Christianize the heathen or civilize the benighted. Faculty members with a modicum of self-respect and dignity resent being treated this way. (Freedman & Associates, 1979, p. x)

Angelo (1993) has also argued that focusing instructional development on the learner will serve to increase the quantity and quality of faculty participation, as well as build a sense of campus community:

> Shift the focus from improving teaching to improving learning. Making improved learning the goal of instructional development focuses everyone's attention on the desired outcome and encourages a wider range of approaches to achieve that goal. A focus on learning can bring together administrators, student affairs personnel, faculty, and students in a common enterprise—rather than singling out faculty for "development." (p. 6)

Under the rubric of "understanding the learner," the following topics and issues are recommended for discussion in the new-student seminar instructor training program.

- *The importance of the first year as a critical period of development in the college experience.* This topic could include discussion of (a) personal adjustments common to first-year students, (b) the "seven vectors" of student development (Chickering, 1969), (c) common first-year student fears, and (d) incidence, causes, and "cures" of first-year attrition.
- *Characteristics of today's first-year students.* This topic could include coverage of (a) entering students' level of academic skill development, (b) Perry's (1970) model of college students' cognitive development, (c) historical factors that have shaped the lives of today's first-year students' attitudes and values, (e) student motives for attending college, (f) needs of today's first-year students, and (g) reading habits and preferences of contemporary first-year students. Chapter 2 of this monograph provides a profile of today's changing college student.
- *Institution-specific student characteristics.* A "student profile" of the institution's first-year class should be presented, containing such information as (a) age, (b) gender, (c) race or ethnicity, and (d) socioeconomic background. Learning styles associated with different student subpopulations could be presented along with this demographic information. The importance of such a student profile is underscored by the increasing generational and demographic differences between traditionally educated college faculty—who tend to be homogeneous with respect to race, gender, and age (i.e., the majority of whom are middle-aged white males) and today's students—who tend to be heterogeneous or diverse with respect to age, gender, and race.

For instance, re-entry (returning adult) students now represent the fastest growing segment of American higher education (The College Board, 1996); by the year 2000, the traditional 18 to 22 year-old student will comprise only 16% of the American college-student population (Levitz, 1989). Adult learners may require different instructional approaches than those historically employed with traditional-age students (Knowles, 1984; Wlodkowski, 1985). For example, relative to traditional-age students, adult learners are more likely to display the following characteristics: (a) lower levels of competitiveness toward other students; (b) more interest in participating with others; (c) more inclination to assume personal responsibility for their learning; and (d) more willingness to work independently of instructor supervision (Eison & Moore, 1980; Fuhrmann & Jacobs, 1980; Kraft, 1976). Faculty development offered via the new-student seminar's instructor training program may be one viable method for preparing college instructors to meet effectively the unique needs of these nontraditional learners.

Other demographic shifts in the college student population discussed in Chapters 2 and 3 are the increases in enrollments of racial and ethnic minorities and international students. A decline in the level of academic preparedness also characterizes the current generation of college students (Astin, 1966-1984). The research on the changing college student points strongly to the conclusion that college instructors might be well served by faculty development efforts designed (a) to help them work with the "new breed" of college students, and (b) to encourage them to perceive and respond to the academically underprepared student as an instructionally stimulating challenge rather than as a morale-sapping liability.

Understanding the Institution

This component of the instructor training program has two related objectives: (a) to increase faculty awareness of institutional resources and support services that are available to promote student development, and (b) to increase student utilization of these support services (e.g., via more frequent and effective faculty referrals of students to appropriate support services).

To most effectively realize these objectives, it is strongly recommended that an orientation to student support services be included as a major component of the instructor training program. This would include orientation to such key student support services as (a) the learning center, (b) the library, (c) student health services and counseling center, (d) career services, (e) student activities, (f) residence life, and (g) service learning (volunteer) programs. Representatives of these services should be present so that seminar instructors can associate a live person or face with each service. Also, phone numbers and exact campus locations of all these services should be presented to instructors in a well organized and easily accessible fashion (perhaps in the form of a flat sheet or brochure) in order to facilitate student referrals.

Ideally, some discussion of the art and science of making student referrals should also be incorporated into this segment of the instructor training program. Practical tips on how instructors might encourage or ensure that first-year students will utilize these services could be offered by campus-service representatives—for example: (a) referring students to a person rather than an office, (b) providing students with the phone number of a person to contact, (c) walking with students to the support service, or (d) developing class assignments or extra-credit options that would stimulate student involvement with key support services.

Research strongly suggests that colleges and universities should not offer support services passively (i.e., waiting for students to come and take advantage of them); instead, institutions should reach out to students and deliver support programs intrusively (Beal & Noel, 1980). If left to their own devices, those students who need programmatic support are less likely to seek it out on their own (Friedlander, 1980). For example, among students who withdraw from college due to academic difficulties, approximately two out of every three never used the institution's academic support services (Williams, Gcrononger, & Johnson, in Daubman et al., 1985).

The importance of student involvement with out-of-class support services and activities for student retention and academic achievement is highlighted by research reviewed by Pascarella and Terenzini (1991):

> The environmental factors that maximize persistence and educational attainment include a peer culture in which students develop close on-campus friendships, participate frequently in college-sponsored activities, and perceive their college to be highly concerned about the individual student, as well as a college emphasis on supportive services. It is worth noting that some of these environmental influences on educational attainment persist even after college size and student body selectivity are taken into account. (p. 604)

It is noteworthy that national survey research indicates that one of the most frequently cited goals of new-student seminars is to increase student use of campus resources and facilities (Barefoot & Fidler, 1996). Thus, one essential element of a comprehensive instructor training program should be to orient new-student seminar instructors to (a) the full range of student-support resources on campus, (b) the professionals who deliver these resources, and (c) effective strategies for encouraging student use of support services.

Reporting on the University of South Carolina's instructor training program, Gardner (1980) notes that one beneficial by-product of the training experience is that faculty "learn much more about the institution. This is especially helpful for new faculty who join the university and have some orientation problems not at all dissimilar to those of students" (p. 7). Like Gardner, Turner and Boice (1987) discuss the transition issues of new faculty. They report that a substantial number of beginning college teachers are overwhelmed by their new professional responsibilities, spending excessive amounts of time preparing lecture material and attempting to "cover" course content, with relatively little time spent focusing on effective ways to involve students in the learning process. New faculty are also those who are most likely to express concern about their teaching effectiveness and ability to relate to students (Baldwin & Blackburn, 1981). These negative findings concerning the experiences of new faculty become especially significant when viewed in light of the anticipated rush of new-faculty hiring in the late 1990s to replace large numbers of retiring faculty (Bowen & Schuster, 1986; Schuster, Wheeler, & Associates, 1990); it is estimated that 75% of faculty members will be replaced between 1995 and 2010 (Kerr, 1994).

Thus, new-faculty orientation and development may represent an unprecedented opportunity not only to facilitate the adjustment of first-year faculty, but also to promote proactively the development of a new faculty "culture" on campus—one that is more student-centered and *initially* equipped to engage in effective teaching. One way to capitalize on this opportunity may be to offer an intensive and comprehensive new-faculty orientation and development experience—delivered as part of, or in conjunction with, the seminar's instructor training program.

Selection of Course Content

A third component of a comprehensive instructor training program is a discussion of potential course content for the new-student seminar and consensus-building with respect to decisions about topic selection and sequencing. When making decisions about content coverage in the new-student seminar, it is important to remain cognizant of the fact that one key potential advantage of the course is that it can provide first-year students with a focused, in-depth alternative to the heavy dose of survey-oriented introductory courses that are delivered during the first year (Gardner, 1993). The new-student seminar may be the single course during the first year in which the instructor lectures less and "covers" less factual material, but where students write more, interact more, do more, and perhaps *learn* more because covering everything is not as important as ensuring that students become actively engaged and deeply process the more limited content. Unlike many first-year introductory courses, the new-student seminar should not focus excessively on breadth of coverage at the expense of depth of coverage. As critical thinking pioneer Richard Paul (1994) argues,

> Let us explicitly recognize the misleading nature of expressions like "this is what we need to cover!" Let us recognize that the key question is "How can we design what we 'cover' so that students must thoughtfully and deeply master it?" The addicting delusion of coverage must end. (p. 10)

The relevance of Paul's argument for the teaching of first-year students is reinforced by Erickson and Strommer (1991) in *Teaching College Freshmen:*

> Compulsions to cover so much material in class are usually counterproductive, but they are especially destructive in freshman courses. They reinforce the passive listening, verbatim note-taking, and superficial information-processing strategies that many bring to college. Students need to learn course content, to be sure, but freshmen also need to be weaned away from their conviction that it cannot be important if it was not covered in class—and we need to give up our apparent belief that students cannot learn it unless we say it. (pp. 96-97)

Moreover, less compulsion to cover vast amounts of content via lecturing often allows instructors to focus more attention on the learning process and student development, as well as allowing them more opportunity to experiment with innovative teaching techniques. The small class size and less content-driven nature of the new-student seminar may make it the ideal place for faculty to begin to experiment with nontraditional, student-centered teaching techniques.

It is further recommended that final decisions concerning the nature and number of course topics covered in the new-student seminar—and their relative degree of emphasis—should be governed, in large part, by the demographic characteristics and special needs of the institution's first-year class. As Barefoot and Fidler (1992) conclude from their national research on the form and content of new-student seminars: "The freshman seminar will likely have multiple features depending on the specific characteristics and needs of institutions and their students" (p. 65).

Consistent with this argument is the recommendation offered by Terenzini and Associates (1993) on how to facilitate students' transition to college, based on research conducted under the aegis of the National Center for Teaching, Learning, and Assessment,

> Faculty members need to be aware of their students' characteristics—both of the student body in general and of the students who attend their classes. Institutional data centers should produce and disseminate this information as soon as students register. With these data in hand, instructors can better prepare courses to meet student needs. (p. 9)

This advice reinforces the importance of the aforementioned recommendation of including an institution-specific "student profile" as a core component of the instructor training program. "Who are our students?" and "What are their needs?" are questions that should precede discussion of course topics, and the answers to these two student-centered questions should serve to guide final decisions about course content. A good illustration of this recommendation is a practice employed at William Jewell College. At this institution, a "Freshman Preview" is provided to faculty and staff at the beginning of the academic year for the purpose of promoting insight into the needs and ability levels of their first-year students so that this information may be used to tailor specific components of the institution's first-year program to meet the specific needs of the institution's entering class (Terry, 1992).

> The new-student seminar may be the single course . . . in which the instructor . . . "covers" less factual material, but where students write more, interact more, do more, and perhaps *learn* more because . . . students become actively engaged and deeply process the more limited content.

Student needs do change with time so particular course topics and units may have to be added or deleted in response to emerging social issues. For instance, the rise of AIDS and related sexually-transmitted diseases among young adults may necessitate that this issue now be addressed in the new-student seminar. This has been done at the University of South Carolina, where a sexuality component was added to its new-student seminar, and course research indicates that it has had a positive impact on the use of condoms and abstinence among first-year students who take the course (Turner, Garrison, Korpita, Waller, Addy, Hill, & Mohn, 1994). If the content of the new-student seminar is viewed as fluid, flexible, and revisable in light of emerging student and institutional priorities, the course may then take on the capacity to be the one place in an otherwise ossified undergraduate curriculum that is most sensitive and immediately responsive to contemporary student adjustments.

Whatever particular content is chosen for the new-student seminar, research suggests that new-student seminars which cover content that either has an academic-skills emphasis or a personal development (social-emotional) emphasis are equally effective in terms of promoting positive effects on student retention and academic achievement—relative to control groups of students who do not take any type of new-student seminar (Cannici & Poulton, 1990). These results suggest that final decisions about whether the new-student seminar will focus primarily on one or the other of these forms of course content may not be of major consequence, since either focus should have a salutary effect on important student outcomes.

However, course content which reflects a healthy balance of both academic and personal development topics might have a multiplicative or synergistic effect on positive student outcomes. Drawing upon their national experience with new-student seminar courses, Upcraft and Gardner (1989) maintain that the most effective new-student seminars are those which are designed to facilitate first-year student success in both academic and non-academic facets of college life. National survey research also indicates that the majority of new-student seminars have "multiple goals and support a holistic definition of freshman success" (Barefoot & Fidler, 1992, p. 63).

At institutions with very diverse student bodies,

course content may need to be tailored specifically to meet the unique needs of student subgroups. One strategy for accomplishing this demanding task is to offer special sections of the course for different subgroups—in which course content is selected to meet the students' special needs—and for which course instructors have been specially trained. Survey research indicates that such special sections of the new-student seminar are being offered for such student subgroups as re-entry (adult) students, international students, racial/ethnic minority students, athletes, women, commuters, and students with disabilities (Barefoot & Fidler, 1992).

Lastly, whatever content is chosen for inclusion in the course, and whether or not it is uniform or different for special students in special sections, it is recommended that individual instructors (and perhaps even students) be provided with at least some degree of personal control or decision-making power with respect to what they cover in their particular course section. Research strongly suggests that when individuals have some degree of control or element of choice with respect to a task, they have a higher level of intrinsic motivation for engaging in that task (Zuckerman, Porac, Lathin, Smith, & Deci, 1978).

One strategy for allowing individual instructors and students some control of course content while still maintaining consistency in content coverage across course sections is for instructors to reach consensus on a set of course goals or objectives and, perhaps, a circumscribed number of target topics (core content). These key course objectives and core topics become the standardized "skeleton syllabus," and the remainder of the syllabus is then "fleshed out" or filled in with specific subtopics and issues that reflect the personal preferences or professional experiences of individual instructors (Hunter, 1996).

Sequencing of Course Content

One issue that has received little or no attention in the scholarly literature on the new-student seminar is the order or sequence in which course topics should be arranged. In the absence of any research literature to guide decisions about the timing of topic delivery, perhaps the best guideline to offer prospective seminar instructors is to introduce course topics at times when students are most likely to encounter them during their first semester in college. For instance, the "meaning and value of general education" might be a topic that would be most effectively positioned at the very beginning of the course because new students have recently registered for their first semester of college courses, most of which will be lower-level, introductory and/or skill-building courses that may be perceived as distressingly similar to their compulsory high school curriculum. Also, a topic such as "strategies for lecture comprehension and note-taking" might warrant early introduction because first-year students will be immediately immersed in these academic tasks during the first week of class. On the other hand, delivery of such topics such as "test-taking strategies" and "stress management" may be more timely if introduced prior to midterms or finals, when both tests and stress are likely to peak.

It might be a useful instructor-training exercise to engage participants in the process of identifying whether there is a natural rhythm of "critical periods" or "teachable moments" during the first semester of college life on which they can capitalize to guide their decisions about topic sequencing for the new-student seminar. If the rhythm of course topics in the syllabus can approximate the rhythm of first-year student experiences during their initial semester of college life, then it may be possible to maximize the probability that seminar topics will be introduced at times when students are most receptive or "ready" to learn them. If such synchrony can be achieved, or at least approximated, then the perceived relevance and educational impact of the new-student seminar might be enhanced.

Instructor training programs tied to the new-student seminar provide a valuable means for improving the quality of undergraduate education. While the focus of training may be geared toward effective delivery of the new-student seminar, the positive impact on instructional development is not limited to these courses. Faculty and staff gain an understanding of student needs and learning styles and a knowledge of institutional resources upon which they can draw in their other courses and in their encounters with students outside the classroom. The increased knowledge of student characteristics and the institution lays the groundwork for the content, sequencing, and instructional strategies instructors adopt in the new-student seminar. Learner-centered pedagogies taught in instructor training programs may also redefine the way faculty teach other courses, not just the new-student seminar. Finally, because the content of the new-student seminar tends to be dynamic, tailored to institutional concerns and the needs of a changing student population, the course can provide faculty with a model of how to relate more static curricular areas to local concerns and needs.

References

Angelo, T. A. (1993). A "teacher's dozen": Fourteen general, research-based principles for improving higher learning in our classrooms. *AAHE Bulletin, 45*(8), 3-17.

Association of American Colleges and Universities. (1985). *Integrity in the curriculum: A report to the academic community*. Project on redefining the meaning and purpose of baccalaureate degrees. Washington, DC: Author.

Astin, A. W. (1966-1984). *The American freshman: National norms.* Los Angeles: University of California-Los Angeles, Higher Education Research Institute.

Astin, A. W. (1982). *Minorities in American higher education: Recent trends, current prospects, and recommendations.* San Francisco: Jossey-Bass.

Baldwin, R. G., & Blackburn, R. T. (1981). The academic career as a developmental process: Implications for higher education. *Journal of Higher Education, 52*(6), 598-614.

Barefoot, B. O. (Ed.). (1993). *Exploring the evidence: Reporting outcomes of freshman seminars* (Monograph No. 11). Columbia, SC: National Resource Center for The Freshman Year Experience and Students in Transition, University of South Carolina.

Barefoot, B. O., Warnock, C. L., Dickinson, M. P., Richardson, S. E., & Roberts, M. R. (1998). *Exploring the evidence: Reporting outcomes of first-year seminars, Volume II* (Monograph No. 25). Columbia, SC: University of South Carolina, National Resource Center for The First-Year Experience and Students in Transition.

Barefoot, B. O., & Fidler, P. P. (1992). *Helping students climb the ladder: 1991 national survey of freshman seminar programs.* (Monograph No. 10). Columbia, SC: University of South Carolina, National Resource Center for The Freshman Year Experience and Students in Transition.

Barefoot, B. O., & Fidler, P. P. (1996). *The 1994 survey of freshman seminar programs: Continuing innovations in the collegiate curriculum* (Monograph No. 20). Columbia, SC: University of South Carolina, National Resource Center for The Freshman Year Experience and Students in Transition.

Beal, P., & Noel, L. (1980). *What works in student retention: A report of a joint project of the American College Testing Program and the National Center for Higher Education Management Systems.* (ERIC Reproduction No. 197 635). Iowa City, IA: American College Testing Program.

Berman, D. (1997). On the road with University 101: Where are we now? *The Freshman Year Experience Newsletter, 10*(1), 2-3.

Bok, D. C. (1986). *Higher learning.* Cambridge, MA: Harvard University Press.

Bowen, H., & Schuster, J. (1986). *American professors: A national resource imperilled.* New York: Oxford University Press.

Boyer, E. L. (1987). *College: The undergraduate experience in America.* New York: Harper & Row.

Cannici, J. P., & Poulton, J. (1990). Personal competency training as a preventive intervention. *Journal of The Freshman Year Experience, 2*(2), 31-43.

Chickering, A. W. (1969). *Education and identity.* San Francisco: Jossey-Bass.

Cohen, P. A. (1981). Student rating of instruction and student achievement: A meta-analysis of multisection validity studies. *Review of Educational Research, 51,* 281-309.

The College Board. (1996). Students over 24 becoming the norm at US colleges. *College Board News, 24*(4), 1.

Daubman, K. A., Williams, V. G., Johnson, D. H., & Crump, D. (1985). Time to withdrawal and academic performance: Implications for withdrawal policies. *Journal of College Student Personnel, 26*(6), 518-523.

Eble, K. E., & McKeachie, W. (1985). *Improving undergraduate education through faculty development*. San Francisco: Jossey-Bass.

Eison, J., & Moore, J. (1980, September). *Learning styles and attitudes of traditional age and adult students*. Paper presented at the annual convention of the American Psychological Association, Montreal, Canada.

Erickson, B. L., & Strommer, D. W. (1991). *Teaching college freshmen*. San Francisco: Jossey-Bass.

Freedman, M., & Associates (1979). *Academic culture and faculty development*. Berkeley, CA: Montaigne Press.

Friedlander, J. (1980). Are college support programs and services reaching high-risk students? *Journal of College Student Personnel, 21*(1), 23-28.

Fuhrmann, B. S., & Jacobs, R. (1980). *The learning interactions inventory*. Richmond, VA: Ronne Jacobs Associates.

Gaff, J. (1978). Overcoming faculty resistance. In J. Gaff (Ed.), Institutional renewal through the improvement of teaching (pp. 43-56). *New Directions for Higher Education, 24*. San Francisco: Jossey-Bass.

Gardner, J. N. (1980). *University 101: A concept for improving university teaching and learning*. (ERIC Reproduction No. 192 706). Columbia, SC: University of South Carolina, National Resource Center for The Freshman Year Experience.

Gardner, J. N. (1993, January). *Structural problems in the first college year*. Presentation made at the Freshman Year Experience Resource Seminar, Irvine, CA.

Gardner, J. N., & Hunter, M. S. (1994, July). *First-year seminar instructor training*. Preconference workshop presented at The Seventh International Conference on The First-Year Experience, Dublin, Ireland.

Group for Human Development in Higher Education. (1974). *Faculty development in a time of retrenchment*. New York: Change Publications.

Hoyt, D. P., & Howard, G. S. (1978). The evaluation of faculty development programs. *Research in Higher Education, 8*, 25-38.

Hunter, M. S. (1996). *Who trains the trainers?* Postconference workshop presented at the Second National Conference on Students in Transition, San Antonio, Texas.

Institute of International Education. (1992). *Open doors 1990/91*. New York: IIE Books.

Kerr, C. (1994). Knowledge ethics and the new academic culture. *Change, 26*(1), 8-15.

Knefelkamp, L. L. (1980). Faculty and student development in the '80's: Renewing the community of scholars. *Current Issues in Higher Education, 2*(4), 13-26.

Knowles, M. S. (1984). *Andragogy in action*. San Francisco: Jossey-Bass.

Kraft, R. E. (1976). An analysis of student learning styles. *Physical Education, 20*, 140-142.

Lacey, P. A. (1988). Faculty development and the future of college teaching. In R. E. Young & K. E. Eble (Eds.), College teaching and learning: Preparing for new commitments (pp. 57-70). *New Directions for Teaching and Learning, 33*. San Francisco: Jossey-Bass.

Levinson-Rose, J., & Menges, R. J. (1981). Improving college teaching: A critical review of research. *Review of Educational Research, 51*, 403-434.

Levitz, R. (1989). The "new majority." *Recruitment and Retention in Higher Education, 4*(2), 3.

Levitz, R. (1994) Pointers on success courses. *Recruitment and Retention in Higher Education, 8*(3), 5-7.

Menges, R. J., & Brinko, K. T. (1986). *Effects of student evaluation feedback: A meta-analysis of higher education research.* Paper presented at the annual meeting of the American Educational Research Association, San Francisco, CA.

National Endowment for the Humanities. (1984). *To reclaim a legacy.* Study Group on the State of Learning in the Humanities in Higher Education. Washington, DC: Author.

Noel, L. (1985). Increasing student retention: New challenges and potential. In L. Noel, R. Levitz, D. Saluri, & Associates (Eds.), *Increasing student retention* (pp. 1-27). San Francisco: Jossey-Bass.

Pascarella, E. T., & Terenzini, P. T. (1991). *How college affects students: Findings and insights from 20 years of research.* San Francisco: Jossey-Bass.

Paul, R. W. (1994). Educational vision: We changed our name but not our ideals. *Education Vision, 2*(1), 5, 10.

Perry, W. G. (1970). *Forms of intellectual and ethical development during the college years.* New York: Holt, Rinehart & Winston.

Pickering, J. W., Calliotte, J. A., & McAuliffe, G. J. (1992). The effect of noncognitive factors on freshman academic performance and retention. *Journal of The Freshman Year Experience, 4*(2), 7-30.

Schuster, J. H., Wheeler, D. W., & Associates. (1990). *Enhancing faculty careers.* San Francisco: Jossey-Bass.

Stevens, J. J., & Aleamoni, L. M. (1985). The use of evaluative feedback for instructional improvement: A longitudinal perspective. *Instructional Science, 13,* 285-304.

Terenzini, P. T., & Associates. (1993). *The transition to college: Easing the passage.* The Pennsylvania State University: National Center on Postsecondary Teaching, Learning, and Assessment.

Terry, E. F. (1992). The freshman year experience as environmental press: The William Jewell experience. *College Student Journal, 26*(1), 110-118.

Tinto, V. (1993). *Leaving college: Rethinking the causes and cures for student attrition* (2nd ed.). Chicago: University of Chicago Press.

Tracey, T. J., & Sedlacek, W. E. (1985). The relationship of noncognitive variables to academic success: A longitudinal comparison by race. *Journal of College Student Personnel, 26,* 405- 410.

Turner, J. L., & Boice, R. (1987). Starting at the beginning: The concerns and needs of new faculty. In J. Kurfiss (Ed.), *To improve the academy: Resources for student, faculty, and institutional development* (pp. 41-47). Stillwater, OK: New Forums Press, The Professional and Organizational Development Network in Higher Education.

Turner, J. C., Garrison, C. Z., Korpita, E., Waller, J., Addy, C., Hill, W. R., & Mohn, L. A. (1994). Promoting responsible sexual behavior through a college freshman seminar. *AIDS Education and Prevention, 6*(3), 266-277.

Upcraft, M. L., & Gardner, J. N. (1989). A comprehensive approach to enhancing freshman success. In M. L. Upcraft, J. N. Gardner, & Associates, *The freshman year experience* (pp. 1-12). San Francisco: Jossey-Bass.

Wlodkowski, R. J. (1985). *Enhancing adult motivation to learn.* San Francisco: Jossey-Bass.

Zuckerman, M., Porac, J., Lathin, D., Smith, R., & Deci, E. L. (1978). On the importance of self-determination for intrinsically motivated behavior. *Personality and Social Psychology Bulletin, 4,* 443-446.

Teaching and Today's Changing First-Year Students

M. Lee Upcraft and Pamela S. Stephens

College students have changed. Most of us associated with higher education recognize this fact, but the magnitude of changes becomes apparent when we compare college students of today with those of 40 years ago. A condensed description of a typical college student provided by Schoch (1980) highlights the extent of those changes.

> Remember Joe College? The young man who, after working hard in high school arrived at Berkeley, where he set out to sample the rich and varied intellectual feast at the University of California. Joe was independent, self-motivated, and academically well prepared. About his junior year, Joe settled on a major field of study, which he pursued with diligence and increasing confidence in order to graduate four years after his arrival. (p. 1)

Joe doesn't live here any more, Schoch concludes, and a look at the 1998 entering class at Berkeley confirms his conclusion. That class was 40.9% Asian, 31.4% White, 13.2% Hispanic, 6.1% African American, 7.2% unknown, and 1.2% American Indian. In other words, at least 68.6% of students were non-White (Berkeley Office of Student Research, 1998).

But racial and ethnic diversity is only one indicator of how much students have changed in the last 40 years. This chapter reviews the many ways in which students have changed, including the challenges faculty face because of students' changing physical and psychological health, their family dynamics, and other factors. The chapter concludes by exploring some of the instructional implications of these changes for our dealings with students both inside and outside the classroom.

CHAPTER 2

The Changing Demographics of Today's Students

Racial/Ethnic Diversity

The number of racial/ethnic groups accessing higher education has grown dramatically. In 1996, minorities constituted 25.2% of total enrollments, compared to 17.9% in 1986. Put another way, from 1986 to 1996, while overall enrollments increased by 14.4%, American-Indian enrollment increased by 48.9%, Asian-American by 83.8%, African-American by 38.6%, Hispanic by 86.4%, and international student by 34.8%. Compare that with a 3.1% increase in White enrollment (Wilds & Wilson, 1998). If these trends continue, racial/ethnic minorities soon may constitute almost one third of our student population.

To be sure, racial/ethnic group participation is quite uneven by type of institution and geographic location. For example, 68.1% of American Indians, Hispanics, Asians, and African Americans attend two-year institutions, compared to 30.3% of

Whites. In fact, half of American Indians (50.0%) and a majority of Hispanics (55.9%) attend two-year institutions (*The Chronicle of Higher Education Almanac*, 1998). States with more than a quarter of minority enrollment in higher education include, in rank order: Hawaii (71.0%); California (48.8%); Washington, DC (45.7%); New Mexico (44.9%); Texas (37.4%); Florida (32.9%); Louisiana (32.8%); Mississippi (32.7%); Maryland (32.2%); New York (31.6%); Georgia (30.8%); New Jersey (29.5%); Illinois (28.4%); and Alabama (27.0%) (*The Chronicle of Higher Education Almanac*, 1998).

Interestingly, differences within minority groups may be as great as differences between them. For example, there are four major Hispanic/Latino groups in higher education—Mexican Americans, Puerto Ricans, Cubans, and Central/South Americans—each with different histories, traditions, and cultures (Justiz & Rendón, 1989). Within-group diversity is also evident with Asians, Native Americans, African Americans, and others, which means we must be very cautious in reaching conclusions about students based on gross categorizations of race and ethnicity.

All this evidence suggests that Joe College has passed on or away, replaced by a population of students that are so demographically diverse that a . . . stereotype . . . is out of the question.

Gender

The opportunity for higher education first belonged only to men. Women were not allowed to enroll in college until the mid-19th century. But in this century, by around 1980, more women than men were enrolled in college. Since 1978, women have outnumbered men among first-time enrollees. In 1995, 55.6% of students enrolled in postsecondary education were women (Wilds & Wilson, 1998).

Enrollment Status

Today more of our students enroll part-time. In 1995, 35.7% of all undergraduate students were enrolled part-time, compared with 29.0% in 1976. Part-time students are more likely to be women over 24 years of age who are enrolled at two-year institutions. Nearly two thirds of part-time students (63.3%) are 25 years or older. Of male undergraduates enrolled part-time, 59.6% are 25 years or older, while among females, 60.0% are 25 years or older (*The Chronicle of Higher Education Almanac*, 1998).

As a consequence of their part-time enrollment, fewer students are completing bachelor's degrees in four years. According to a survey by the National Collegiate Athletic Association, only 56% of full-time, first-year students graduate within six years. By racial/ethnic group, 64.0% of Asians graduated within six years, followed by 59% of Whites, 45% of Hispanics, 38% of African Americans, and 37% of American Indians (Wilds & Wilson, 1998).

"Stopping out" (the practice of dropping out and re-enrolling at a later date) is also a more frequent occurrence. According to the National Center for Education Statistics (1998), nearly one third of all undergraduates depart institutions of higher education in their first year. In 1989-90, 15% of all students stopped out, with students enrolled at public two-year institutions stopping out at nearly twice the rate of those enrolled at four-year institutions.

Age

Since World War II and the GI Bill, older student enrollments have steadily increased to the point where they represented 42.2% of all students enrolled in 1996. Students over 25 are more likely to be women, to enroll part-time, and to attend two-year institutions (*The Chronicle of Higher Education Almanac*, 1998). The proportion of students over the age of 40 has increased substantially in the last 30 years. In 1970, students 40 years of age or older constituted 5.5% of total enrollments. Between 1970 and 1993 that number increased by 235% to 1.6 million students, making them the fastest growing age group on American campuses (*The Chronicle of Higher Education*, 1996).

Residence

Given the fact that more students are older, studying part-time, and enrolling in two-year institutions, it is not surprising that more of them are commuting and living off campus. Hodgkinson (1985) reports that only about one in six students in postsecondary education is (a) studying full time, (b) 18 to 22 years of age, and (c) living in the residence hall. Yet our popular stereotypes reflect the opposite: traditional-aged students, studying full-time, and living on campus. In fact, these students are a very distinct minority of today's students.

Students with Disabilities

Students with disabilities had little access to higher education until the passage of the 1973 Rehabilitation Act. Section 504 of that act mandated equal opportunity for qualified handicapped people in the educational programs of institutions receiving federal assistance. Since then, enrollments of students with disabilities (impairments of mobility, vision, hearing, speech, learning, or others) have risen steadily, to the point where it is estimated that 9.0% of all students in 1994 had some disability (Henderson, 1995).

Sexual Orientation

Today's students are more open about their sexual orientation. According to some estimates, as many as 10% of today's students are gay, lesbian, bisexual, or transsexual, although most of them choose to remain "in the closet." Those who are open about their different sexual orientation frequently experience violence and discrimination, and those who are closeted live in fear of their sexual orientation being disclosed (Evans & Levine, 1990).

International Students

International student participation in higher education rose 48.6% from 1984 to 1995. Countries sending the most international students to the United States are, with one exception, exclusively Asian—Japan, China, Korea, Taiwan, Canada, Malaysia, Thailand, Indonesia, and Hong Kong (*The Chronicle of Higher Education Almanac*, 1998). International students face various difficulties because of cultural differences. Among these difficulties are the emphasis on discussion in the classroom, the challenge of completing a heavy workload, departmental preferences for applied research, and the informality of the teacher-student relationship (Hu, 1997). In addition to these differences, international students also encounter difficulties resulting from prejudice, stereotyping, frustration, isolation, and low self-esteem. Furthermore, many international students are not accustomed to planning their own courses of study and are not familiar with the practice of academic advising (Do, 1996).

All this evidence suggests that Joe College has passed on or away, replaced by a population of students that are so demographically diverse that a proper stereotype to replace dear old departed Joe is out of the question. But demographics tell only part of the changing student story. Our students have also changed in other ways.

Changing Characteristics of Today's Students

Above and beyond these dramatic demographic shifts, other significant changes in college students are occurring. They include changes in student attitudes and values, their family dynamics, their physical and psychological health, their academic preparation, and sources of financing their education.

Changing Attitudes and Values

Since 1966, the Cooperative Institutional Research Program (CIRP) at the University of California, Los Angeles has tracked the attitudes, values, and aspirations of traditional-aged high school students entering college. Students of today, compared to those in the mid-1960s are politically more conservative; less interested in "developing a meaningful philosophy of life;" more interested in making money; more concerned about getting a job after college; more interested in the fields of business, computer science, and engineering; and less interested in the humanities, fine arts, and the social sciences. On the other hand, there has been little change in the percentage of entering students who list "obtain a general education" (about three in five) as a very important reason for deciding to go to college (*The Chronicle of Higher Education Almanac*, 1998).

Depending on their age, today's students have been shaped by events including the Great Depression, World War II, the Korean War, the Civil Rights movement, the Kennedy and King assassinations, the Vietnam War, the Reagan years, the Challenger explosion, the collapse of the Soviet Union, the fall of the Berlin Wall, various economic booms and recessions (although traditional-aged students may only remember the current run of expanding economic prosperity), the Gulf War, the Clinton years, and many other important events.

Changing Family Dynamics

The American family is undergoing a transformation that is already having a significant impact on today's students. The divorce rate increased rapidly through the 1960s and 1970s. The rate of divorce in 1985 was 5.0 per 1,000 people compared with a rate of 2.2 divorces per 1,000 people in 1960 (Friedberg, 1998). According to the Stepfamily Association of America (1998), 35% of all children born in the 1980s will experience approximately five years of life in a single-parent family before their 18th birthday. Additionally, students who are themselves divorced and/or single parents make up a significant part of our adult learner population.

But changing family stability is only part of the picture. Families characterized by physical violence, sexual abuse, alcohol and other drug abuse, and other problems are on the rise (Gannon, 1989). Consequently, we are seeing more students today who are affected by family instability and dysfunction. Henton, Hayes, Lamke, and Murphy (1990) found that students who lack family support have a more difficult time adjusting in college. Likewise, many students from dysfunctional families have relationship problems and low self-esteem, as well as higher suicide-attempt rates, sexual dysfunction, social alienation, physical ailments, and psychological trauma (Hoffman & Weiss, 1987).

Changes in Mental and Physical Health

Thirty years ago, students seeking help from college counseling centers presented problems clearly related to their college experiences, such as roommate conflicts, career indecision, academic difficulty, or relationship problems—in other words, "normal" students with "normal" problems. Today, students with problems present a very different picture. Witchel (1991) describes a substantial increase in psychological disturbance among today's college students. Waiting lists for treatment in college counseling centers are at an all-time high and are very much a sign of the times. There is an increase in the number of students suffering from serious emotional distress, including self-destructive behavior, violence against others, anxiety, depression, and eating disorders, as well as those dealing with the aftermath of date and acquaintance rape, courtship violence, family or spouse abuse, and family drug and alcohol abuse. Many of these conditions result not from students' collegiate experience but from their lives prior to or outside the collegiate environment.

Physical health problems are also on the increase, often closely linked to some mental health problems. For example, eating disorders result from psychological problems, but they can become serious physical problems very quickly. Drug and alcohol abuse can also create significant physical and psychological problems, as can various kinds of violence such as date rape. Further, the age diversity of today's students means that health issues reflect the spectrum of ailments, rather than those associated only with late adolescence.

An even more alarming trend is the increase in sexually transmitted diseases among students, the most serious of which is AIDS. The HIV-positive rate among today's college students is approximately 2.4 per 1,000, compared to 1.0 per 1,000 in 1983 (E. Jurs, personal communication, 1997). Much of this increase is attributable to the spread of the disease to heterosexuals, particularly women. Among younger age groups, the proportion of women infected with the HIV virus is approaching that of men (*The Chronicle of Higher Education*, 1992).

Changing Academic Preparation

Perhaps no trend is more disturbing to faculty in higher education than the lack of academic preparation of today's students. A 30-year decline in the Scholastic Aptitude Test (SAT) scores between

1957 and 1987 has been well documented (Forrest, 1987), although in recent years this trend appears to have leveled off (*The Chronicle of Higher Education Almanac*, 1998). Great discrepancies exist in scores by gender, race, and ethnicity, with men scoring higher than women, and majority students generally scoring higher than minorities, with the exception of Asians.

Perhaps even more important for faculty, more of today's students require remediation in basic reading, writing, and computational skills. According to a recent national report, "approximately 29% of college first-year students enrolled in remedial reading, writing, or math in 1995, about the same percentage that enrolled in 1989. Of those students in remedial classes, 46% were 22 years of age or older, and 25% over the age of 30" (*The Chronicle of Higher Education*, 1998, p. A72).

> There is an increase in the number of students suffering from serious emotional distress, including self-destructive behavior, violence against others, anxiety, depression, and eating disorders. . . .

Changing Sources for Financing an Education

Before 1955, virtually all students paid for their education with their own or their parents' resources, or with limited academic scholarship aid. (A major exception was veterans who received GI Bill benefits after World War II and the Korean War.) In 1989, 56.4% of all undergraduates received some form of financial aid, including 70.4% of students enrolled in private institutions. Today, only about 20% of undergraduates between the ages of 18 and 22 are pursuing a parent/student-financed education (*National On-Campus Report*, 1992).

Recent trends continue to put more financial pressure on students and their families. For example, according to the National Commission on the Cost of Higher Education (1998), since the 1980s, college tuition has increased annually at the rate of two to three times the rate of inflation. Between 1981 and 1995, tuition at four-year public colleges and universities increased 234%, while during the same time period, the median household income rose 82%, and the consumer price index rose only 74%. Further, the typical bill for tuition, fees, room, board, books, and incidentals at public institutions is $10,069, a whopping 23% of the average American family's household income (*Time*, 1998). At one Ivy League institution, tuition in 1976 was $3,790. Two decades later that same tuition bill is $21,130, nearly a six-fold increase (Larson, 1997). To be sure, by 1997 the average increase had dropped to a more manageable 5%, and a few brave institutions actually lowered tuition, but the damage has been done (*Time*, 1998).

However, as costs have risen, so have the strategies that students and families use for dealing with them. They include government-sponsored incentives (e.g., Education IRAs) to encourage families to start saving early for college, institution-based programs (e.g., prepaid tuition plans which lock in tuition rates at current levels), and federal and state loan programs and other financial aid (Upcraft, 1999). According to the College Board, in 1996-97 a total of 55.7 billion dollars was spent on student aid, of which approximately 54% was federal loans, 19% institutional grants, and 15% federal or state grants (Cabrera, 1998). Today's students must cobble together a financial aid package which is complex, difficult to access, and more dependent upon loans than ever before.

In addition to all these issues, more and more students must work in order to contribute to their college education. It is estimated that 8 out of 10 students work while studying for their undergraduate degrees. Two thirds of working undergraduates must be employed in order to finance their education. Most of these students are attending classes full-time, under 24 years of age, and financially dependent upon their families (*The Chronicle of Higher Education*, 1998). The problem, of course, is that when students work too much, they are much more likely to drop out, and much less likely to earn good grades (Pascarella & Terenzini, 1991).

Implications for Learning Inside the Classroom

Implications for teaching and learning that spring from the changing personal experiences of today's students can be considered as they relate to student experiences both in and out of the classroom. As will be noted subsequently, the distinction is a convenient one in that it differentiates between spaces in which student experiences occur, but it is an artificial separation when it comes to explaining how, when, and under what circumstances learning occurs. Despite the fact that we cannot propose a precise and specific set of implications, we do have relevant experiences and useful knowledge. They provide a foundation on which to build a pedagogy that does respond to increased diversity among our students. No literature base better illustrates this than our growing knowledge of learning styles.

Work on learning styles began 20 years ago with Whitkin and Moore (1975), who first distinguished between field-dependent learners (who respond best in collaborative environments that take into account their needs, feelings, and interests) and field-independent learners (who prefer environments that focus on tasks, objectives, analysis, and independence). Since then, a variety of other research has expanded our understanding of the different kinds of cognitive processing that learners use. In Chapter 3, we identify several ways of looking at differences in the ways in which students learn; those studied and described include Perry (1970), Kolb (1984), Gardner (1993), Baxter-Magolda (1992), and King and Kitchener (1994).

In a nutshell, if different students learn in different ways, then faculty must teach in different ways... our teaching ought to be as diverse as our students.

This research on learning styles is general and applies to all learners, but there is also work that attempts to describe differences between and among groups. For example, there is considerable evidence that men may learn differently than women (Baxter-Magolda, 1992), that older students may learn differently than those of traditional student age (Cross, 1981; Pearson, Shavlick, & Touchton, 1989), and that racial/ethnic minorities may learn differently than majority students (Shade, 1989; Tharp, 1989).

Differences spelled out by this research and the literature that explores its implications (see, for example, Svinicki & Dixon, 1987) are specific and concrete. In a nutshell, if different students learn in different ways, then faculty must teach in different ways. Said in the context of this chapter, our teaching ought to be as diverse as our students.

Again, the realities of higher education (at least as most of us experience them) preclude a specific and individual response to each student. But the common approach of yesteryear, (one teaching style fits all) when faculty lectured and gave two objective exams, is doomed to failure with today's diverse student population.

To illustrate and drive home the point, McCarthy (1980) documents that teachers often teach everyone the same way, most often using lecture/discussion methods. From Kolb's (1981) perspective, teaching methodologies tend to cluster according to fundamental differences in the nature of the discipline taught. That is, many faculty tend to be field-independent, analytical, verbal, and observational learners ("assimilators" in the Kolb framework) who learn best from lectures and discussion (Kolb & Smith, 1986). However, use of the lecture/discussion method with learners whose primary style is relational, field-dependent, visual, and intuitive may connect with only about 30% of the students (McCarthy, 1980). This mismatch becomes even more of a problem at institutions with high racial/ethnic enrollment because learning styles of racial or ethnic minority students tend to be more relational, field-dependent, intuitive, and involving (Cox & Ramirez, 1981).

There is another important reason for diversifying styles of instruction. As noted earlier, an increasing number of students come to college academically underprepared. We can no longer assume that all students in our classes have the required level of reading, writing, and other basic skills to succeed, and this creates some very difficult instructional challenges.

The first challenge is what to do about students with basic-skills deficiencies. Leaving them alone condemns them to almost certain failure. Most of us are not qualified and lack the necessary time to teach them basic skills. The only option left is to refer them to campus basic-skills centers, if such centers exist. Even in those circumstances, referrals take time, and there must be close coordination with academic tutors.

The second challenge comes from the breadth of preparedness in our classes that is an inevitable outcome of seeing more academically underprepared students. In previous times, we could assume a much more normal curve of preparedness, with a few gifted students at the one margin and a few underprepared students at the other. We provided individual help for these students and focused our instructional methodologies on the "mass middle" of the preparedness curve, all of whom were at least minimally prepared to succeed in our classrooms. In today's classes, the curve has flattened, or at worst become bimodal. At best, we end up with about the same number of underprepared, prepared, and gifted students; at worst, we have a class with no mass middle at all. If we persist in teaching to the middle of the preparedness curve, we may not be teaching to anyone. In classes with great diversity of preparation, there must be greater diversity of instruction.

To sum up, then, the first implication of changing student demography and characteristics is a call for a more diverse and varied style of instruction. Although it is true that an instructor cannot be all things and do all things for all students, we tend to err on the side of consistency as opposed to diversity. We can and should use more instructional techniques, strategies, and activities in our teaching. The research and literature on learning styles are helpful in cultivating a clearer and more complete understanding of the various approaches to learning, which allows for a more thoughtful and systematic inclusion of alternatives.

But that is not the only implication that arises from changes in student demography and characteristics. We also know from a variety of sources and contexts (see, for example, Erickson & Strommer, 1991) that beginning college students, especially those not as academically well prepared, do better in learning environments that are structured and organized—where expectations are clearly articulated. This structure is relevant and positive whether the referent is a whole course or individual assignments.

Most of us who teach college students today are impressed (sometimes distressed) by their lack of confidence in their ability as learners. They seem unable to take control of situations and act much more like victims to whom things happen not of their choosing. Many of today's college students need to be empowered, convinced that learning is something over which they can exercise control. The implication here is a call for a change in faculty role in terms of relationships with students. Faculty who help these students succeed act more like guides and coaches and less like guards and judges. This new role may mean significant changes in the way we view teaching, as well as how we teach.

Still another potential implication is the assumption that even though students may be very different from their teachers, they do have much in common with their fellow students. They can and should be encouraged to learn with and from each other. Not only can they better help each other connect knowledge with their own experiences, but having a voice, a say, a role in their own learning can be an empowering experience. Much of the current interest in cooperative and collaborative learning derives from the growing diversity of our students and our culture. Education makes an important contribution when it teaches diverse people how to live and work together in communities of respect. As previously noted, teachers cannot be expected to respond to all the differences, but students can be enlisted in the effort.

These implications give us places to start our exploration of the ways to adapt, modify, and change instruction so that it better connects with our students. Existing research and literature lead us to believe that courses charted in these directions will lead to desired destinations, but nothing suggested here or in subsequent chapters is surefire. As noted earlier, we are traversing uncharted waters. At every step in our efforts to change, we need to solicit and respond to learner feedback. It is not a question of doing what students want but of understanding how they are experiencing education and then modifying what we do so that learning outcomes improve.

Implications for Learning Outside the Classroom

One of the most significant implications of changing student demography and characteristics is that *all* student experiences influence whatever learning does or does not occur (see Chapter 3). Faculty may think of their classrooms as secure castles, protected by moats and thick walls, but students bring all manner of unwanted and counterproductive forces into those chambers of learning. They sit in class worried about the next tuition bill; they wonder about children in day care; they fight fatigue and have eight hours of work still ahead; they don't understand why the professor requires them to attend an evening lecture; they can't believe how long it takes to do the reading; they don't have time to work on the group project, and on and on. What occurs in the classroom, as important as it is, happens as part of something larger. More so than previously, today's college students are forcing faculty to see what happens inside the classroom as a consequence of what happens outside.

Research, including that summarized by Pascarella and Terenzini (1991), documents that students' experiences outside the classroom may contribute just as much to their success as their performance inside the classroom. In general, students who get involved in activities, participate in orientation, make use of support services, establish effective interpersonal relations with other students and faculty, live in residence halls, belong to student organizations, and attend cultural events are more likely to graduate than students without such involvement (Kuh, Douglas, Lund, & Ramin-Gyurnek, 1994).

Having someone else, such as a family member, friend, or faculty/staff member, take an interest in and care about one's success is also very important (Schlossberg, Lynch, & Chickering, 1989). Contact with faculty, both inside and outside the classroom, plays a positive role in the experiences of beginning students (Terenzini, Rendón, Millar, Upcraft, Gregg, Jalomo, & Allison, 1994).

The weight of this research stands somewhat in opposition to what has been described as experiences of college students today. Most of them do not live on campus; they commute. Limited time on campus means fewer opportunities to connect with other students and faculty. It means less chance of getting involved with the academic life of the college. Since research implies that success depends to a large degree on student involvement, the challenge for faculty becomes how to help students structure their out-of-class experiences to promote learning goals.

Again, this means a change in faculty role—the need to see oneself more as a designer, arranger, facilitator, and manager of learning experiences. For example, assignments can be designed which tie out-of-class experiences to learning goals. Practica and internships can be used to help students apply what they've learned in the classroom. Volunteer service that relates to academic goals offers another vehicle for involvement. Can part-time work experiences, common to so many college students, be somehow connected to their classroom experiences? Engaging students in faculty scholarship and research can also get students involved and provide that invaluable contact with faculty.

There is no question that institutions must work harder to create academic communities that connect with today's college students. Classrooms are about the only place on campus where you can be assured that all students will be present, including those who commute and work. This puts faculty at the vanguard of efforts to get students involved in the intellectual life of the campus.

In addition to this new and expanded role for faculty with respect to out-of-class learning, changes in students spell out implications in two other areas as well. As diversity among our students increases, the composition of the faculty and staff must change to more accurately reflect the students they serve. Ultimately, we are unsure of the impact of the changing student population on teaching and learning. Not only is it absolutely essential that faculty keep their fingers on the pulse of classes, but institutions too must understand the impact and effectiveness of programming with respect to changing students.

Summary and Conclusions

Changes in students mean we must change the ways we think about learning and teaching. We must also recognize that the in-class and out-of-class experiences of students are inextricably intertwined. Our success with students depends upon our clear understanding of how today's college students have changed, an acceptance of those differences, and a willingness to adapt our teaching to meet these new realities. Life in the classroom needs to be changed, we suspect, in some pretty dramatic and significant ways.

Change is often thrust upon us at what seems like inopportune times—when things are going along just fine, when we'd just as soon not have to change, or when we don't have enough money to change. That is how many people in higher education feel. But there are those among us who have caught a sense of what these changes can mean. We have the opportunity to educate students for whom the college experience can be life-altering. We are also in a unique position to meet the serious and significant needs of an increasingly complex and diverse society. It is a time when our work in higher education can really and truly make a difference.

References

Baxter-Magolda, M. B. (1992). *Knowing and reasoning in college: Gender-related patterns in students' intellectual development.* San Francisco: Jossey-Bass.

Berkeley Office of Student Research. (1999). http://www.uga.berkeley. edu/ouars/ level_2/ camp_over.html.

Cabrera, A. F. (1998). *Estimated student aid by source, 1996-97.* University Park, PA: Unpublished Paper.

Can you pay his way through college? (1998, August 17). *Time, 152*(7).

The Chronicle of Higher Education. (1992, December 12). *39*(17), p. A2.

The Chronicle of Higher Education. (1996, October 25). *43*(9), p. A44.

The Chronicle of Higher Education. (1998, May 1). *44*(34), p. A72.

The Chronicle of Higher Education Almanac. (1998, August 28). *45*(1).

Citizens for Responsible Education Reform. (1998). *National commission on the cost of higher education.* Washington, DC: Author.

Cox, B., & Ramirez, M., III. (1981). Cognitive styles: Implications for multiethnic education. In J. A. Banks (Ed.), *Education in the 80s* (pp. 66-71). Washington, DC: National Education Association.

Cross, K. P. (1981). *Adults as learners: Increasing participation and facilitating learning.* San Francisco: Jossey-Bass.

Do, V. T. (1996, January/February). Counseling culturally different students in the community college. *Community College Journal of Research and Practice, 20,* 9-21.

Evans, N., & Levine, H. (1990). Perspectives on sexual orientation. In L.V. Moore (Ed.), *Evolving theoretical perspectives on students. New Directions for Student Services Sourcebook, 51.* San Francisco: Jossey-Bass.

Erickson, B. L., & Strommer, D. (1991). *Teaching college freshmen.* San Francisco: Jossey-Bass.

Forrest, A. (1987). Managing the flow of students through higher education. National Forum: *Phi Kappa Phi Journal, 68,* 39-42.

Friedberg, L. (1998). *Did unilateral divorce raise divorce rates?: Evidence from panel study.* Cambridge, MA: National Bureau of Economic Research.

Gannon, J. R. (1989). *Soul survivors: A new beginning for adults abused as children.* Englewood Cliffs, NJ: Prentice-Hall.

Gardner, H. (1993). *Multiple intelligences: The theory in practice.* New York: Basic Books.

Henderson, C. (1995). *College freshmen with disabilities: A triennial statistical profile.* Washington, DC: Health Resource Center, American Council on Education.

Henton, J., Hayes, L., Lamke, L., & Murphy, C. (1990). Crisis reaction of college freshmen as a function of family support systems. *Personnel and Guidance Journal, 58*, 508-510.

Hodgkinson, H. L. (1985). *All one system: demographics of education, kindergarten through graduate school.* Washington, DC: Institute of Educational Leadership.

Hoffman, J., & Weiss, B. (1987). Family problems and presenting problems in college students. *Journal of Counseling Psychology, 2*, 157-163.

Hu, H. (1997, March). *Crossing the river by touching the stones: The experiences of first-year Asian graduate students at a midwestern university.* Paper presented at the American Educational Research Association, Chicago, IL.

Jurs, E. (1997, November 6). Personal Communication with P. S. Stephens, University Park, PA.

Justiz, M., & Rendón, L. (1989). Hispanic students. In M. L. Upcraft, & J. N. Gardner (Eds.), *The freshman year experience: Helping students survive and succeed in college* (pp. 261-276). San Francisco: Jossey-Bass.

King, P. M., & Kitchener, K. (1994). *Developing reflective judgment: Understanding and promoting intellectual growth and critical thinking in adolescents and adults.* San Francisco: Jossey-Bass.

Kolb, D. A. (1981). Learning styles and disciplinary differences. In A. Chickering (Ed.), *The modern American college* (pp. 232-255). San Francisco: Jossey-Bass.

Kolb, D. A. (1984). *Experiential learning: Experience as the source of learning and development.* Englewood Cliffs, NJ: Prentice-Hall.

Kolb, D. A., & Smith, D. M. (1986). *User's guide for the learning style inventory: A manual for teachers and trainers.* Boston: McBer.

Kuh, G. D., Douglas, K. B., Lund, J. P., & Ramin-Gyurnek, J. (1994). *Student learning outside the classroom: Artificial boundaries.* ASHE-ERIC Higher Education Report No. 8. Washington, DC: The George Washington University, School of Education and Development.

Larson, E. (1997, March 17). Why colleges cost too much. *Time, 149*(11).

McCarthy, B. (1980). *The 4Mat system: Teaching learning styles with right/left mode techniques.* Chicago: Excel.

National Center for Educational Statistics. (1998). *Stopouts or stayouts? Undergraduates who leave college in their first year.* Washington, DC: US Department of Education, Office of Educational Research and Improvement.

National On-Campus Report. (1992, September 15). *20*(18), p. 5.

Pascarella, E.T., & Terenzini, P.T. (1991). *How college affects students: Findings and insights from twenty years of research.* San Francisco: Jossey-Bass.

Pearson, C. S., Shavlick, D. L., & Touchton, C. (Eds.). (1989). *Educating the majority: Women challenge tradition in higher education.* New York: American Council on Education, MacMillan.

Perry, W. G., Jr. (1970). *Forms of intellectual and ethical development in the college years.* New York: Holt, Rinehart, & Winston.

Schlossberg, N. K., Lynch, A. Q., & Chickering, A. W. (1989). *Improving higher education environments for adults: Response programs from entry to departure.* San Francisco: Jossey-Bass.

Schoch, R. (1980). As Cal enters the 80s, there'll be some changes made. *California Monthly, 90*(3), 1-3.

Shade, B. J. R. (Ed.). (1989). *Culture, style, and the educative process.* Springfield, IL: Thomas.

Svinicki, M. D., & Dixon, N. M. (1987). The Kolb model modified for classroom activities. *College Teaching, 35*(4), 141-146.

Terenzini, P. T., Rendón, L. I., Millar, S. B., Upcraft, M. L., Gregg, P. L., Jalomo, R. Jr., & Allison, K. W. (1994). Making the transition to college. In R. J. Menges, M. Weimer, & Associates

(Eds.), *Teaching on solid ground.* San Francisco: Jossey-Bass.

Tharp, R. C. (1989). Psychocultural variables and constraints: Effects on teaching and learning in schools. *American Psychologist, 44*(2), 349-359.

Stepfamily Association of America. (1998). http://stepfam. org.

Upcraft, M. L. (1999). Affordability: Responding to the rising cost of higher education. In C. S. Johnson, & H. E. Cheatham (Eds.), *Higher education trends for the next century.* Washington, DC: American College Personnel Association.

Whitkin, H. A., & Moore, A. C. (1975). *Field-dependent and field independent cognitive styles and their educational implications.* Princeton, NJ: Educational Testing Service.

Wilds, D. J., & Wilson, R. (1998). *Minorities in higher education 1997-98, sixteenth annual status report.* Washington: American Council on Education.

Witchel, R. I. (1991). The impact of dysfunctional families on college students' development. In R. I. Witchel (Ed.), Dealing with students from dysfunctional families. *New Directions for Student Services, 54.* San Francisco: Jossey-Bass.

What We Know about Students and How They Learn

M. Lee Upcraft and Jennifer L. Crissman

CHAPTER 3

In the previous chapter, we made the case for the necessity of teaching today's students differently because of their diverse backgrounds and characteristics. In this chapter, we will explore this diversity in greater detail, focusing on not only who they are, but why they behave and learn in the many different ways they do.

Telling faculty that they should "know their students" is, at first glance, like telling Eskimos they should "know snow." After all, we spend most of our waking time each day thinking about and preparing for how to teach them; in fact, many of us have spent our entire careers either being or teaching students. So what is left to know?

Well, to be candid, a whole lot. Sure, we spend our time with students and their problems. But in many ways our view is a limited one, narrowed by the time and context within which we see them. Our perception is narrow for three reasons. First, we tend to see students in our classrooms and offices, and sometimes in other contexts such as social gatherings, academically related student organizations, and the occasional meeting while crossing campus. Most of us, however, do not spend time with students outside the classroom to see them in *their* environments. For traditional students, we seldom see them interacting in their residence halls or off-campus apartments, letting off steam on the intramural playing fields, partying with their friends, or engaging in other out-of-class activities. For nontraditional students, we rarely see them relating to their families or working part-time or full-time to make ends meet.

Second, our focus is also narrow because we tend to see students as academic entities engaged in the sometimes harrowing process of attending class, studying for exams, preparing papers, and doing their best to earn decent grades. Beyond these more mundane requirements, we may even see them struggling to master a concept, solve a problem, think critically, make reflective judgments, and do all the other things that an academic education is all about. Most of us are very good at helping students progress in the classroom and structuring their class preparation time outside the classroom to achieve these goals. What more can we do? After all, the students are ultimately responsible for their own learning.

Third, in spite of the time we spend teaching students in our classrooms, how much do we really know about how they learn? How do students master content? How can we teach critical thinking, reflective judgment, problem solving, and the other learning processes we claim to develop in our classrooms? Does the much used and frequently overused lecture method really contribute to learning outcomes? Are we comfortable in using multiple teaching methods to meet the needs of diverse student learning styles? We may know about teaching (or think we do), but how much do we know really know about student learning?

We would strongly concur that students must be responsible and held accountable for their own learning. We would also agree that "knowing" students in our offices and classrooms and "knowing" them as academic entities is essential to their learning. Without such "knowing" it would be hard to imagine that any kind of education could take place. But we would also argue that learning can be enhanced even more if we take the time to "know" more about how students learn in the classroom, how they learn in their many environments outside the classroom, and to "know" them not only as academic beings, but also as emotional, psychosocial, moral, ethical, developing, and maturing human beings. Substantial research evidence exists to demonstrate that students' experiences inside and outside the classroom, along with their levels of development and maturation as human beings, directly and indirectly influence their success in the classroom. Put another way, if we give greater attention to students in their many contexts and their many stages of development, they will learn more of what we are trying to teach them in our classrooms.

> ... we spend our time with students and their problems. But in many ways our view is a limited one, narrowed by the time and context within which we see them.

This chapter will review that evidence and point to a fairly substantial body of theory and literature that helps us better understand the students' environments and development. We will look at students' intellectual/cognitive and psychosocial/moral development, how that development may be conditioned by age, gender, race/ethnicity, disability, sexual orientation, and other characteristics, and how learning plays out in the many campus and non-collegiate environments within which they live and learn.

Student Learning Inside the Classroom

Much of this monograph focuses on teaching and learning inside the classroom, so only a few basic principles will be discussed here. We do know that students learn best when they are actively involved, have an opportunity to function in different learning activities consistent with their learning styles, believe that their instructors are both invested in their learning and care about them, and receive frequent feedback on their performance.

Student Learning Outside the Classroom

We start with the assumption that what students experience outside the classroom has an effect on their learning inside the classroom. Most of us would readily acknowledge that learning occurs beyond our classroom doors, but we tend to believe that such learning is unrelated to classroom learning. For example, if we ask our graduating seniors what they learned in college, most would say things like "I learned to get along better with people," or "I learned more about myself," or "I grew up." In other words, through the rough and tumble of the college years, they learned about "life." In fact, however, these "learnings" are not independent of what they learned in the classroom, but are intimately connected to classroom learning.

The simplest way of putting this is that when students are successful in coping with their life outside the classroom, they do better in the classroom. For example, there is evidence that joining a fraternity actually *decreases* critical thinking in the first year of college, even when other factors that might affect this important academic skill are taken into account (Pascarella, Edison, Whitt, Nora, Hagedorn, & Terenzini, 1996). Other student experiences which enhance student learning *in the classroom* and are associated with persistence and educational attainment include living in on-campus residence halls (especially those with living/learning programs), participating in co-curricular activities, working part-time on campus, joining academically related student organizations, participating in orientation, having faculty contact outside the classroom, spending time studying, and using student support services (Kuh, Douglas, Lund, & Ramin-Gyurnek, 1994). To be sure, some out-of-class activities contribute negatively to these learning outcomes, including time spent socializing with friends, fraternity membership, and personal/family problems (Kuh et al., 1994). The bottom line is that if we want our students to learn more, we need to pay attention to their out-of-class experiences and their personal development.

Students' Cognitive Development

Much has been written and theorized about students' cognitive development. Understanding this literature is important to student success, and consists of several different approaches.

1. *Intellectual development.* Probably the most well-known and widely researched theory of intellectual development is that of Perry (1970). Perry believed that students move through nine stages, from a simplistic, categorical view of the world to a more relativistic, committed view. According to Perry, first-year students start out with an unquestioning, dualistic conceptual framework (right-wrong, good-bad, beautiful-ugly) and grow to a realization of the contingent nature of knowledge, values, and truth. As they move through the stages of intellectual development, they integrate their intellects with their identities, gain a better understanding of the world, and find personal meaning through an affirmation of their own commitments. Perry has been criticized by Gilligan (1982) as describing male intellectual development, and by many adult learning theorists as failing to account for adult intellectual development.

2. *Reflective judgment.* King and Kitchener (1994) describe a hierarchical, seven-stage sequence of students' assumptions about knowledge (what can be known, how knowledge is gained, certainty of knowledge claims) and how those assumptions are related to the way students justify their beliefs. Students progress from Stage 1, when all knowledge is certain, to Stage 2, when all knowledge is certain but not always observable, to Stage 3, when temporary uncertainty emerges, using one's own biases until absolute knowledge is possible. In Stage 4, some knowledge is permanently uncertain, while in Stage 5, knowledge is uncertain and subjective interpretation is based on rules of inquiry in a particular context. Students then move from Stage 6, when knowledge is constructed, and beliefs are based on generalized rules of inquiry, to Stage 7, when objective knowledge is obtainable, and beliefs are better or worse approximations of reality based on evidence.

3. *Epistemological reflection.* Baxter-Magolda (1992) studied students' perceptions of the nature of knowledge, and the role of gender in their changing patterns of reasoning. She described four different kinds of "knowers."

- *Absolute knowers* view knowledge as certain and authorities as having access to absolute truths. Women are more likely to be receivers of knowledge in the patterns of reasoning, while men are more likely to master such knowledge.

- *Transitional knowers* view knowledge as absolute in some areas but not others. Women are more likely to be interpersonal in their patterns of reasoning, while men are more likely to be impersonal.

- *Independent knowers* view knowledge as mostly uncertain. In this type of knower, the two patterns of reasoning were interindividual, used frequently by women, and individual, used more frequently by men.

- *Contextual knowers* view some knowledge claims as better than others in a particular context, with no gender differences.

4. *Field dependency/independency.* Whitkin and Moore (1975) first focused on the degree to which individuals are heavily influenced or relatively uninfluenced by their surrounding context. They distinguished between field dependent learners (those who respond best in collaborative learning environments that take into account their needs, feelings, and interests) and field independent learners (those who prefer environments that focus on tasks, objectives, analysis, and independence). Field dependent learners tend to see situations globally, seeing the whole instead of its parts, while field independent learners see situations more analytically, separating the parts from the whole.

5. *Learning styles.* Kolb (1984) identified four basic approaches derived from student learning preferences which are abstract or concrete, active or reflective.

- *Divergers* learn best by "feeling and thinking," taking in information through concrete experience and transforming it though reflective observation. They are open to people's feelings, listen with an open mind, and use their imagination.

- *Assimilators* learn best by "thinking and watching," taking in information through abstract conceptualization and transforming it through reflective observation. They like to organize information, build conceptual models, test theories and ideas, and analyze quantitative data.

- *Convergers* learn best by "thinking and doing," taking in information through abstract conceptualization and transforming it through active experimentation. They like to create new ways of thinking, experiment with new ideas, set goals, and make decisions.

- *Accommodators* learn best by "feeling and doing," taking in information through concrete experience and transforming it through active experimentation. They like to commit to objectives, seek and exploit opportunities, influence and lead others, and deal with people.

6. *Multiple intelligences.* Gardner (1987, 1993, 1997) posits a theory of multiple intelligences which includes eight distinctive ways people process information, or "domains of intelligence," which he believes are largely independent of one another. They include linguistic, logical-mathematical, musical, spatial, bodily-kinesthetic, interpersonal, intrapersonal, and naturalistic. Gardner argues that traditional teaching approaches focus too heavily on linguistic and logical-mathematical intelligences, to the detriment of students whose strengths lie in other domains.

7. *Psychological types.* There are many models of categorizing basic personality types, but one often applied to students is the Myers-Briggs Type Indicator. The MBTI tries to document differences based on perceptual functions (the ways individuals tend to take in information) and judgment functions (the ways in which individuals make decisions). The perceiving and judging functions are categorized into four polar dimensions, introversion/extraversion, sensing/intuition, thinking/feeling, and perceiving/judging, which, when combined, yield 16 different personality types.

While the MBTI was originally used to profile different personality types, Schroeder (1993) has argued that personality types are related to learning styles. For example, extraverts tend to learn best by trial and error, introverts by watching and observing. Sensors tend to learn best by moving from the concrete to the abstract, intuitors through their imagination. Thinkers tend to learn best through logical analysis; feelers need personal encouragement in the learning environment. While judgers prefer more structured learning environments, perceptors prefer an open and spontaneous learning environment.

What does all this mean for faculty who teach first-year students? It means that we must use these theories and models to expand our narrow way of thinking about students' cognitive development. It also means we must reassess our teaching strategies based upon this broadened perception. In order to accomplish this, we must commit ourselves to achieving an in-depth understanding of the developmental models briefly described here.

Students' Psychosocial Development

As noted earlier, students' psychosocial development affects their learning. What exactly is psychosocial development? Is it "touchy-feely" fluff or does it have academic merit? Psychosocial theory attempts to describe developmental tasks over a person's life span and to define how a person responds to and resolves these tasks (Pascarella & Terenzini, 1991; Rodgers, 1989). The theories which attempt to explain students' psychosocial development are as diverse as college students themselves.

1. *Involvement.* Astin's (1985) theory of involvement proposes that student learning is enhanced by becoming involved, which he defined as "the amount of physical and psychological energy that the student devotes to the academic experience" (p. 297). Involved students learn more by participating in the many out-of-class activities available to them, as well as through interaction with peers, faculty, staff and administrators, and other students. Faculty members can enhance student learning by talking to students before, during, and after class; during office hours about both academic and nonacademic subjects; and perhaps while joining students in the dining hall for a meal. There is evidence that the higher the level of

involvement, the more likely the student is to succeed both personally and academically (Astin, 1993).

2. *Validation.* While getting involved in the college experience is beneficial to students' personal and academic success, they also need someone, inside or outside the collegiate environment, who has a vested interest in their success and confirms their academic worth. Validation, as defined by Rendón (1994), is when some individual (e.g., faculty, advisor, coach, student affairs professional) either in or out of class takes an active interest in the student. Students want to feel affirmed and supported in their collegiate experience. Faculty have opportunities to validate their students and thus enhance student learning. Rendón suggests that faculty validate students, especially first-year students, early in the semester and continue to validate them through the college year. She also recommends that faculty connect with students, structure student learning experiences so they can see themselves as capable and powerful learners, and create supportive caring classrooms without being patronizing. Rendón summarizes her theory when she states, "the validating classroom empowers students, connects faculty with students, and creates an atmosphere of trust, respect and freedom to learn" (p. 47).

While getting involved in the college experience is beneficial to students' personal and academic success, they also need someone, inside or outside the collegiate environment, who has a vested interest in their success and confirms their academic worth.

3. *Mattering/marginality.* The degree to which students *matter* is the premise of Schlossberg, Lynch, and Chickering's theory (1989). Similar to Rendón's (1994) validation theory, students want and need to feel that they are important to other members of the academic community, that their contributions matter, and that people (faculty and family) care about them. As the newest members of an institution, students want to feel included in and connected to the campus community. If students do not feel accepted or appreciated, they will feel marginalized and will be less likely to succeed.

4. *Support and challenge.* Finding a balance between support and challenge during the first semester is the premise of Sanford's (1979) theory. He argues that being in a community provides opportunities for support and challenge, which are necessary conditions for development. Students are faced with myriad dilemmas during college, especially during the first year. Being part of a larger community provides the support needed for students to face these developmental challenges, to confront the challenges in a supportive environment, and to find appropriate ways of resolving these crises. Too much challenge in students' lives is overwhelming, whereas too much support is debilitating.

5. *Rites of Passage.* The transition one makes from previous environments to the college setting is another way of looking at first-year student learning. Tinto (1993) views new students' development within the framework of Van Gennep's (1960) concept of "rites of passage." This process involves three stages: separation, transition, and incorporation. First-year students must learn to separate themselves from past associations (high schools, community groups, and family) both physically and emotionally. Commuting students may not feel the separation as much as residential students. Commuters may continue to live at home, work at their job, and maintain their friendships. In making the transition to college, most students experience some type of adjustment. Ways of the past are no longer the norm, yet new ways are unclear and unfamiliar. It is at this point that first-year courses are successful in helping new students make the transition to college. Once students have gone through the separation and transition stages, they are now ready to embrace and accept the collegiate way. To successfully achieve the level of incorporation, students must become members of both the academic and social communities within the college or university.

6. *Vectors of development.* Chickering and Reisser (1993) believe students move through non-sequential but related "vectors" which include (a) developing intellectual, physical, and interpersonal competence; (b) managing emotions; (c) moving through autonomy toward interdependence; (d) developing mature interpersonal relationship; (e) establishing identity; (f) developing purpose; and (g) developing integrity. They argue that Vectors 1 through 4 deal primarily with issues of first-year students, while the other vectors apply to upper-level students. They also argue that students can be dealing with more than one vector at a time and may revisit vectors as new challenges emerge.

7. *Identity development.* According to Erikson (1959), "Who am I?" is the recurring question in identity development. He was the first to look at personality development in a social context and to define the process of identity development of youth. In each of his eight stages of development, a crisis occurs which must be successfully resolved if the person is to move to the next stage. Erikson believed that the task of establishing one's identity is particularly critical during the college years—a time when youth must redefine themselves. During Stage 5 (youth), students are discovering facets of their personality and attempting to define their personal identity. Students may be trying out new roles and assuming different personality traits as they attempt to answer the question, "Who am I?"

8. *Spiritual development.* The spiritual development of students is often overlooked and ignored in the literature. Fowler (1981) formulated seven stages of spiritual development.

Stage 1: undifferentiated (a "prestage" in infancy)

Stage 2: intuitive-projective (early childhood)

Stage 3: mythical-literal (childhood and beyond)

Stage 4: synthetic-conventional (adolescence and beyond)

Stage 5: intuitive-reflective (young adulthood and beyond)

Stage 6: conjunctive (mid-life and beyond)

Stage 7: universalizing (midlife and beyond)

For traditional-aged college students, Stage 3 and Stage 4 are the most relevant. Synthetic-conventional faith (Stage 3) becomes a basis for one's personal identity and synthesizes one's personal and family values. Stage 4, intuitive-reflective faith, occurs when individuals recognize the need to take responsibility for their commitments, lifestyles, beliefs, and attitudes.

9. *Wellness.* A more holistic view of students' psychosocial development is Hettler's (1980) wellness model, based on six dimensions: emotional, intellectual, physical, social, occupational, and spiritual. Emotional wellness focuses on a person's feelings about one's self, handling stress, and relationships with others. Intellectual wellness emphasizes learning activities both in and out of the classroom and utilizing as many resources as are available. Physical wellness stresses familiarity with exercise and nutrition, discourages the use of tobacco and drugs and excessive alcohol consumption, and warns against the dangers of sexually transmitted diseases. Social wellness is concerned with a sense of belonging to a community; it strives to achieve respect, tolerance, and cooperation among community members. Occupational wellness is about career exploration and planning. It entails finding a career suited to one's strengths and skills. Spiritual wellness is a lifelong process that involves "seeking meaning and purpose in human existence" (Leafgren, 1993, p. 446).

Student Learning and Today's Diverse Students

As discussed in the Chapter 2, our students are becoming increasingly diverse, which brings about new challenges to our conventional ways of teaching. This increased diversity also results in serious challenges to our ways of thinking about cognitive and psychosocial development. It was argued that these conventional theories fail to explain fully the development of underrepresented groups such as women; racial and ethnic groups; older students; international students; gay, lesbian, and bisexual students; student athletes; honors students; commuters; students with disabilities; and others (Upcraft, 1995).

For example it is now acknowledged that while students of color are in many ways similar to other students in their cognitive and psychosocial development, they are also different. Traditional theories make certain assumptions about the commonality of environments, cultures, and backgrounds of students that simply do not apply to many students of color. Being raised in a minority culture within a majority-dominated society may create different developmental outcomes for persons of the minority culture. Parental roles, child rearing practices, cultural values, community commitments and obligations, and other culture-related factors combine to produce different developmental dynamics for minority students (Upcraft, 1995). A brief synopsis of ways of looking at student learning from the perspective of the diversity of students is, therefore, essential.

1. *Multi-Racial development.* Because race is no longer just a Black/White issue but rather a multiracial issue, new models are needed to address the diversity of today's students. Atkinson, Morten, and Sue (1993) developed a five-stage model for students not in the majority. The model is a continuous process in which the stages blend together. Stage 1, the conformity stage, begins when students deny their cultural heritage and embrace the majority group's values. Dissonance, Stage 2, occurs when students' denial of their culture begins to breakdown. In Stage 3, the resistance and immersion stage, students feel guilty about having "sold out" in the past, feel angry about being oppressed, and search for information about their own heritage. As students move into Stage 4, introspection, they gain comfort with their sense of identity but also may experience some conflict. Students have a sense of loyalty and commitment to the minority group but are also trying to establish some autonomy. The synergistic stage is the final phase in the model. Students accept, embrace, and identify with their own culture; have a strong sense of self and self-esteem; and trust dominant-group individuals who also seek to eliminate discrimination and racism.

2. *African Americans.* Cross (1991) developed a five-stage model for Black identity formation. Stage 1 (preencounter) happens when a student views the world through a majority world perspective. The student has not dealt with his or her racial identity. Stage 2 (encounter) happens when the student experiences an event and becomes aware of his or her racial identity. This encounter does not need to be negative. In Stage 3 (immersion-emersion), the student searches for new meaning as a Black person, becoming immersed in African-American culture and values to the exclusion of other cultural norms. Stage 4 (internalization) has four possible outcomes: (a) continuation and rejection, (b) continuation and fixation at Stage 3, (c) internalization that brings satisfaction to the self but not a willingness to commit to the larger community, and (d) movement to Stage 5. In Stage 5 (commitment), the student has emerged with a new sense of self, committed to preserving the culture and values of the Black community.

3. *Native Americans.* Little research is available concerning the smallest minority group on campuses, American Indians. As noted in Chapter 2, American Indians account for less than 1% of all students in higher education. Those studying American-Indian development include Heinrich, Corbine, and Thomas (1990); Johnson and Lashley (1988); and Wright (1985). What we do know about American-Indian students is that most have inadequate academic preparation and believe in community-dominated values instead of individual ones. They also may not view White education as being as important as understanding the history, culture, and traditions of their tribe. Wright (1985) developed five ways to assist American-Indian students with their adjustment and development. These include: academic support services, counseling support services, ethnic studies, student centers and organizations, and hiring minority faculty and administrators to serve as role models.

4. *Hispanics.* The term "Hispanic" encompasses a diverse group that includes Cubans, Puerto Ricans, Mexicans, Chicanos, Central Americans, South Americans, Spaniards, and many others. Demographically, Hispanics are the fastest growing minority group on college campuses. We must be careful, though, not to lump all the groups together and assume that they have the same needs. Several people are studying Hispanic development including Martinez (1988) and Nora (1987).

Justiz and Rendón (1989) discuss barriers to Hispanic students' development. Many are first-generation college students who do not understand higher education or its benefits. Many come from low socioeconomic backgrounds, are poorly prepared academically, may not have adequate English writing and speaking skills, and bring the cultural belief that education is valued for males but not females.

5. *Asians.* Great diversity also exists within the Asian population. Several different groups in this category are Chinese, Japanese, Vietnamese, Korean, Filipino, Samoan, and many others. Psychosocial development of Asians has been researched by Sue and Morishima (1982) and Sue and Zane (1985), while Suzuki (1994) addressed academic development and achievement. Compared to White students, Asians "exhibit greater deference, abasement, and external locus of control and show less dominance, aggression, preference for ambiguity, and autonomy" (Sue & Morishima, 1982, p. 272). Many Asians also experience stress and alienation, study long hours, and are more lonely and anxious than other students (Sue & Zane, 1985). Adding to Asians' stress is an increase in racial harassment incidents. Suzuki (1994) found that Asians had high persistence rates but that their verbal and linguistic skills were underdeveloped.

Traditional theories make certain assumptions about the commonality of environments, cultures, and backgrounds of students that simply do not apply to many students of color.

6. *Adult learners*. Returning adult students differ from the traditional undergraduates in that the adults typically attend part-time, hold jobs, have family responsibilities, live at home, and have very different needs from traditional-aged students. Cross, in her landmark publication, *Adults as Learners* (1981), was one of the first to challenge the age bias of our student development theories. She asserted that adult students start with a self-evaluation which leads them to desire more education if their prior experiences were positive. They establish appropriate goals and expectations that may be based on life transitions—either gradual or related to traumatic events such as loss of a job, divorce, or the death of a friend or family member. They gather information about potential learning activities while they consider special opportunities and overcome barriers. Finally, they participate in some learning activity.

Schlossberg, Lynch, and Chickering (1989) view adult learning as a transition process that extends from the moment one thinks about returning to college to the time when the experience is complete and integrated into one's life. They break down the transition process for adult learners into three main parts: (a) moving into the learning environment, (b) moving through it, and (c) moving on, preparing to leave. For adult learners, the transition process may extend over many years—generally much longer than for traditional-aged students.

7. *Gender.* Until the early 1980s, most theorists assumed that men and women developed and learned in the same ways. Gilligan (1982) was one of the first to challenge that assumption and theorized that women are more concerned with the well-being of others and thus use a "voice of care." Men, on the other hand (or in another voice), are more likely to focus on justice and rights. Belenky, Clinchy, Goldberger, and Tarule (1986) also studied women's intellectual development and noted that women had five ways of knowing:

- silence (have no independent thoughts and are controlled by external sources)
- received knowledge (able to learn from external sources but unable to generate original thoughts)
- subjective (knowledge is personal, private, and based on intuition)
- procedural (learning based on procedures and rules)
- constructed (viewed themselves as creators of knowledge)

Further, Baxter-Magolda (1992) presents evidence that men learn differently from women.

For example, women may tend to be experiential, collaborative learners, while men may be inclined to work more analytically and individually.

8. *Students with disabilities.* With the passage of the Americans with Disabilities Act in 1990 and Section 504 of the Rehabilitation Act of 1973, colleges and universities have seen the enrollment of an increasing number of students with all types of disabilities. Institutions have two major responsibilities to these students: (a) they must not discriminate against the students, and (b) they must give meaningful access to them. Jarrow (1993) has identified three types of barriers for people with disabilities: architectural, attitudinal, and programmatic. Institutions must not only make buildings and facilities accessible (Nathanson v. Medical College of PA, 1991), but they must also ensure that these students have opportunities to learn. In addition, Section 504 mandates that auxiliary aids and services be provided if needed and that tests be structured to accommodate all types of learners' abilities. The key to working with students who have disabilities is communication. Students should notify the appropriate people of their learning disabilities so that the necessary provisions can be made. Faculty should be aware of the circumstances so that they can provide alternative teaching methods and testing procedures.

9. *Sexual orientation.* Models dealing with gay/lesbian/bisexual issues began emerging in the 1970s and 1980s. The main focus of these developmental models explain how gay, lesbian, and bisexual students come to terms with their sexual orientation. One of the most widely used models is Cass's (1979) homosexual identity formation. It is comprised of six stages (identity confusion, identity comparison, identity tolerance, identity acceptance, identity pride, identity synthesis). It begins with confusion about one's sexual identity, continues with an exploration and examination of the lifestyle, and ends with an acceptance and commitment to this identity. Others who address these issues include Evans and Wall (1991), Minton and McDonald (1984), and Coleman (1981-1982).

Student Learning Environments

All learning occurs in an environmental context. Students experience two primary environmental contexts: the classroom and the world outside of the classroom. Earlier in this chapter, we reviewed how components of these environments affect student learning, but a substantial body of theory also exists to help us understand how environments exert their influence. According to Upcraft (1995), in the late 1960s several sociologists argued that in order to have a complete understanding of how students develop and learn, one has to look not only at students, but also at the environments in which they live. They focused on the interpersonal aspect of the campus environment, with a special emphasis on the powerful influence of the peer group. The first notions about peer group influence were articulated by Newcomb and Wilson (1966), when they demonstrated peer group influence on first-year students during the first six weeks of college.

According to Feldman and Newcomb (1969), peer groups influence student learning in the following ways:

- helping students achieve independence from home and family
- supporting or impeding the institution's educational goals
- offering students general emotional support and fulfilling needs not met by the curriculum, classroom, or faculty
- giving students practice in getting along with people, particularly those whose backgrounds, interests, and orientations differ from their own
- providing students support for changing or for remaining the same
- affecting decisions about staying in or leaving college

In the 1970s, according to Upcraft (1995), the study of student environments expanded beyond the peer group to a more generalized concept of campus ecology. We began to look at the influence of campus environments on student learning, focusing on the relationship between the student and his or her environment and the impact of that interaction on academic success and personal development.

In 1973, the Western Interstate Commission for Higher Education outlined some of the basic assumptions of the ecological perspective based on research about college students. Students enter college with their own backgrounds, personalities, and experiences, facing an environment never before encountered. This environment can have a powerful impact on students, particularly traditional-aged first-year students, whose need to identify and affiliate with others is strong. This influence, however, cuts both ways. Students can also influence environments, and upper-class or older students appear to be less susceptible to environmental influences. College environments are mutable as well and can be influenced and channeled by the institution to enhance student success (Western Interstate Commission, 1973). When there is congruence between the student and his or her environment, the student is more likely to learn and succeed in college.

It should be noted, however, that campus climate influence may be minimal for older and part-time students, for whom the collegiate environment may be limited to the classroom. There is some evidence to suggest that certain classroom climates may be more conducive to adult learners than others. For example, Ennis et al. (1989) studied classroom environments and concluded that instructors who were seen by adult learners as most conducive to their learning were those who were open to discussing issues, had good communication patterns, put learning in a context relevant to their lives, and established mutual trust.

Additionally, for adult learners, home, family, and work may be their most influential environments, and the extent to which these environments are supportive of or detrimental to student learning is critical. For example, Darkenwald and Merriam (1982) found that among the factors which accounted for not participating in an educational activity were family problems and child care. Likewise, conflicts between work and education can be detrimental to adult student learning.

More recently, campus climate has become a volatile issue because there is some evidence that collegiate environments may have an adverse effect on underrepresented groups (Evans & Wall, 1991; Fleming, 1984) and women (Sandler, Silverberg, & Hall, 1996). Incidents of racial harassment, discrimination, and violence are, unfortunately, all too frequent in today's collegiate environment. So, too, are incidents of discrimination and violence against women, as well as against gay, lesbian, and bisexual persons. These students have an added burden placed on their ability to learn if they are in environments that are openly or implicitly hostile to them.

In the light of what appears to be a deterioration of campus communities, the Carnegie Foundation for the Advancement of Teaching (1990) offers a framework within which campus environments can be viewed. The foundation identifies five principles upon which to base a campus community committed to student learning.

1. It should be a *purposeful* community, a place where the intellectual life is central and where faculty and students work together to strengthen teaching and learning.

2. It should be a *just* community, where the dignity of all individuals is affirmed and where equality of opportunity is vigorously pursued.

3. It should be an *open* community, where freedom of expression is uncompromisingly protected and where civility is powerfully affirmed.

4. It should be a *disciplined* community, where individuals accept their obligations to the group and where well-defined governance procedures guide behavior for the common good.

5. It should be a *caring* community, where the well-being of each member is sensitively supported and where service to others is encouraged.

The bottom line for faculty teaching first-year students is that students function in various out-of-class environments that will influence their in-class learning. Becoming more knowledgeable about these environments and knowing ways of making these environments more conducive to student learning should be a critical role of faculty if we wish to maximize learning in our classrooms. There is evidence to suggest that faculty who spend time with students outside the classroom enhance the learning of students in their classrooms (Wilson, Gaff, Dienst, Wood, & Bavry, 1975).

Implications for Practice

The more we know about how students learn, both inside and outside the classroom, the greater the likelihood that they will learn more, and in greater depth. We can no longer naively believe that learning is simply a function of student ability and motivation. To be sure, these factors are important, but represent only two of many powerful factors that contribute to student learning. It is our responsibility as faculty to "know students," but we must know them in the more complex and multiple ways described in this chapter.

References

Astin, A. (1985). *Achieving educational excellence: A critical assessment of priorities and practices in higher education*. San Francisco: Jossey-Bass.

Astin, A. (1993). *What matters in college? Four critical years revisited*. San Francisco: Jossey-Bass.

Atkinson, D. R., Morten, G., & Sue, D. W. (1993). *CounselingAmerican minorities: A cross-cultural perspective* (4th ed.). Dubuque, IA: Brown & Benchmark.

Baxter-Magolda, M. B. (1992). *Knowing and reasoning in college: Gender-related patterns in students' intellectual development*. San Francisco: Jossey-Bass.

Belenky, M. F., Clinchy, B. M., Goldberger, N. R., & Tarule, J. M. (1986). *Women's ways of knowing: The development of self, voice, and mind*. New York: Basic Books.

Carnegie Foundation for the Advancement of Teaching. (1990). *Campus life: In search of community*. Lawrenceville, NJ: Princeton University Press.

Cass, V. C. (1979). Homosexual identity formation: A theoretical model. *Journal of Homosexuality, 4*, 219-235.

Chickering, A. W. (1969). *Education and identity*. San Francisco: Jossey-Bass.

Chickering, A. W., & Reisser, L. (1993). *Education and identity* (2nd ed.). San Francisco: Jossey-Bass.

Coleman, E. (1981-1982). Developmental stages of the coming out process. *Journal of Homosexuality, 7*, 31-43.

Cross, P. K. (1981). *Adults as learners*. San Francisco: Jossey-Bass.

Cross, W., Jr. (1991). *Shades of black: Diversity in African American identity*. Philadelphia: Temple University Press.

Darkenwald, G. G., & Merriam, S. B. (1982). *Adult education: Foundations of practice*. New York: Harper & Row.

Ennis, C. D., et al. (1989). Educational climate in elective adult education: Shared decision making and communication patterns. *Adult Education Quarterly, 39*, 76-88.

Erikson, E. (1959). Identity and the life cycle. *Psychological Issues Monograph, 1*(1), 1-171.

Evans, N. J., & Wall, V. A. (Eds.). (1991). *Beyond tolerance: Gays, lesbians and bisexuals on campus*. Washington, DC: American College Personnel Association.

Feldman, K. A., & Newcomb, T. M. (1969). *The impact of college on students*. San Francisco: Jossey-Bass.

Fleming, J. (1984). *Blacks in college: A comparative study of students' success in Black and White colleges*. San Francisco: Jossey-Bass.

Fowler, J. W. (1981). *Stages in faith: The psychology of human development and the quest for meaning*. San Francisco: Jossey-Bass.

Gardner, H. (1987). The theory of multiple intelligences. *Annals of Dyslexia, 37*, 19-35.

Gardner, H. (1993). *Multiple intelligences. The theory in practice*. New York: Basic Books.

Gardner, H. (1997). Are there additional intelligences? *Gifted Education Press Quarterly, 11*(2), 2-5.

Gilligan, C. (1982). *In a different voice: Psychological development and women's development*. Cambridge, MA: Harvard University Press.

Heinrich, R. K., Corbine, J. L., & Thomas, K. R. (1990). Counseling Native Americans. *Journal of Counseling and Development, 69,* 128-132.

Hettler, W. (1980). Wellness promotion on a university campus. *Family and Community Health Promotion and Maintenance, 3*(1), 77-95.

Jarrow, J. (1993). Beyond ramps: New ways of viewing access. In Responding to Disability Issues in Student Affairs (pp. 5-16). *New Directions for Student Services, 64.* San Francisco: Jossey-Bass.

Johnson, M. E., & Lashley, K. H. (1988). Influence of Native Americans' cultural commitment on preference for counselor ethnicity. *Journal of Multicultural Counseling and Development, 17*(30), 115-122.

Justiz, M., & Rendón, L. (1989). Hispanics. In M. L. Upcraft, J. N. Gardner, & Associates (Eds.), *The freshman year experience: Helping students survive and succeed in college* (pp. 261-276). San Francisco: Jossey-Bass.

King, P. M., & Kitchener, K. (1994). *Developing reflective judgment: Understanding and promoting intellectual growth and critical thinking in adolescents and adults*. San Francisco: Jossey-Bass.

Kolb, D. A., (1984). *Experiential learning: Experience as the source of learning and development*. Englewood Cliffs, NJ: Prentice-Hall.

Kuh, G. D., Douglas, K. B., Lund, J. P., & Ramin-Gyurnek, J. (1994). *Student learning outside the classroom: Transcending artificial boundaries*. ASHE-ERIC Higher Education Report No. 8. Washington, DC: The George Washington University, School of Education and Human Development.

Leafgren, F. (1993). Wellness as a comprehensive student development approach. In R. Winston, Jr. (Ed.), *Housing and residential life*. San Francisco: Jossey-Bass.

Martinez, C. (1988). Mexican Americans. In L. Comas-Diaz & E. E. H. Griffith (Eds.), *Cross-cultural mental health*. New York: Wiley.

Merriam, S. B., & Caffarella, R. S. (1991). *Learning in adulthood: A comprehensive guide*. San Francisco: Jossey-Bass.

Minton, H. L., & McDonald, G. J. (1984). Homosexual identity formation as a developmental process. *Journal of Homosexuality, 9*(2-3), 91-104.

Newcomb, T. M., & Wilson, E. K. (1966). *College peer groups: Problems and prospects for research*. Chicago: Aldine.

Nora, A. (1987). *Campus-based aid programs as determinants of retention among Hispanic community college students*. Houston: University of Houston, Institute for Higher Education Law and Governance.

Pascarella, E. T., Edison, M., Whitt, A., Nora, L., Hagedorn, L., & Terenzini, P. T. (1996). Cognitive effects of Greek affiliation during the first year of college. *NASPA Journal, 33*(4), 242-259.

Pascarella, E. T., & Terenzini, P. T. (1991). *How college affects students: Findings and insights from 20 years of research*. San Francisco: Jossey-Bass.

Perry, W. G., Jr. (1970). *Forms of intellectual and ethical development in the college years*. New York: Hold, Rinehart, & Winston.

Rendón, L. I. (1994). Validating culturally diverse students: Toward a new model of learning and student development. *Innovative Higher Education, 19*(1), 33-51.

Rodgers, R. (1989). Student development. In U. Delworth, G. Hanson, & Associates (Eds.), *Student services: A handbook for the profession* (2nd ed.). San Francisco: Jossey-Bass.

Sandler, B. R., Silverberg, L. A., & Hall, R. M. (1996). *The chilly classroom climate: A guide to improve the education of women*. Washington, DC: National Association for Women in Education.

Sanford, N. (1979). Freshman personality: A stage in human development. In N. Sanford & J. Axelrod (Eds.), *College and character*. Orinda, CA: Montaigne Press.

Schlossberg, N. K., Lynch, A. Q., & Chickering,

A. W. (1989). *Improving higher education environments for adults: Responsive programs and services from entry to departure*. San Francisco: Jossey-Bass.

Schroeder, C. C. (1993, September/October). New students—new learning styles. *Change, 25*(4), 21-26.

Sue, S., & Morishima, J. K. (1982). *The mental health of Asian Americans*. San Francisco: Jossey-Bass.

Sue, S., & Zane, N. W. S. (1985). Academic achievement and socioemotional adjustment among Chinese university students. *Journal of Counseling Psychology, 32*(4), 570-579.

Suzuki, B. H. (1994). Higher education issues in the Asian American community. In M. Justiz, R. Wilson, & L. Bjork (Eds.), *Minorities in higher education*. Phoenix, AZ: Oryx Press, American Council on Education.

Tinto, V. (1993). *Leaving college: Rethinking the causes and cures of student attrition* (2nd ed.). Chicago: University of Chicago Press.

Upcraft, M. L. (1995). Insights from theory: Understanding first-year student development. In M. L. Upcraft, & G. L. Kramer (Eds.), *First-year academic advising: Patterns in the present, pathways to the future* (Monograph No. 18) (pp. 15-22). Columbia, SC: University of South Carolina, National Resource Center for The Freshman Experience and Students in Transition.

Van Gennep, A. (1960). *The rites of passage* (M. Vizedon & G. Caffee, Trans.). Chicago: University of Chicago Press.

Western Interstate Commission for Higher Education (1973). *The ecosystem model: Designing campus environments*. Boulder, CO: Author.

Whitkin, H. A., & Moore, C. A. (1975). *Field-dependent and field-independent cognitive styles and their educational implications*. Princeton, NJ: Educational Testing Service.

Wilson, R. C., Gaff, J. G., Dienst, E. R., Wood, L., & Bavry, J. L. (1975). *College professors and their impact on students*. New York: Wiley-Interscience.

Wright, B. (1985). Programming success: Special student services and the American Indian college student. *Journal of American Education, 24*(1), 1-71.

Teaching First-Year College Students: Ten Tips for Success

Diane W. Strommer

CHAPTER 4

Few tasks in higher education prove more difficult than sustaining a first-year seminar course that is both rewarding for faculty who teach it and valuable for the students who take it. Whether the course focuses on student success, an introduction to the college or university, an interdisciplinary theme, or the basics of an academic discipline, many instructors encounter unexpected classroom challenges. Some have not taught a first-year student for a decade or more. The English professor's nostalgic image of engaging students in meaningful chats about life issues while perched on the edge of a desk evaporates against a row of bored faces. The microbiologist frets about teaching course content outside of what she *knows*, her area of specialization. The economist is as disquieted by discussing date rape as he would be discussing his sex life with the department chair.

Delivering the course as a requirement for all entering students, as increasing numbers of institutions do, also often means drawing upon faculty resistant to the very idea of a first-year seminar. To them, such a seminar smacks of "mollycoddling," "hand-holding," "high school stuff," or worse. Others more sympathetic to its aims nonetheless find teaching the course an imposition thrust upon them, a task that detracts from their higher purposes and offers them nothing in return for their expenditure of time and effort.

Even faculty both sympathetic to and clear about course objectives are not always certain of how to achieve them. Their first classroom experiences with new students may make them less so. Faculty unused to first-year students or those who know them only through large lectures are often disconcerted—even shocked—when they encounter student passivity, disengagement, resistance to discussion, and curious indifference to the content of a course specifically designed to meet their needs.

It does not need to be this way. As many faculty have discovered, teaching the first-year seminar can be a rejuvenating, exciting experience. By drawing upon what we know about first-year students and what we know about how students learn best, we can transform the seminar for first-year students into the campus model of the best practices to facilitate student learning. Teaching the first-year seminar can be a way for faculty to develop—and practice—new strategies and approaches to teaching, providing an extended opportunity to improve their craft that most faculty members welcome. Although the ten tips that follow introduce some of the more important principles in teaching the first-year seminar, faculty will soon discover that most readily transport to any college classroom.

1. Understand Your Students

The problem at the beginning of the semester is that the prof just didn't understand the students. I mean, she tried to relate to them, but she didn't understand where they were coming from and they didn't know the stuff she talked about. It was like they lived in two different worlds.

—Upper-class student mentor

Because different types of institutions tend to attract different types of students—community colleges enrolling more mature students, for example—generalizations about student populations can be risky. In an ideal environment, all of the data that colleges and universities collect about their students before and during their first college year would find their way to faculty and serve as a basis for discussions about teaching and learning, and faculty would know what they need to know about students at their institution. Gathering and reflecting on information about students are important not only because one cannot really teach *those* you don't know any more than you can teach *what* you don't know, but also because student generations change at an ever-accelerating rate, reflecting the rate of change in the larger society. Chapters 2 and 3 focus on the characteristics of today's students and issues related to their development and learning styles.

The social environment our students inhabit, what they learn (or don't) in high school, the skills and habits of study they have acquired, and the attitudes that they have about learning differ from those of earlier generations. How they learn, how they spend their time, how they think about learning, higher education, and their future—all of these matters influence their becoming effective learners. Faculty need to understand the worlds their students already inhabit, the experiences they have already had, in order to develop effective links from where they are to where we want them to be. We need to understand our students in order to provide the appropriate challenges and supports within our classrooms and to create an environment that fosters learning.

While students' worlds differ considerably from campus to campus, several key differences between today's new college students and their parents' generation are important to note, given a national average faculty age of over 50. The most obvious difference, of course, is that younger students were raised in a very different social environment with changing family patterns (the number of families headed by a single parent increased four percent in just the eight years between 1985 and 1993, for example). Some of the other major changes suggest societal failures: increased numbers of children raised in poverty and an increased gap between the poorest and the wealthiest, increased violence affecting young people, tensions and conflicts in communities and high schools between young people of different racial and ethnic groups, dating violence and date rape, substance abuse, teen pregnancy, and the lack—both real and perceived—of economic opportunity. Most commentators on our society agree that life is more difficult for young people today, and much of what they live with, especially unstable families and the influence of television, probably has a negative effect on learning, particularly on the ability to read and comprehend college-level texts.

As we have widened access and expectation for entering college, we have also welcomed new populations of students with new and different learning needs to our campuses. Nationally, the new majority in higher education are older students, part-timers, and community college-goers. But even among the traditional-age and middle-class student population, the college years no longer signify a unique, carefree period of life in which a "gentlemanly C" and an exposure to the great books and ideas are sufficient preparation for a career and for life—if indeed they ever were.

Few students today view college as a kind of finishing school but rather as a means to acquire the skills, knowledge, and experiences essential for survival in a society changing at a dizzying pace. Because many rely on work and loans to support their college years, their hectic schedules deny them the very involvement in campus life that has so richly benefitted many in previous generations and that we know positively affects student learning.

The disengagement and passivity that often distress faculty do not begin in the college classroom. Students come to us with assumptions about how learning occurs based on their high school experiences, which vary enormously from inner city to affluent suburb. Students from some communities might know more about information technology than their faculty; others have never turned on a computer. Just as their level of basic skills is more uneven than that of past student generations, so too is the way in which almost all of today's high school students spend their time. Nearly three quarters of high school seniors work, and many of them work long hours at dead-end jobs. No one should be surprised that seven or eight hours of flipping hamburgers or delivering pizza lead, as one study found, to less time spent on homework, fewer extracurricular activities, and less commitment to school. With less time on homework, little reading for pleasure, and more time spent working and watching television, students' decreased involvement in learning is well established by the end of high school (Erickson & Strommer, 1991; Gallo, 1997).

To consider the text, assignments, classroom activities, and even tests and quizzes as supporting course goals rather than as the goals themselves is an important shift in planning.

Knowing this and given the importance of time on task, involvement, and motivation to effective learning, what happens in our college classrooms should be no surprise. Many of our students are ill-prepared for college-style classrooms because they are used to frequent testing on brief bits of material and few, if any, cumulative exams; problem solving that does not necessarily progress to greater degrees of difficulty; the lack of the need to read difficult material and aids like extensive glossing by the teacher; and academic "credit" for nonacademic behaviors such as a pleasant classroom demeanor or extra work.

Understanding our students' backgrounds, however, should not lead us to lower our expectations, dumb down our curriculum, or have students avoid their responsibility. We need to understand them in order to create connections in our seminars and other classrooms—between what they know and what they need to know, to find links to motivate, encourage, and support them, but certainly not to doubt their ability to meet high standards or to lower our expectations of their performance.

Institutional research, the daily paper and weekly news magazines, as well as the annual freshman surveys by the Cooperative Institutional Research Program at UCLA (a summary is published mid-January in the *Chronicle of Higher Education*) are rich sources of information about today's students and their culture. The best source of all, of course, is the students themselves, and one of the delights and benefits of teaching the first-year seminar is the opportunity it affords faculty really to know their students.

2. Clarify Course Objectives

I think one of the problems with this course is that it just tries to do too much for one credit. I mean, we're trying to make the freshmen feel comfortable with one another and the university, teach them the computer and the library, and then there's all this other stuff, too. And it's only one credit.

—Upper-class student mentor

However the first-year seminar is structured, most have an agreed-upon set of course objectives. Sometimes, however, these objectives relate to the institution ("increase student retention") rather than to the students, and almost always they are overly ambitious. In designing the first-year seminar so that it will satisfy both academic liberals and conservatives, we often attempt to pack too much in, especially if the course is for just one credit. In course planning, one needs to consider the time available to meet course goals, time both for classroom activities and for student preparation.

Most of us find writing clear course goals enormously difficult because we have been trained to think about our courses in terms of covering content (with the hidden goal of the course being to get through the text) rather than in terms of what students will be able to do at its conclusion. To consider the text, assignments, classroom activities, and even tests and quizzes as supporting course goals rather than as the goals themselves is an important shift in planning. The critical issue for learning in any course is not what or how much content is covered but rather what students will achieve—what they will come to understand, what they will know or have memorized, what they will be able to do, and the behaviors they will perform, such as recalling ideas, recognizing examples, applying general principles to specific examples. These constitute the outcomes of the course.

Along with being less than precise about our course goals, most of us also underestimate what it takes to achieve them. Because students need considerable practice, we need to build practice into both in-class and out-of-class activities and assignments. One cannot, for example, assume that once we have "covered" e-mail by talking about it in class or by spending an hour using it in the computer lab that our students will be able to get on-line by themselves. If we want them to know how to use e-mail with ease, we need assignments that provide practice and plenty of it, like submitting journal entries on e-mail.

A good course syllabus thus includes statements of course goals to indicate the outcomes of instruction, which is not the same as the instructional methods or assignments. For example, "You'll become more familiar with campus resources" becomes "You'll identify two or three campus clubs of interest, learn when they meet, and attend one meeting to decide whether to pursue active involvement." "Lecture on using the World Wide Web" changes to "You'll be able to find at least three articles related to your major on the World Wide Web." Only when course goals are absolutely clear can the course's success be ascertained; only when the seminar program as a whole precisely states the ways in which it is trying to change student behavior and foster student learning can the program's effectiveness be accurately measured.

3. Attend to the First Class

This first class was definitely the most effective because this was to set the tone for all the coming classes. If the students didn't like this class, they might have dropped it. The first class is always one of the most important. You can tell a lot on the first day.

—Upper-class student mentor

Like the appetizer for a meal, the first day of class predicts what is to come. Is it to be tantalizing or flat? The first day makes students hunger for more or spoils their appetite. Handing out the syllabus and dismissing the students after 10 or 15 minutes gives students a powerful message: It announces that this class is not very important.

Most faculty experienced with the first-year seminar emphasize the importance of spending the first class period on two essential matters: (a) introducing students to the course and getting acquainted with one another by sharing some information about oneself, and (b) an icebreaker activity. One simple icebreaker asks pairs of students to gather information about one another, then to introduce one another to the rest of the class. One of our faculty members takes Polaroid shots of his students on the first class day. The students assemble a class collage that remains on view for most of the semester, helping everyone become quickly acquainted, and serving as a reminder of "where we were" at the end of the course. Another distributes name tags with the first name of another student to students as they enter. The recipient's task is to locate the name tag's "owner." A few weeks later the last name is added and sometimes the student's major, the residence hall, or another identifying piece of information.

An icebreaker that divides students into pairs or trios usually makes students more comfortable. One that several of our faculty have used successfully asks students in small groups to share (and record) not just their names and other personal information, but also some information related to the course—three ways in which they expect college to be different from high school (or the work force), for example. Within the larger group, the commonalties in these expectations are recorded for future discussion. With sufficient time, students might be asked to note the different skills they will need for success in college. Another exercise to identify common experiences is adapted from an article by Levine (1993). In pairs or small groups, students list the four or five "defining events" of their childhood and early adolescence, then share them with the entire class. Their answers typically identify their common experiences, reveal some interesting differences among them, and provide the instructor with an insight into the students' lives.

Such first-day activities lead naturally into a discussion of course goals and the significance to college-level learning of being actively involved and interacting with one's peers. Beginning students tend to be intellectual dualists, looking to the professor (or the text) as the source of all wisdom and truth. They are often impatient with group work and discount the views of their peers. By providing an example of how much they can learn from one another early in the course, they better understand not only why much of the world's work is done in cooperative groups but also how important to their learning peers are.

A syllabus that gives essential course information and a list of course goals but not a fixed week-to-week schedule allows students to participate in setting course priorities. When students can rank the course objectives in order of their importance to them, their sense of participation and ownership in the course increases, setting the stage for continued involvement.

4. Establish a Climate for Learning

There must be a comfort zone in these classrooms to ensure a productive class.

—Upper-class student mentor

Learning depends on more than intellectual ability. Motivation and self-confidence, the latter often in short supply among new college students, determine academic success as much as, or more than, native intelligence. As faculty, we tend to forget how hard learning can be. Most of us enjoyed unusual success in learning, at least in our own disciplines. Stephen Brookfield (1996), who has written extensively about teaching, observes that as faculty we lack the "autobiographical experience of struggle" (p. 5). He comments:

> Most teachers have never been in the same unfortunate position that many of their own students are in—the position of 'just not getting it'.... You are powerless to help your own students who are in this position because you have never lived through their experience of being blocked and unable to grasp the fundamentals of your discipline. (pp. 4-5)

Becoming a learner again, especially learning something personally difficult, can capture or recapture these emotional responses. Brookfield (1996) recommends to faculty that on "an annual basis we will deliberately put ourselves in the position of being a student who 'just doesn't get it'" (p. 5), as he did when, in his mid-40s and terrified of the water and failure, he decided to take swimming lessons. When we venture out of the comfort of what we know and into an area new and hard for us, we begin to feel what our first-year students feel and more readily grasp what we need to do (or to avoid) to help our students learn.

For good reason, one of the quality movement's first principles is "drive out fear." Parker Palmer (1983) in his book *To Know as We Are Known* sums up the reasons why the classroom must be a safe haven for students:

> A learning space needs to be hospitable not to make learning painless but to make the painful things possible, things without which no learning can occur—things like exposing ignorance, testing tentative hypotheses, challenging false or partial information, and mutual criticism of thought. (p. 74)

Student interaction also establishes the classroom as a "comfort zone." One way to ensure that students connect with one another is to set up classroom *base groups*. These four- to-five-student cooperative learning groups serve as a support group for their members. Johnson, Johnson, and Smith (1991), who outlined the functions and procedures for base groups, suggest that members sit together during class and that class time be allotted for members to check with one another, making sure no one is under undue stress, each is appropriately prepared for the class, progressing in learning the course material and developing academic skills, and becoming better acquainted. Class base group members also help one another by exchanging phone numbers, e-mail addresses, and other information to do assignments or study together or to swap information about missed classes.

Some research on learning also suggests that a class begun with music or with a brief activity to foster reflection (*pair up and decide the most important thing you learned from our last class, write for a couple minutes on two or three things the assigned article made you think of*) helps students focus their attention and become ready to learn.

5. Abandon the Non-Stop Lecture

The only real problem I saw was lecturing. To better impact these freshmen, we need activity. College is not just books and tests; it is growing and experiencing. To be told about the library or the history of the university or how to register for classes successfully is one thing—boring. To go on a tour, do a scavenger hunt around campus, or set up a mock registration where students can actually experience what college is all about is another—successful.

—Upper-class student mentor

Most research suggests that if one could simultaneously visit all undergraduate classrooms, in close to 80% one would see an instructor lecturing. What might be harder to discern is that "students are attentive to what is being said only about 50% of the time and retain only about 50% of what they actually pay attention to" (Pascarella & Terenzini, 1991). Non-stop lecturing is seldom effective instruction. The notion that it is effective is one of the myths exposed by Pascarella and Terenzini (1995) through their analysis of 20 years of research on the effects of college on students.

Having a variety of teaching strategies in our repertoire gives each student the opportunity to learn from their strengths from time to time. That, in turn, creates a climate in which diversity can thrive.

The other most common instructional methodology, the discussion, does not fare much better. A recent study of discussion in the college classroom (Nunn, 1996) confirmed earlier findings that the professor's talk occupied 80% of class time, leading the author to conclude that "learning at the college level is a 'spectator sport.'"

To *learn*—that is, to be able to use information by retrieving, applying, synthesizing, categorizing, or generating inferences from it—we must break new information into meaningful chunks, or categories, and make connections between them and things we already know. When a new concept is introduced, therefore, students must not only be able to link it to a framework they already understand (linking new information to the wrong framework is a source of most wildly erroneous student ideas), but they also need practice in thinking in terms of that concept. That means generating their own examples of the concept, summarizing it, explaining it to someone else, and applying it. Doing so works with the mind's natural processes, and that in turn improves learning.

Research in cognitive science has clarified much about how people learn and the many differences among us in such matters as multiple intelligences and learning styles. Research on the Myers-Briggs Type Indicator, for example, suggests that extroverted sensors (ES), active/concrete learners and thinkers, represent 50% or more of high school seniors and introverted intuitives (IN), or abstract/reflective thinkers and learners, appear only in about 10% of high school seniors. Other studies show that the largest group of college students also consists of concrete/active learners, who learn best from direct experiences that engage their senses, that begin with practice and end with theory. As Schroeder (1993) points out, the majority of college faculty, however, apparently prefer the IN (abstract/reflective) pattern. The typical result is that faculty teach as they like best to learn, but not as their students learn best.

Differences in learning style mean, primarily, that we differ in which activities seem natural and come easily and which feel awkward, require more concentration, and take longer to do. Despite having a preference, however, we all can learn in a variety of ways. Paying attention to learning styles in the first-year seminar by administering and discussing the Kolb Learning Style Inventory or the Personal Style Inventory in Gardner and Jewler (1992) can help students better understand themselves as learners and encourage them to expand their approaches to learning.

No faculty member can be expected to teach to every student's preferred learning style, but understanding learning styles provides a basis for developing the class assignments and activities to teach the diverse students in our courses. Having a variety of teaching strategies in our repertoire gives each student the opportunity to learn from their strengths from time to time. That, in turn, creates a climate in which diversity can thrive.

Given the knowledge explosion, our notions of what students need to know are also changing. As one prominent British educational leader (Marchese, 1996) put it, "people world-wide need a whole series of new competencies" to cope with change, to work collaboratively, to learn continuously, and to solve problems. These competencies are more readily acquired when students are actively engaged in learning.

At least four good reasons exist to abandon the non-stop lecture and to rely instead on classroom activities and assignments that encourage student activity and involvement: (a) research on attention span, (b) evidence about how we learn from cognitive science, (c) learning style difference, and (d) the new competencies essential for lifelong learning.

6. Involve Students with Varied Activities[1]

Just because the professor isn't lecturing doesn't mean that the class can be unstructured. We found breaking the class into small groups and having specific activities related to the topic to be an effective teaching style. This became the game-plan for most classes.

—Upper-class student mentor

Although the benefits more than make the effort worthwhile, the shift to active learning strategies requires planning and preparation. Students expect and sometimes welcome the passive role lectures encourage and look on their faculty as the sole classroom authority, so they need to understand the reasons for a different approach. In order to establish the climate for cooperation, Prescott (1996) suggests that faculty do the following in their courses:

1. Explain that research on learning shows that students learn more when they work actively and collaboratively in groups in class.

2. Discuss the relationship of developing skill in working in groups to their current or future employment.

3. Tell them that the content in the group tasks is directly related to the content that will be on exams, papers, and projects.

4. Lead a discussion on specific skills that help to facilitate pair or group work.

5. Make sure that partners or group members have a chance to connect with one another. (p. 11)

One way to bring students' concerns about pair or group work to the fore is to make group work itself the topic for a small group discussion, following the steps suggested below. Further discussion can lead to developing class rules or guidelines to ensure successful group work. A case study that briefly chronicles a group project gone awry, "A College Classroom Discussion Group" (Cagen & Wright, 1986), provides another method to raise concerns about group work and to set classroom standards collaboratively.

Small Group Discussion

The ideal of the discussion method implies that the instructor poses provocative questions that elicit responses from the entire class. As we have noted, that ideal is far from the reality. A few fearless or assertive students participate; the rest sit passively, disengaged; the instructor winds up talking almost as much as in a lecture. Dividing students into pairs, trios, or small groups of four to six increases the participation of individual class members. Individual students will pose questions, make suggestions, and raise issues in small groups when they would remain silent in a larger group.

The instructor typically follows these steps for a small group discussion:

1. Divide students into pairs, trios, or small groups of four to six students.

2. Pose a question or assign a task to be completed with a prepared group response in an allotted period of time (putting the assignment in writing as a hand-out or an overhead avoids confusion).

3. Move from group to group during the discussion to ensure that students remain on task and to observe participation and any points of confusion that may require clarification then or later.

4. End group discussion for reports to the whole class.

5. Record group responses and assist students in drawing conclusions or synthesizing the results of the discussion to provide closure for the activity.

Pairs or trios work best for short or impromptu assignments while small groups work best for longer activities. Some assignments can begin with pairs and then have each pair join another for a further step. Small group discussion activities must be carefully structured and timed. A sampler of open-ended structures appropriate for pair or small group work in the first-year seminar follow:

- *Application cards.* Instructors distribute index cards and ask students to write down a real-world example or application for a concept, principle, theory, or procedure they are studying. Angelo and Cross (1993) provide several examples of this technique that encourages students to connect new material to prior learning and experience and to assume responsibility for seeing the relevance of what they are studying. After writing down their example or application, students form pairs or trios to discuss their examples.

- *Guided reciprocal peer questioning.* In this activity, the instructor provides a set of generic question stems for students to use as a guide for generating their own specific questions on course material. With the help of question stems, each student individually writes two or three thought-provoking questions in five minutes or less. Students do not need to be able to answer the questions they pose. They then form groups of three or four and take turns querying one another. Generic question stems include:

  What is the main idea of. . . . ?
  What if. . . . ?
  How does . . . affect. . . . ?
  What is the meaning of. . . . ?
  What is a new example of. . . . ?
  Explain why. . . .
  Explain how. . . .
  How does this relate to what we've learned before?
  What conclusions can I draw about. . . . ?
  What is the difference between . . . and. . . .?
  How are . . . and. . . . similar?
  What are the strengths and weaknesses of. . . . ?
  What is the best . . . and why?

  At the end of the allotted time, students report their insights, examples, and other matters that arose in their group to the class (Cottell & Millis, 1994).

- *Minute paper.* Near the end of the class period, instructors distribute index cards and ask students to respond briefly to two questions: "What was the most important thing you learned in this class?" and "What important question remains unanswered?" (Angelo & Cross, 1993). This writing-to-learn exercise can become a pair activity by asking students to share their responses and then attempt to answer each other's unanswered questions. Any unanswered questions can be posed to the whole class. Angelo and Cross (1993) suggest variations that ask for (a) the most illuminating example, (b) the most powerful image, (c) the most convincing argument or counterargument, (d) the most surprising information, (e) the most memorable character, or (f) the most disturbing idea.

- *Muddiest point.* Instructors ask students to jot down a quick response to the question "What was the muddiest point in today's class (or reading or film or discussion)?" (Angelo & Cross, 1993). Then students form pairs or small groups to see if they can clarify one another's questions. Instructors collect the cards, identifying points that remain "muddy," and begin the next class with an activity to clarify them.

- *Popular media logs.* Students scan popular media—newspapers, magazines, television—for stories and events related to course content. Students must first summarize key issues or ideas discussed in the article. Then, depending on the type of article, students discuss the impact of the event(s) reported, assess conflicting positions on an issue, or evaluate the credibility and arguments used in attempts to persuade (Johnson & Johnson, 1993). Students' media logs can be the basis of a small group discussion, with members of the group selecting the best example to share with the entire class.

- *Paired discussions.* In three to five minutes students discuss something with the person next to them (summarize; react to theory, concepts, or information presented; relate today's material to past learning; come up with additional examples; and so on). For best results, the discussion topic should be as specific as possible (Kalish, 1996).

- *Question and answer pairs.* Outside of class, students develop questions relating to the assignment (a reading, an event, or another activity) that deals with the major points raised. At the beginning of class, students form pairs. One student asks his first question, the partner answers. The first student may correct the answer or give additional information. Then the second student asks her question and the first answers. The instructor monitors the process, interacting when it seems appropriate (Johnson, Johnson, & Smith, 1991).

- *Reaction sheet.* After presenting a controversial topic, instructors ask pairs or small groups to answer these three questions: (a) What ideas do you question? (b) What ideas are new to you? and (c) What ideas really hit home? Follow up with whole class discussion (Kalish, 1996).

- *Think-Pair-Share.* In Think-Pair-Share, the instructor poses a question or problem and gives students a minute or two to think through a response. Students then pair with a neighbor to share and discuss their responses. In a third stage, pairs may also be invited to share their responses with another pair or with the entire class. Think-Pair-Share explicitly sets time for students to think before discussion begins, which may be important for students who need time to collect their thoughts. Discussing their responses in pairs enables all students to test their ideas and receive feedback from at least one other person in a relatively short amount of time (King, 1993).

- *Truth statements.* Ask students in small groups to decide on three things they know to be true about some particular issue. This is useful when introducing a new topic that students think they know well, but about which their assumptions need to be examined (Kalish, 1996).

- *Value lines.* Students line up according to how strongly they agree or disagree with a proposition or how strongly they value something. This gives a visual reading of the continuum of the feelings in the group. Next, sort students into heterogeneous groups for discussion by grouping one from either end with two from the middle. Ask students to listen to differing viewpoints in their group and to paraphrase opposing positions fairly (Kalish, 1996).

Case Studies, Simulations, and Role Plays

First used in medicine and law and, more recently, in business schools, case studies have been shown to be effective learning tools. Because they are concrete and realistic, they are particularly effective in engaging students who are concrete/active learners. As Meyers and Jones (1993) point out, another value of case study is the opportunity it provides for students to become involved in higher-order levels of reasoning as they analyze and evaluate situations and form judgments. Although an effective case cannot be written on the spot, they are not difficult to put together. The key is to find a real or plausible event or situation that tells a story, illustrates the issue you wish to discuss, allows identification with the characters, contains conflict, and is sufficiently ambiguous and open-ended to prompt lively discussion and different points of view. For the first-year seminar at one university, case studies based on actual campus situations involving alcohol abuse have proven an effective way to engage students often weary of yet another pass at alcohol education.

Brief cases of a few paragraphs can be distributed in class; longer ones should be assigned for reading ahead of time with a list of questions to consider in a small group discussion. So that students focus on the broad issues that a case presents, the questions should guide their initial discussion to ensure understanding of the basic facts of the case. The next step is typically to determine (a) those points in the narrative when alternative courses of action were possible to reach different outcomes or make different decisions, and (b) what courses of action the characters should follow. As with all small group discussion, allowing sufficient time for summary and closure is important.

Role plays and simulations are closely related. In role-playing activities, students receive an outline of a real or hypothetical situation and a description of the character they are to play. Students then improvise dialogue and actions to fit their views of the situation and the character they are playing. Role plays of interactions (a) between faculty and a student concerning an advising session, a disagreement about a grade, or a class absence; (b) between roommates about having guests overnight; or (c) between students and parents about a change of major all provide practice in handling situations often problematic for new students.

A variation on role play developed for the first-year seminar by one of our faculty begins by asking students to write on separate index cards three conflicts faced since entering college. Then through small group discussions, the class attempts to resolve the conflicts. Finally, each group is assigned an unresolved conflict to present at the next class meeting as a skit. While a group is acting, another member of the class who thinks he or she sees a solution to the conflict may interrupt the action by calling out "Freeze!" and changing places with one of the actors.

The goal is, as always, to engage students in learning actively and to afford occasions for application and practice.

Simulations may be longer versions of an improvised role play or one of the many simulation games developed in several disciplines. Many excellent simulation games from the field of intercultural studies are appropriate for engaging students in discussions of diversity in the first-year seminar. The following example, "Tag Game," is taken from *Intercultural Sourcebook: Cross-Cultural Training Methods* (Fowler & Mumford, 1995). It can be used as an ice breaker or as an introductory exercise before a discussion of diversity issues:

> Students are given tags of different shapes and colors and told to walk around silently observing each other. Then they are instructed to form groups, still remaining silent. After a time, they are asked to form different groups. After at least four rounds of forming new groups, they trade their original tags for new, unique tags. Again they observe, but do not talk, while they decide how to form groups during four more rounds. After the game, participants are asked to first discuss on what basis they formed groups and then to list all the obvious similarities and differences among people they can think of. Eventually, they begin to identify deeper-seated, more intangible abstract similarities and differences. The discussion usually prompts discussion of in-group/out-group issues and the recognition that people have a stronger attachment to likeness than to diversity.

Debate

Formal or informal debates are another good way to involve students in understanding multiple sides of a complex issue and to foster the development of critical thinking skills. Bean (1996) provides a useful list of suggestions for holding a fairly formal classroom debate on a controversial proposition, one adaptable to most courses. Small groups can also debate an issue. They might be asked to identify the four best arguments for (or opposed to) a proposition by sharing their views and brainstorming (i.e., without evaluation or criticism) to make a list of all the arguments of which they can think. When they have exhausted their ideas, they then select the four best to share with the entire the class.

A strategy called "Forced Debate" asks all students who agree with a proposition to sit on one side of the room and all opposed on the other side. Hanging signs describing the proposition helps. It is important that students physically take a position and that the opposing sides face each other. After they have sorted themselves out, the instructor switches the signs, forcing students to argue for the position with which they disagree (Kalish, 1996).

Other Methods

Field trips (even to other places on campus), serious games, and media (particularly film and video clips) all vary classroom activities and engage students. Some cautions are in order, however. The single, all-purpose library field trip rarely accomplishes its purpose. Providing too much information irrelevant to the immediate needs of first-year students wastes time and teaches little. Consider instead three or four short course assignments that build basic library skills. And while excellent videos and video clips exist on many topics pertinent to the first-year seminar, a 50-minute video can have the same soporific result as a 50-minute lecture. Showing or playing only key scenes in a video and planning a small group discussion or a writing-to-learn follow-up activity ensure student involvement. The goal is, as always, to engage students in learning actively and to afford occasions for application and practice.

7. Provide Opportunity for Reflection

I think the best time in our class was when we all talked about our community service project and what it had meant to us. We really came together as a group and learned a lot from one another and from what we did.
—Upper-class student mentor

While commentary on higher education frequently refers to students' need to become "lifelong" or "self-directed" learners, how this is supposed to occur is seldom specified. All too rarely do we offer students opportunities to connect what they have learned with their lives or to reflect on how they are learning. Yet in these ways they develop critical thinking skills and expand their notion of learning as something other than memorization.

Perry's (1970) study of students' intellectual development and those of others in the field (Belenky, Clinchy, Goldberger, & Tarule, 1986) remind us that many college students are in the intellectual position of dualism. That is, they view knowledge as facts, information, and right answers and their instructors and texts as the authorities who will provide what they need to know. They understand their role as students primarily as one of learning what is passed on—that is, to memorize the facts and to respond correctly on tests. Students in this intellectual position tend to discount their own experiences and the experiences of their peers; they do not necessarily make a connection between "learning" and "life." To become self-directed learners, they need to understand better how they learn. Increasing the opportunities for reflection about learning aids students' intellectual development.

For this reason, some first-year seminars assign a journal. If not carefully guided, however, the result is likely to be a diary, a list of problems or grievances, or a recounting of events, rather than the student's analysis and reflection. When one reflects about something, one adds to observations and experiences and considers their meaning in a larger context. It is the meaning of an experience that the journal entry should convey. Because this is not easy to do, particularly when one has not had much practice, instructors need to make clear journal assignments, provide examples of good entries, and guide initial submissions.

Succumbing to student arguments that if a journal is a student's thinking about the meaning of experiences, then one journal is as good as another, faculty sometimes shy from grading journals. But journals do differ in terms of quality and can be evaluated on some fairly objective bases. The following criteria fit many journal assignments:

1. *The care and quality of the writing.* Are the entries slap-dash, or does the writer put them together thoughtfully? Are they well-organized and grammatical, with accurate spelling and punctuation?

2. *The nature of the subject.* Do the entries suggest that some serious thought has been given to deciding which issues and topics to raise, or does the author select only the most obvious topics to write about?

3. *The nature of the reflection.* Has the writer given consideration to the issues and topics raised, or does he or she immediately respond with the trite and hackneyed (e.g., "well of course, 'boys will be boys'")?

4. *The demonstration of growth.* Does the journal progress, or is the author noting pretty much the same matters at the end as he or she did at the beginning? Have his or her reflections broadened and deepened, or are they at the same level as at the beginning of the semester?

While journals are a fairly standard method for encouraging reflection, activities such as portfolios, concept maps and other visual displays, and classroom assessment techniques like the "minute paper" or "ethical dilemmas" (Angelo & Cross, 1993) also encourage students to pause and mull over what is happening to them intellectually.

8. Take Risks

Although it is good to keep open to new ideas and developing topics, it is important to have a planned structure for the class. The class needs to be full of information and activities or you will encounter bored students and dull responses.

—Upper-class student mentor

Faculty who have taught the first-year seminar for many years often report that it takes about three years of experience to get it right. If one is used to teaching solely in an area in which one is an expert, it is risky to start talking about career development, binge drinking, or even a new interdisciplinary field. If one is used to lecturing behind a podium, moving around a class observing small groups at work feels strange. If one normally teaches to anonymous large classes, having students discuss details of their lives can be discomforting. If one is used to teaching only upper-class majors or graduate students in the discipline, the diversity of freshmen can be bewildering.

Under their bravado, new students often enter our classrooms convinced they are dopier than most, more likely to make fools of themselves, and less likely to find friends. But, as Palmer (1983) reminds us,

> teachers, too, enter the classroom with fears; at least I do. I am afraid of being inadequately prepared, of having my own ignorance exposed, of meeting the glazed eyes and bored expressions of some of my students. Behind my role and my expertise, I wonder what they think about me as a person. They may be afraid of my power over their lives, the power of the grade and credential, but I am afraid of the negative or ambivalent feelings my power creates in them. I need their affirmation as much as they need mine; I need a sense of community with them that our roles make tenuous. (p. 74)

So it is not unusual to spend the first year as a seminar instructor sorting through one's diverse reactions to the experience, determining what one's role will be as perhaps a different kind of classroom teacher than one had been trained to be. One tries out new things—some case studies perhaps, a simulation game, some small group work. One abandons a well-wrought class plan to attend to an immediate issue. Some things fail, and they are discarded; others are successes, and they remain.

It is a risky business, teaching the first-year seminar. But year after year, faculty learn that it can be the beginning of a whole new phase in their academic careers, one they would not give up for anything. Although the small community formed in these seminars differs in many ways from more conventional classes, at their best they model the ideal of teaching the whole person and being a whole person when we teach.

9. Include Upper-Class Students

I couldn't have gotten through the semester without my student mentor. Not only did she understand the freshmen, she also understood an amazing amount about teaching. I can't tell you how much I learned from her.

—First-year seminar instructor

While the first-year seminar provides an invaluable window on the new student's world, seeing clearly through that window is easier when you have an experienced student to help. Many first-year seminar programs include an experienced student as part of the instructional team. Some students are paid; others receive course credit. They need to be trained, however, but that is a matter beyond the scope of this chapter.

What needs to be emphasized here is that working effectively with a student mentor is itself a skill. Time spent clarifying the mentor's classroom role is important to a successful relationship. Because students who seek the mentor role genuinely care about helping first-year students adjust to higher education and expect opportunities to offer that guidance, they are frustrated when faculty give them little responsibility.

Classes based on small group discussion and activities rather than lecture enable student mentors to exercise their leadership. Mentors can often assume responsibility in guiding students with library assignments, with computer skills like e-mail or creating a Web page, and in leading small group discussions. Mentors are an invaluable resource to the first-year seminar when trained and empowered as part of a teaching team.

10. Develop a Support Group

Steal liberally from the activities and ideas that others use. Find out what's working well for other instructors. Talk with them often.

—First-year seminar instructor

Training workshops, periodic meetings throughout the semester, listservs, or other communication from directors of first-year seminar programs smooth the way for the new first-year seminar instructor. We all need a little help from our friends, and if your institution does not offer opportunities to meet periodically with others involved in the seminar program, create them. During the first year of the seminar program on our campus, several small groups of faculty met regularly to plan activities and share ideas for handling the course material. Not only did the students benefit from and enjoy a number of the results—a field trip, a spirited contest among sections—but the faculty enjoyed the opportunity to work with people on campus they might otherwise never have known. As one colleague revealed at the end of the course, "This has been one of the richest teaching experiences of my life. Not only did I learn more about students and teaching than I ever imagined possible, but I've also made new friends on the faculty." Weekly or monthly brown bag lunches with fellow instructors focused on topics pertinent to the first-year seminar sustain and renew the most experienced among us.

References

Angelo, T., & Cross, P. (1993). *Classroom assessment strategies.* San Francisco: Jossey-Bass.

Bean, J. C. (1996). *Engaging ideas: The professor's guide to integrating writing, critical thinking, and active learning in the classroom.* San Francisco: Jossey-Bass.

Belenky, M. F., Clinchy, B. M., Goldberger, N. R., & Tarule, J. M. (1986). *Women's ways of knowing: The development of self, voice, and mind.* New York: Basic Books.

Brookfield, S. (1996). Through the lens of learning. In L. Richlin (Ed.), *To improve the academy: Vol. 15* (pp. 3-15). Stillwater, OK: New Forums Press and the Professional and Organizational Development Network in Higher Education.

Cragan, J., & Wright, D. W. (1986). *Communication in small group discussion: An integrated approach.* St. Paul, MN: West.

Erickson, B. L., & Strommer, D. W. (1991). *Teaching college freshmen.* San Francisco: Jossey-Bass.

Fowler, S. M., & Mumford, M. G. (Eds.). (1995). *Intercultural sourcebook: Cross-cultural training methods.* Yarmouth, ME: Intercultural Press.

Gallo, N. (1997, February 1). How the work ethic works against teens: Special report. *Family Circle.*

Gardner, J. N., & Jewler, A. J. (1992). *Your college experience: Strategies for success.* Belmont, CA: Wadsworth.

Johnson, D. W., & Johnson, R. T. (1993). Creative and critical thinking through academic controversy. *American Behavioral Scientist, 37*(1), 40-53.

Johnson, D. W., Johnson, R. T., & Smith, K. A. (1991). *Cooperative learning: Increasing college faculty instructional productivity.* Washington, DC: The George Washington University School of Education and Human Development.

Kalish, A. (1996). A change-up sampler. *The National Teaching and Learning Forum, 5*(2).

King, A. (1993). From sage on the stage to guide on the side. *College Teaching, 41*(1), 30-35.

Levine, A. (1993). The making of a generation. *Change, 25*(4), 8-15.

Marchese, T. (1996, March) The search for next-century learning. *AAHE Bulletin*, 3-6.

Meyers, C., & Jones, T. H. (1993). *Promoting active learning: Strategies for the college classroom.* San Francisco: Jossey-Bass.

Nunn, C. (1996) Discussion in the college classroom: Triangulating observational and survey results. *Journal of Higher Education, 67*(3), 244-266.

Palmer, P. J. (1983) *To know as we are known: A spirituality of education*. New York: Harper Collins.

Pascarella, E., & Terenzini, P. (1995). The impact of college on students: Myths, rational myths, and some other things that may not be true. *NACADA Journal, 15*(2), 26-33.

Pascarella, E., & Terenzini, P. (1991). *How college affects students: Findings and insights from 20 years of research.* San Francisco: Jossey-Bass.

Perry, W. G., Jr. (1970). *Forms of intellectual and ethical development in the college years: A scheme.* New York: Holt, Rinehart, and Winston.

Prescott, S. (1996). Memorandum. *Cooperative Learning and College Teaching, 6*(3), 10-11.

Schroeder, C. C. (1993). New students—new learning styles. *Change, 25*(4), 21-26.

Notes

[1]I wish to acknowledge the contribution of my friend and colleague Betty LaSere Erickson to this section. She first identified and adapted some of the activities described here for the Instructional Development Program at the University of Rhode Island. She has given me permission to include them here.

Approaches to Group Learning in the New-Student Seminar

Joseph B. Cuseo

CHAPTER

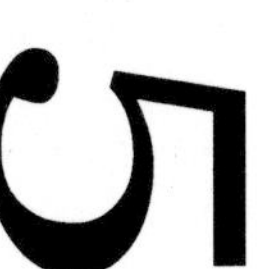

Barefoot and Fidler (1996), working under the aegis of the National Resource Center for The First-Year Experience, conclude from their national research and professional experience with new-student seminars that "'Successful' seminars—those that enjoy strong broad-based institutional support and long life—are those [in which] instructors are trained in basic methods of group facilitation and active learning pedagogies: Course "process" becomes as important as course 'content'"(p. 61). One such method for facilitating the active involvement of the group is collaborative learning, an umbrella term for a variety of pedagogical practices that are gaining momentum in American higher education. As evidence of this trend, the number of scholarly publications concerning collaborative learning has increased dramatically during the 1990s, as has the number of professional conferences and workshops devoted to this topic (Cooper, 1996).

The terms collaborative learning and cooperative learning are often used interchangeably, but subtle differences exist between the two in actual practice. Collaborative learning is a much broader term, encompassing a variety of approaches to group learning methods. Unlike students in the traditional classroom, students in the collaborative classroom exercise greater autonomy and take on greater responsibility for goal setting, for designing learning tasks and monitoring progress toward completion, and for assessing their own learning success. The hallmarks of the collaborative classroom are shared knowledge among teachers and students, shared authority among teachers and students, mediated learning where teachers serve as mediators rather than authorities, and heterogeneous groupings of students (Tinzmann, Jones, Fennimore, Bakker, Fine, & Pierce, 1990). The term cooperative learning, on the other hand, was originally developed with reference to the K-12 classroom. In the cooperative setting, group learning activities occur in small "base" groups that are highly structured by the classroom instructor. In addition to content mastery, a primary goal of cooperative learning is to help students master appropriate problem-solving skills through active engagement in the learning process (Davis & Murrell, 1993).

This chapter will review the research that supports the educational value of student collaboration and then will examine specific instructional strategies for implementing collaborative or more structured cooperative learning in college courses, particularly first-year courses, such as the new-student seminar.

Research Supporting the Value of Collaborative Learning

Empirical support for the effectiveness of collaborative learning in promoting college students' academic achievement is provided by research on peer tutoring which indicates that both the peer learner and the peer teacher (peer tutor) learn significantly from such collaborative experiences (Whitman, 1988). College students display deeper levels of understanding for concepts they that teach to their peers (Bargh & Schul, 1980; Benware & Deci, 1984), and they achieve greater mastery of course content (Johnson, Sulzer-Azaroff, & Mass, 1977). Based on their review of teaching and learning research in higher education, McKeachie, Pintrich, Lin, and Smith (1986) conclude that, "The best answer to the question of what is the most effective method of teaching is that it depends on the goal, the student, the content, and the teachers. But the next best answer is `Students teaching other students'" (p. 63).

Perhaps the most dramatic evidence supporting the value of collaborative learning for college achievement is that generated by Alexander Astin's (1993) national, four-year longitudinal study of students at 159 four-year institutions. This large-scale research project revealed that the form and content of the general education curriculum had no significant effect on a wide range of student outcomes related to general education; what did have the most significant impact on student achievement and development was student-student interaction. This empirical finding strongly suggests that classroom pedagogical practices which promote meaningful collaboration among students should make a significant contribution to student achievement, particularly in general education courses that predominate during the first year of college.

Research strongly suggests that two essential elements of effective retention are active involvement in the learning process and social integration with other members of the college community (Astin, 1993; Tinto, 1993).

The opportunity to gain access to other students' perspectives and to learn from peers, rather than from the instructor only, may be particularly important for promoting the cognitive development of first-year college students. Longitudinal research conducted by Perry (1970) on college students' developmental stages indicates that recent high school graduates enter college at an initial stage of cognitive development characterized by two general dispositions: (a) a tendency to view academic issues in polar terms (right versus wrong), with right answers being seen as absolute and known by an authority (e.g., the teacher—whose job is to teach students these absolute truths), and (b) a tendency to perceive multiple viewpoints and diversity of opinion (e.g., differing theories or methodologies) as bothersome, representing unwarranted confusion generated by inept or unqualified authorities. Participation in small peer-learning groups may be effective for stimulating student progress to more advanced stages of cognitive development characterized by an appreciation of contextual relativism and a tolerance for multiplicity. The peer learning group periodically removes the instructor from center stage, reducing the likelihood that the teacher is perceived as the ultimate or absolute authority. It also exposes students to the perspectives of other students, increasing their appreciation of multiple viewpoints and different approaches to learning and thinking.

One reason why students learn so effectively from their peers may be that peers are better able to explain certain concepts than the instructor because the peer teacher and learner are at a more similar stage of cognitive development than teacher and student (Vygotsky, 1978). Another reason may be that peers have greater similarity in levels of experience with respect to the concept being learned (Whitman, 1988). Also, the perceived similarity of the peer teacher by the peer learner may result in greater identification with the teacher, resulting in a greater likelihood that effective learning strategies modeled by the peer teacher will be emulated by the learner (Bandura, 1977).

Collaborative learning groups comprised of three to six peers may multiply the advantages associated with peer tutoring because multiple peer-teaching models are available when students work together in groups. Astin (1993) offers a similar explanation for the effectiveness of small-group learning in his research-based book, *What Matters in College?*:

> Under what we have come to call cooperative learning methods, where students work together in small groups, students basically teach

> each other, and our pedagogical resources are multiplied. Classroom research has consistently shown that cooperative learning approaches are superior to those obtained through traditional competitive approaches, and it may well be that our findings concerning the power of the peer group offer a possible explanation. (p. 428)

Furthermore, research at the college level suggests that effective learning strategies acquired from peers during *in-class* collaborative learning activities tend to transfer positively or "spill over" to study strategies used individually by students *outside of class* (Larson, Dansereau, O'Donnell, Hythecker, Lambiotte, & Rocklin, 1984). This research also suggests that collaborative learning activities used in class tend to increase the likelihood that students will join together to study collaboratively outside of class (Wheeler, 1992). Thus, collaborative learning procedures can be expected to magnify the effectiveness of the peer tutoring process—both inside and outside the classroom.

Collaborative learning also represents an effective instructional strategy for promoting student retention. Student attrition is alarmingly high in American colleges and universities. Approximately 40% of all students who begin college never complete a degree program (Tinto, 1993), and the attrition rate is significantly higher for commuter students (Astin, 1977; Pascarella & Terenzini, 1991) as well as for students who are members of underrepresented racial or ethnic groups (Carroll, 1989; Ottinger, 1991).

Research strongly suggests that two essential elements of effective retention are active involvement in the learning process and social integration with other members of the college community (Astin, 1993; Tinto, 1993). Collaborative learning implements each of these retention-promoting principles by allowing students to become actively engaged in the learning process and by enabling them to interact with their peers. The opportunity to work regularly in small groups serves to promote social integration, peer networking, and emotional "bonding" among students.

The relevance of collaborative learning for the new-student seminar is underscored by the fact that two of the most frequently cited goals of new-student seminars reported in national surveys are (a) to promote the "social integration of students," and (b) to help students achieve a "felt sense of community" (Barefoot & Fidler, 1996, p. 6). The need to realize these goals early in the college experience is suggested by research indicating that social integration or social adjustment is the most demanding and highest-priority issue experienced by first-year students during their initial weeks on campus (Brower, 1990; Simpson, Baker, & Mellinger, 1980). The new-student seminar pioneered by John Gardner at the University of South Carolina (University 101), which now serves as a national model, has always emphasized small-group interaction as a means of promoting student bonding and retention (Gardner, 1980). Collaborative learning lends itself to fostering social-emotional ties among first-year students because of its emphasis on positive interdependence and frequent small-group interaction.

The peer networking facilitated by collaborative learning should appeal to traditionally aged (adolescent) students because they have strong peer affiliation needs (Conger, 1986). For reentry (adult) students, in-class peer networking might not only be desirable, it may be essential for effective retention. Reentry students have little or no opportunity for out-of-class social interaction with other students because they commute to school, and the only time they may spend on campus is the time they spend in the classroom. Thus, the retention-promoting impact of instructional practices that promote student-student interaction in the classroom could play a pivotal role in promoting the retention of commuter and part-time students, whose numbers are rising on college campuses (U.S. Department of Education, 1994). Research consistently reveals that these students are "at risk" because their college attrition rate is significantly higher than that of full-time residential students (Astin, 1993; Chickering, 1974). Collaborative practices which promote student-student interaction inside the classroom may provide this "curricular" antidote to commuter and part-time students' lack of co-curricular involvement outside the classroom. In-class collaborative learning experiences may provide these students with "intra-curricular" opportunities for peer interaction and social integration which could alleviate their historically high rates of attrition.

The importance of collaborative learning for the retention and achievement of underrepresented students is strongly supported by the work of Uri Treisman (1985) and others (Green, 1989). Treisman studied the effects of collaborative learning on African-American students who entered the University of California, Berkeley as math or science majors. He found that African-American students participating in his collaboratively-taught tutorial sessions received a mean grade-point average of 2.6 in freshman calculus, whereas a comparable group of African Americans who did not attend the collaborative sessions received a mean grade-point average of 1.5. Five-year retention rates at Berkeley for African-American students participating in collaborative learning workshops was 65%, while the retention rate for black non-participants was 41%.

More recently, these findings were replicated in a five-year longitudinal study of underrepresented Latino students enrolled in mathematics, science, or engineering programs at California Polytechnic State University, Pomona. This study revealed that fewer than 4% of the Latino students who participated in out-of-class collaborative learning sessions withdrew or were academically dismissed, compared to 40% of non-participants (Bonsangue, 1993).

Collaborative learning can provide college students with the "education for teamwork" needed to prepare them for the world they will encounter after graduation....

Collaborative learning also has potential for realizing the general-education goal of promoting active and responsible citizenship in a democratic society. In *Renewing Civic Capacity: Preparing College Students for Service and Citizenship*, Suzanne Morse (1989) identifies one major civic competency as "the ability of individuals and groups to talk, listen, judge, and act on issues of common concern" (p. 6). Collaborative learning encourages collective responsibility and the pursuit of a common goal, both of which are consistent with this civic competency. The powerful role that collaborative learning can play in serving democracy and promoting community is well articulated in the following argument made by the late Ernest Boyer (1987):

> If democracy is to be well served, cooperation is essential. The goal of community is essentially related to the academic program and, most especially, to procedures in the classroom. We urge, therefore, that students be asked to participate in collaborative projects, that they work together occasionally on group assignments... and that special effort be made to create conditions that underscore the point that cooperation is as essential as competition in the classroom. (p. 151)

Collaborative learning can also serve to better prepare college graduates for the contemporary workforce. Reports from today's business leaders reveal that they need to provide extensive "in-house" or "on-the-job" training and development for college graduates, particularly in the areas of small-group interaction and teamwork (American Society for Training and Development, 1988; Holton, 1992; Wingspread Group, 1993). College alumni themselves report that the biggest gap in their college preparation involves working "effectively in groups to accomplish goals" (Marchese, 1990, p. 6).

According to Astin (1988), the major reason why college graduates are unprepared to engage in teamwork is the preoccupation of general education with the *content* of the curriculum at the expense of attending to the *process* of learning—one key element of what he calls the "implicit curriculum." This oversight, he argues, may be contributing to the schism between the individualistic, competitive experiences of college students and the collaborative demands of today's workplace:

> The implicit curriculum, at least as it is manifested in the typical undergraduate liberal arts program today, is not designed to foster such qualities [interpersonal trust, teamwork]. On the contrary, it seems more likely to encourage competitiveness, individualism, and a relative lack of interest in co-workers. (p. 10)

Collaborative learning can provide college students with the "education for teamwork" needed to prepare them for the world they will encounter after graduation and, in so doing, will enable higher education to achieve one of its most oft-cited goals: preparing undergraduates for life after college (Cross, 1982).

Instructional Strategies for Promoting Collaborative Learning

The following instructional strategies are recommended for promoting effective collaboration among students in any college course, particularly first-year courses such as the new-student seminar.

1. *Use icebreakers to provide students with early opportunities to get to know each other.*

Given the power of first impressions, the first day of class represents the ideal time to provide students with some opportunity to get to know each other. Icebreakers are effective first-day vehicles for (a) introducing students to each other, (b) reducing students' social anxiety, and (c) building group trust and cohesiveness among classmates. Icebreakers and group building activities are plentiful, from the simplest pairing of two students to exchange information on personal interests to far more elaborate and involved exercises. Effective icebreakers have two very basic characteristics: They are structured in such a way that all group members must be actively involved, and they produce new knowledge of group members through active sharing of ideas and information.

At some institutions, outdoor activities have been used as icebreaker and team-building strategies in the new-student seminar. For example, at Eastern Washington University, rock-climbing instruction, followed by a rock-climbing expedition that requires team coordination, is used as a team-building experience at the outset of the course (Higman, Chase, & Wagner, 1994). Though not all institutions are geographically situated to allow for such "outward bound" experiences, other types of out-of-class informal settings (e.g, the instructor's home or a scenic spot on campus) may provide a retreat-like atmosphere conducive to building class community and a social foundation for future collaboration.

2. *Periodically allow students to work in pairs (dyads) to maximize peer interaction.*

When students work in pairs or dyads, maximum face-to-face interaction is achieved and an optimal level of verbal involvement or interchange between students is realized. (An individual is least likely remain passive or "hide in the crowd" if the "crowd" consists of only two people.) Research also indicates that students' memory for course concepts is enhanced significantly when the instructor occasionally pauses for several minutes to allow students to work in pairs to discuss and rework their notes (Ruhl, Hughes, & Schloss, 1987). Specific practices for promoting paired-peer interaction include the following collaborative learning procedures:

- "Think-Pair-Share": Students think alone about a question or issue, then pair up with a student partner to share their ideas (Lyman, in Kagan, 1992).
- "Think-Pair-Square": Students think alone, pair up with a partner to discuss their individual thoughts, then join another pair of students to a form small group of four ("square") for further discussion (Kagan, 1992).
- "Scripted Cooperation": Students form pairs after listening to a segment of lecture, and one member of the pair summarizes the information presented to the partner who then provides feedback about the accuracy and comprehensiveness of the other's summary. Lastly, the partners jointly attempt to relate the information to their personal experiences or to other course concepts (O'Donnell, 1994).

3. *Occasionally divide the class into three to five member discussion groups to provide students with opportunities for small-group interaction.*

Small discussion groups provide opportunities for the development of oral communication skills which are rarely promoted in the introductory, general education courses typically experienced by first-year students (Gardner, 1993). The importance of occasionally conducting small-group discussion in addition to, or in lieu of, whole-class discussions is suggested by the research of Nunn (1996) who found that only 25% of students in a given class participated in class discussions. Consistent with this finding, Karp and Yoels (1976) observed that in classes of less than 40 students, four to five students account for 75% of all interactions; and in classes with more than 40 students, two to three students account for over half the exchanges. They also discovered that students themselves are acutely aware of this phenomenon because 94% of students surveyed agreed with the statement: "In most of my classes, there are a small number of students who do most of the talking." Moreover, research indicates that students perceive themselves to be less active in class than do their professors (Fassinger, 1995).

The need to redress these disturbing patterns of student participation is underscored forcefully in a national research report released by The Carnegie Foundation for the Advancement of Teaching:

> All students, not just the most aggressive or most verbal, should be actively engaged. It is unacceptable for a few students to participate . . . while others are allowed to be mere spectators. (Boyer, 1987, p. 150)

The potential of small-group discussions to engage these less "aggressive" or less "verbal" students is highlighted by research indicating that students who are most apprehensive about communicating in the classroom have a preference for discussing things in small, rather than large groups (Neer, 1987).

To increase the quality and quantity of student communication during small-group discussions, the following practices are recommended:

- Prior to having students discuss their ideas in small groups, instructors may want to give students some private time to gather their thoughts individually. Having personal reflection time before engaging in verbal interaction should enrich the quality and depth of the ideas exchanged and should also increase the likelihood that shy or verbally apprehensive students will contribute. Research suggests that these students are more likely to do so if they have thought about the topic in advance (Neer, 1987).

- Instructors may ask groups to keep a visible record of the ideas they generate. If possible, each group should be provided with a flip chart or transparency on which their ideas can be recorded and displayed.

- Instructors should notify students that *any* member of the group may be called on to report the group's ideas. This serves as an incentive for all members to listen actively to the ideas of others in addition to their own.

4. Assign group projects that require students to work together outside of class.

The group's final project can be presented collaboratively in the form of a jointly-constructed written report (e.g., term paper) or oral report (e.g., panel presentation). Grades for group projects can be assigned on an individual or group basis, or some combination thereof. For example, the performance of the individual and the group may be graded separately and then combined or averaged to generate each student's grade for the project. However, it should be noted that survey research on students who have participated in group projects indicates that high-achieving students report great dissatisfaction with projects in which each member of the group is given the same undifferentiated grade (Fiechtner & Davis, 1992). These findings suggest that instructors should build at least some degree of individual accountability and individual grading into the evaluation of the group's final overall product.

5. Emphasize the value of peer study groups and facilitate their formation.

The educational value of study groups is supported by research conducted with first-year students at Harvard University which indicates that academic achievement is enhanced appreciably when first-year students engage in collaborative, study-group sessions outside of class (Light, 1990, 1992). In particular, the Harvard-based research reveals that first-year students who work in small study groups outside of class tend to (a) express a substantially higher level of personal interest in their course work, (b) commit more time to their course work, and (c) display more willingness to seek help from others (Buchanan, Feletti, Krupnick, Lowery, McLaughlin, Riesman, Snyder, & Wu 1990).

One way such out-of-class collaboration can be encouraged is for the instructor to offer to construct a class directory containing the phone numbers of students who are interested in working with other students or forming study groups outside of class. Another strategy for encouraging out-of-class study groups is to assign students to groups based on their semester class schedule. Instructors assign students taking the same course(s) to the same group when forming discussion groups or when assigning group projects. Such groupings may increase the likelihood that these same students will get together out of class to work on the other courses they have in common, particularly if the instructor explicitly encourages them to do so.

Since instructors cannot directly observe and monitor study groups because they meet outside of class, it is recommended that specific guidelines be provided to students for the purpose of optimizing the quality of their study-group work. One strategy is to provide study groups with some in-class time to work together. This would enable instructors to observe their patterns of interaction and provide them with constructive feedback.

Cooperative Learning Practices: Maximizing the Impact of Small-Group Work

The highly-structured nature of cooperative learning (CL) practices lends itself to maximizing the effectiveness of small-group work. The primary objective of CL is to structure and "fine tune" group work in a fashion that maximizes its strengths and minimizes its weaknesses (Cooper, Prescott, Cook, Smith, Mueck, & Cuseo, 1990; Johnson, Johnson, & Smith, 1992). More specifically, CL attempts to strengthen the effectiveness of small-group work by means of the following seven procedural features, which when implemented together, distinguish it from other forms of collaborative learning in higher education.

1. Intentional group formation

In contrast to traditional approaches to small-group formation, in which students often select their own group members or groups are randomly formed by the instructor, CL begins with the intentional selection of group members—on the basis of predetermined criteria—in order to potentiate the positive effects of small-group learning. For instance, groups may be deliberately formed to maximize heterogeneity and diversity of perspectives by grouping students of different (a) gender, (b) racial, ethnic, or cultural background, (c) chronological age (e.g., traditional age and reentry students), (d) level of prior academic achievement (e.g., based on performance in high school or on early course exams), (e) learning style (e.g., based on learning-style inventories completed in class), (f) personality profile (e.g., based on the Myers-Briggs Type Indicator), or (g) some combination of any of the foregoing selection criteria.

The particular criterion used to form groups, and whether students are grouped heterogeneously or homogeneously with respect to this criterion, may vary depending on the instructor's objectives or the characteristics of students in the class. However, a thematic procedural principle of CL is that group formation is not left to chance; instead, careful forethought is given to the question of who comprises each learning group, attempting to create an optimal social-learning environment for the instructor's intended educational objective.

2. Continuity of group interaction

In contrast to traditional small-group discussions or "buzz groups" which usually bring students together sporadically for a relatively short period of time (e.g., a single class period or portion thereof), CL groups may meet regularly over an extended period of time (e.g., every class period for five weeks or more). This allows for continuity of interaction among group members and opportunity for social cohesion and "bonding" (emotional ties) to develop among group members. In this fashion, CL groups are given the time needed to evolve into a tightly knit social network or social-support group.

3. Interdependence among group members

Rather than simply allowing students to interact in small groups, and then hoping they will do so in a collaborative manner, CL incorporates specific procedures designed to create a feeling of group identity among students and a sense of collective responsibility (positive interdependence) for one another's learning. The following CL procedures are used to increase the likelihood that a sense of positive interdependence develops within groups.

Group production of a common product at the end of the cooperative learning experience. In contrast to usual small-group discussions that typically involve informal discussion of some course-related issue, each CL group is expected to generate a formal product which represents a concrete manifestation of the group's collective effort—for example, completion of a work sheet, a list or chart of specific ideas, or an overhead transparency which can be displayed to other groups. The objective of working toward a common, tangible outcome is essential for keeping individual students "on task" and focused on the group goal—the creation of a unified product reflecting their group's concerted effort.

Assignment of interdependent roles to different group members. A sense of personal responsibility to the group may be increased if each member has a specific and indispensable role to play in achieving the group's final goal. For instance, individuals within the group could be assigned the following interdependent roles: (a) group manager who assures that the group stays on task and that all members actively contribute, (b) group recorder who keeps a written record of the group's ideas, (c) group spokesperson who is responsible for verbally reporting the group's ideas to the instructor or other groups, and (d) group processor who monitors the social interaction or interpersonal dynamics of the group process (e.g., whether individuals listen actively and disagree constructively).

Specialized roles can also be assigned in terms of (a) different perspectives that each group member contributes to the final product (e.g., historical, ethical, economic, and global perspectives), or (b) different higher-level thinking skills each member contributes to the final product (e.g., application, analysis, synthesis, and evaluation).

Role specialization assures that each individual has an explicit and well differentiated responsibility to the group throughout the learning process. A further advantage of such role specialization is that the quality of each member's contribution to the final product can be readily identified and assessed by the instructor, thus ensuring individual accountability.

Team-building activities designed to produce a sense of group identity and social cohesiveness. Such activities include (a) having groups participate in icebreakers or warm-up activities when they are first formed (e.g., name-learning, personal information-sharing, team photos, team names), and (b) providing groups with explicit suggestions and concrete recommendations for promoting cooperation and teamwork (e.g., phone-number exchange, group review of lecture notes, and study-group formation).

The educational objective of these team-building activities is to create a social-emotional climate conducive to the development of an esprit de corps and sense of intimacy among group members, enabling them to feel comfortable in future group activities that may require them to express their personal viewpoints, disagree with others, and reach consensus in an open (non-defensive) fashion. Small-group learning involves cognitive and social risk-taking, and students are more likely to take such risks in an interpersonal climate characterized by group cohesiveness, mutual trust, and emotional security. Furthermore, explicit attention to the social and emotional foundations of effective small-group interaction may serve to increase students' social integration into the college community—a variable that is strongly correlated with student retention (Pascarella & Terenzini, 1991).

Provision of individual rewards as an incentive for promoting group interdependence. This has been the most hotly debated CL strategy for creating group interdependence because it involves extrinsic rewards for cooperative behavior. For example, group interdependence may be rewarded by a grading policy which grants all group members extra (bonus) points toward their course grades if (a) any individual member improves her score from one exam to the next, or (b) if each group member's performance exceeds a certain criterion (e.g., each member achieves a score of at least 90%).

Some practitioners of CL oppose this strategy because they feel it is unnecessary; they believe that students become intrinsically motivated to cooperate and take responsibility for helping others as long as they are given a well-defined task and the opportunity to work together. Other critics feel that providing extrinsic rewards for helping others tends to destroy intrinsic motivation for behaving cooperatively and altruistically.

However, those who do use incentives feel that, if group-performance rewards are not large—for example, if they represent only "bonus" points, rather than a significant portion of the course grade, then such incentives can significantly enhance group interdependence and promote academic achievement (Slavin, 1989).

Since the issue of whether or not to use extrinsic rewards for promoting interdependent behavior in CL groups is still unresolved, it is perhaps best to consider this strategy as an *optional* rather than essential procedure for promoting group interdependence.

4. Individual accountability

Though procedures for ensuring interdependence and cooperation among group members are essential elements of CL, students receive individual grades, i.e., all group members do *not* receive the *same* "group grade" (as is often the case with group projects). Research at the K-12 level consistently supports the importance of personal accountability and individual grading for realizing the positive outcomes of CL (Slavin, 1990). These precollegiate findings are reinforced at the college level by experimental research in social psychology which documents the phenomenon of "social loafing," i.e., the effort exerted by an individual working in a group will be less than that exerted by the same individual working alone—unless the individual's particular effort or output in the group is not anonymous, but clearly identifiable (Williams, Harkins, & Latane, 1981). These experimental findings are consistent with anecdotal and survey reports from high-achieving students who often contend that they dislike group projects in which all group members receive the same, undifferentiated "group grade" because their individual effort and contribution to the group's final product often exceeds the efforts and contributions of their less motivated teammates—the "social loafers"—all of whom inequitably receive the same grade (Fiechtner & Davis, 1992).

5. Explicit attention to the development of social skills

In contrast to the exclusively "academic" objectives of most small-group work in higher education, a major objective of CL is the intentional development of students' interpersonal communication and human relations skills. To achieve this objective, CL typically involves the following procedures:

Explicit instruction on effective skills for communicating and relating to others is given to students prior to, and in preparation for, their involvement in small-group learning activities. This instruction may include explicit strategies for (a) encouraging and supporting other group members, (b) listening actively, (c) learning to disagree constructively, (d) resolving conflict, and (e) building consensus. Thus, students receive adequate preparation and guidance for handling the social and emotional demands of small-group work, rather than being left entirely to their own devices.

Provision of opportunities for students to reflect on, and to evaluate the social-interaction process. Students' "meta-social" awareness is encouraged by having them assess the group interaction with respect to already-learned principles of effective interpersonal communication. In addition, CL students are sometimes asked to reflect on how their social interaction in groups has affected their individual learning. For example, students may be asked, "Do you find that you learn more or less (a) when you verbalize your thoughts to other group members? (b) when there is disagreement between yourself and another group member? and (c) when you question the reasoning of other group members?" Opportunities to reflect on such questions relating to the impact of the social process on individual learning may serve to promote students' meta-cognitive awareness of the covert thought processes that undergird effective learning.

The importance of such cognitive self-awareness for first-year college students is underscored by Erickson and Strommer (1991) in *Teaching College Freshmen*:

> The distinction between learning *what* to think and learning *how* to think is a subtle one for freshmen; it takes some time to get it. Until they do, reviewing what students gain by participating in these [collaborative] exercises at least reminds them that we have a clear purpose in mind to aid and support their learning. (pp. 120-121)

Effective interpersonal behavior displayed by students within groups is explicitly recognized and verbally reinforced by the instructor, then shared with the entire class to provide them with specific examples or models to be emulated in future group interactions. During CL, the instructor is alert not only to the cognitive aspects of group work, but also to the social aspects. Specific instances of effective interpersonal communication exhibited by students in their learning groups are praised by the instructor and used to reinforce and showcase concrete manifestations of important human relations' principles.

6. *Instructor as facilitator*

In contrast to most small-group discussions and group projects, where students are left on their own to verbalize their ideas and conduct their work, CL involves the instructor as a facilitator and consultant in the group-learning process. Though the instructor does not sit in on individual groups (such intrusiveness might disrupt the student-centered advantage of group learning), he or she will circulate actively among the groups to: (a) offer encouragement, (b) reinforce positive instances of cooperative behavior, (c) clarify task expectations, (d) catalyze dialogue, or (e) issue timely questions designed to promote cognitive elaboration and higher-order thinking. As Erickson and Strommer (1991) suggest,

> Students often need step-by-step prompts, hints, and feedback when they first encounter problems or situations that ask them to think. In fact, we recommend that initial practice exercises be done in small groups *in class* where instructors are available for such guidance. (p. 76)

Being careful not to be overly directive or authoritative, the instructor functions as a learned peer or collegial coach, interacting with students in a much more personal, informal, and dialogic fashion than would be possible in the traditional lecture or whole-class discussion format. Interacting with students in this fashion not only benefits the learner, it also benefits the instructor by enabling him or her to know his students better (e.g., their names, their ways of thinking, their styles of communicating and relating to others).

In contrast to the exclusively "academic" objectives of most small-group work in higher education, a major objective of CL is the intentional development of students' interpersonal communication and human relations skills.

7. *Attention to intergroup dynamics by coordinating interaction between different groups and integrating their separate work products*

The issue of fostering communication between different learning groups and effectively synthesizing their separate work products is an important one because of its potential for (a) bringing a sense of closure to the group-learning experience (Millis & Cottell, 1998), (b) promoting potentially powerful synergy across work generated by individual learning teams, and (c) creating class community or solidarity whereby students perceive the class as an interrelated and unified "group of groups." Though there may be many occasions where small-group work is an end in itself and cross-group interaction is unnecessary, at least periodic attempts should be made to transform the separate experience of small, isolated groups into a larger, unified learning community. This transformation can be achieved by having a representative from each group share his or her group's main ideas with the rest of the class. A second strategy involves the use of "roving reporters" who move from their original group to a new group. Each reporter shares his or her group's ideas with the new group while this group attempts to integrate these ideas with their own. A similar process merges two small groups that share and synthesize their separate work. The final product reflects an amalgamation of their own work and the best ideas gleaned from their successive interactions with other groups.

These different intergroup-interaction strategies have common objectives and advantages, namely (a) providing meaningful synthesis and closure to the learning experience, (b) promoting class synergy by harnessing and pooling the ideas generated by separate learning groups, and (c) allowing students to meet and collaborate with other classmates beyond those who comprise their small group. In this fashion, group-building is augmented by class-building, and a classroom of students that was initially "deconstructed" into separate and isolated subgroups is subsequently "reconstructed" into a single, interdependent learning community.

The foregoing seven features of CL, taken together, distinguish this instructional technique from traditional methods of small-group instruction and student collaboration in higher education (Cuseo, 1992). Large-scale, meta-analyses (quantitative synthesis of many studies relating to a particular educational variable or instructional method) of hundreds of studies at the precollege level provide overwhelming empirical documentation for the cognitive, social, and affective benefits of CL—when its implementation is consistent with the procedural elements described herein (Johnson, & Johnson, 1989; Slavin, 1990.

Research on CL in higher education is much less extensive, but data collected thus far are very consistent with those gathered in precollegiate settings (Cooper & Mueck, 1990; Cuseo, 1996; Johnson, Johnson, & Smith, 1992). Recent evidence for the positive impact of CL is provided by a meta-analysis of its effects on college students' academic performance in science, math, engineering, and technology conducted by the National Institute for Science Education. Over 500 studies of small-group collaboration were included in this meta-analysis, and it was found that CL had a "robust" positive effect on such educational outcomes as (a) academic achievement, (b) student retention, and (c) attitude (like/dislike) toward the subject matter (Cooper, 1997).

Thus, it is reasonable to expect that faithful application of the distinctive procedural features of CL should ensure that its broad spectrum of potential positive outcomes will be realized in higher education as well.

Conclusion

Engaging students in collaborative learning experiences, such as those described in this chapter, enables the new-student seminar instructor to employ first-year students as a social learning resource in the college classroom. Capitalizing on this social resource with instructional methods that foster peer collaboration can provide beginning college students with a welcome alternative to other first-year courses that rely almost exclusively on traditional teacher-centered instructional methods, such as the lecture.

Collaborative learning is a student-centered instructional strategy that can combat higher education's over-reliance on the lecture method—and its tendency to convert college learning into a passive, isolated, individualistic, and often competitive affair—by transforming it into an active, interactive, and interdependent experience.

Furthermore, use of collaborative learning during the first year of college may establish an initial "mental set" or mental habit among beginning students—characterized by active involvement, individual accountability, and collective responsibility—which may be maintained and applied to learning across the curriculum. Moreover, if collaborative-learning methodology is incorporated into the new-student seminar's instructor training program, and this program is offered as a faculty development experience for all instructors on campus, then it may have a positive impact on teaching across the curriculum as well.

References

American Society for Training and Development. (1988). *Workplace basics: The skills employers want*. Washington, DC: U.S. Department of Labor.

Astin, A. W. (1988). The implicit curriculum: What are we really teaching our undergraduates? *Liberal Education, 74*(1), 6-10.

Astin, A. W. (1993). *What matters in college*? San Francisco: Jossey-Bass.

Bandura, A. (1977). *Social learning theory*. Englewood Cliffs, NJ: Prentice-Hall.

Barefoot, B. O., & Fidler, P. P. (1996). *The 1994 survey of freshman seminar programs: Continuing innovations in the collegiate curriculum*. (Monograph

No. 20). National Resource Center for The Freshman Year Experience and Students in Transition, University of South Carolina.

Bargh, J., & Schul, Y. (1980). On the cognitive benefits of teaching. *Journal of Educational Psychology, 72*, 593-604.

Benware, C. A., & Deci, E. L. (1984). Quality of learning with an active versus passive motivational set. *American Educational Research Journal, 21*(4), 755-765.

Bonsangue, M. V. (1993). The effects of calculus workshop groups on minority achievement in mathematics, science, and engineering. *Cooperative Learning and College Teaching, 3*(3), 8-9.

Boyer, E. L. (1987). *College: The undergraduate experience in America.* New York: Harper & Row.

Brower, A. (1990). Student perceptions of life-task demands as a mediator in the freshman year experience. *Journal of The Freshman Year Experience, 2*(2), 7-30.

Buchanan, C. H., Feletti, G., Krupnick, C., Lowery, G., McLaughlin, J., Riesman, D., Snyder, B., & Wu, J. (1990). *The impact of Harvard College on freshman learning. A pilot study conducted in the Harvard Seminar on Assessment.* Cambridge, MA: Harvard University.

Carroll, C. D. (1989). *College persistence and degree attainment for 1980 high school graduates.* Washington, DC: National Center for Education Statistics.

Chickering, A. W. (1974). *Commuting versus resident students.* San Francisco: Jossey-Bass.

Conger, J. J. (1986). *Adolescence and youth* (3rd ed.). New York: Harper & Row.

Cooper, J. L. (1996). Research on cooperative learning in the mid-1990s: What the experts say. *Cooperative Learning and College Teaching, 6*(2), 2-3.

Cooper, J. L. (1997). New evidence of the power of cooperative learning. *Cooperative Learning and College Teaching, 7*(3), 1-2.

Cooper, J. L., & Mueck, R. (1990). Student involvement in learning. *Journal on Excellence in College Teaching, 1*, 68-76.

Cooper, J. L., Prescott, S., Cook, L., Smith, L., Mueck, R., & Cuseo, J. (1990). *Cooperative learning and college instruction: Effective use of student learning teams.* Long Beach, CA: California State University Institute for Teaching and Learning, Office of the Chancellor.

Cross, K. P. (1982). Thirty years have passed: Trends in general education. In L. B. Johnson (Ed.), *General education in the two-year colleges* (pp. 11-20). San Francisco: Jossey-Bass.

Cuseo, J. (1992). Cooperative learning versus small-group discussions and group projects: The critical differences. *Cooperative Learning and College Teaching, 2*(3), 4-10.

Cuseo, J. (1996). *Cooperative learning: A pedagogy for addressing contemporary challenges and critical issues in higher education.* Stillwater, OK: New Forums Press.

Davis, T. M., & Murrell, P. H. (1993). *Turning teaching into learning: The role of student responsibility in the collegiate experience.* ASHE-ERIC Higher Education Report, No. 8. Washington, DC: The George Washington University, School of Education and Human Development.

Erickson, B. L., & Strommer, D. W. (1991). *Teaching college freshmen.* San Francisco: Jossey-Bass.

Fassinger, P. A. (1995). Understanding classroom interaction: Students' and professors' contributions to students' silence. *Journal of Higher Education, 66*, 61-69.

Fiechtner, S. B., & Davis, E. A. (1992). Why some groups fail: A survey of students' experiences with learning groups. In A. S. Goodsell, M. Maher, & V. Tinto (Eds.), *Collaborative learning: A sourcebook for higher education*(pp. 59-67). University Park, PA: National Center on Postsecondary Teaching, Learning, and Assessment, The Pennsylvania State University.

Gardner, J. N. (1980). *University 101: A concept*

for improving university teaching and learning. Columbia, SC: National Resource Center for The Freshman Year Experience, University of South Carolina. (Eric Reproduction No. 192 706).

Gardner, J. N. (1993, January). *Structural problems in the first college year*. Presentation made at the Freshman Year Experience Resource Seminar, Irvine, CA.

Green, M. G. (Ed.). (1989). *Minorities on campus: A handbook for enhancing diversity*. Washington, DC: American Council on Education.

Higman, P., Chase, M., & Wagner, L. (1994, July). *Outdoor experience freshman seminar at Eastern Washington University*. Paper presented at The Seventh International Conference on The First-Year Experience, Dublin, Ireland.

Holton, E. (1992, Spring). Teaching going-to-work skills: A missing link in career development. *Journal of Career Planning and Employment, 52*(3), 46-51.

Johnson, D. W., & Johnson, R. T. (1989). *Cooperation and competition: Theory and research*. Edina, MN: Interaction Book Company.

Johnson, D. W., Johnson, R. T., & Smith, K. (1992). *Cooperative learning in college: The state of the art*. ASHE-ERIC Higher Education Report No. 4. Washington, DC: Association for the Study of Higher Education.

Johnson, K., Sulzer-Azaroff, B., & Mass, C. (1977). The effects of internal proctoring upon examination performance in a personalized instruction course. *Journal of Personalized Instruction, 1*, 113-117.

Kagan, S. (1992). *Cooperative learning*. San Juan Capistrano: Resources for Teachers, Inc.

Karp, D. A., & Yoels, W. C. (1976). The college classroom: Some observations on the meanings of student participation. *Sociology and Social Research, 60*, 421-439.

Larson, C. O., Dansereau, D. F., O'Donnell, A., Hythecker, V., Lambiotte, J. G., & Rocklin, T. (1984). Verbal ability and cooperative learning: Transfer effects. *Journal of Reading Behavior, 16*(4), 289-295.

Light, R. L. (1990). *The Harvard assessment seminars*. Cambridge, MA: Harvard University Press.

Light, R. L. (1992). *The Harvard assessment seminars, second report*. Cambridge, MA: Harvard University Press.

Marchese, T. (1990). A new conversation about undergraduate teaching. *AAHE Bulletin, 42*(9), 3-8.

McKeachie, W. J., Pintrich, P., Lin, Y., & Smith, D. (1986). *Teaching and learning in the college classroom: A review of the research literature*. Ann Arbor: University of Michigan, NCRIPTAL.

Millis, B. J., & Cottell, P. G., Jr. (1998). *Cooperative learning for higher education faculty*. Phoenix: Oryx Press, American Council on Education.

Morse, S. W. (1989). *Renewing civic capacity: Preparing college students for service and citizenship*. ASHE-ERIC Higher Education Report No. 8. Washington, DC: The George Washington University, School of Education and Human Development.

Neer, M. R. (1987). The development of an instrument to measure classroom apprehension. *Communication Education, 36*, 154-166.

Nunn, C. E. (1996). Discussion in the college classroom: Triangulating observational and survey results. *Journal of Higher Education, 67*(3), 243-266.

O'Donnell, A. M. (1994). Facilitating scripted cooperation through the use of knowledge maps. *Cooperative Learning and College Teaching, 4*(2), 7-10.

Ottinger, C. (1991). College going persistence and completion patterns in higher education: What do we know. *ACE Research Briefs, 2*(3), 1-10.

Pascarella, E. T., & Terenzini, P. T. (1991). *How college affects students: Findings and insights from twenty years of research*. San Francisco: Jossey-Bass.

Perry, W. G. (1970). *Forms of intellectual and ethical development in the college years.* New York: Holt Rineheart.

Ruhl, K. L., Hughes, C. A., & Schloss, P. J. (1987). Using the pause procedure to enhance lecture recall. *Teacher Education and Special Education, 10,* 14-18.

Simpson, C., Baker, K., & Mellinger, G. (1980). Conventional failures and unconventional dropouts: Comparing different types of university withdrawals. *Sociology of Education, 53*(4), 203-214.

Slavin, R. E. (1989). Cooperative learning and student achievement. In R. E. Slavin (Ed.), *School and classroom organization*. Hillside, NJ: Erlbaum.

Slavin, R. E. (1990). *Cooperative learning: Theory, research, and practice.* Englewood Cliffs, NJ: Prentice-Hall.

Tinto, V. (1993). *Leaving college: Rethinking the causes and cures for student attrition* (2nd ed.). Chicago: University of Chicago Press.

Tinzmann, M. B., Jones, B. F., Fennimore, T. F., Bakker, J., Fine, C., & Pierce, J. (1990). *What is the collaborative classroom?* Oak Brook, IL: North Central Regional Education Laboratory. Online. http://www/ncrel.org/srdr/areas/rpl_esys/collab.htm.

Treisman, P. U. (1985). A study of the mathematics performance of Black students at the University of California, Berkeley (Doctoral dissertation, University of California, Berkeley, 1986). *Dissertation Abstracts International, 47,* 1641-A.

U.S. Department of Education, National Center for Education Statistics. (1994). *Digest of education statistics.* Washington, DC: Government Printing Office.

Vygotsky, L. S. (1978). Internalization of higher cognitive functions. In M. Cole, V. John-Steiner, S. Scribner, & E. Souberman (Eds. & Trans.), *Mind in society: The development of higher psychological processes* (pp. 52-57). Cambridge, MA: Harvard University Press.

Wheeler, D. L. (1992, June 17). Teaching calculus to minority students helps them stay in college. *The Chronicle of Higher Education,* p. A15.

Whitman, N. A. (1988). *Peer teaching: To teach is to learn twice.* ASHE-ERIC Higher Education Report No. 4. Washington, DC: Association for the Study of Higher Education.

Williams, K., Harkins, S., & Latane, B. (1981). Identifiability as a deterrent to social loafing: Two cheering experiments. *Journal of Personality and Social Psychology, 40,* 303-311.

Wingspread Group. (1993). *An American imperative: Higher expectations for higher education.* Racine, WI: The Johnson Foundation.

Facilitating A Group

Constance Staley

CHAPTER 6

Faculty training for the first-year seminar is much more than *simply* faculty training. Commitment to training is the measure of an institution's commitment to its first-year seminar program. A campus that spends time, energy, and resources preparing its faculty to teach this unique course is truly invested in its faculty and students, and first-year seminar programs with well-trained faculty will *survive* and *thrive* within these institutions. This chapter will not only provide straightforward, practical suggestions to help trainers cultivate effective group facilitation skills, but it will also offer guidelines to help program administrators select promising training facilitators.

Identifying Training Facilitators: Qualifications and Characteristics

In training faculty to teach the first-year seminar, there is perhaps no variable more important than the training facilitator. Facilitators should be selected with three key qualifications in mind: *reputation, readiness,* and *relating* (communication) *skills* (Staley, 1998). Like classroom teaching, the ability to hold the interest of a roomful of people is a rare talent, but one which can be cultivated and improved. While some trainers, like teachers, seem to be born with the ability to facilitate a group, the truth is that people can develop facilitation skills with guidance and practice. To be a successful facilitator, both *prerequisite* characteristics (reputation and readiness) and *requisite* (relating) skills are important.

Reputation

Internal trainers should be highly respected individuals on campus. Ideally, faculty should train other faculty since persons from within a particular professional group have more inherent credibility (i.e., doctors training doctors, engineers training engineers, etc.) than do individuals from outside the group. However, whether the facilitator is faculty, administrator, or staff, this individual should be well-respected and perceived as neutral in terms of campus politics.

Readiness

Readiness refers to an individual's willingness to facilitate a group, which is based on interest, and to some extent, on his or her personality. Successful facilitators are willing and able; they are outgoing, friendly, and confident people who are truly interested in others and eager to share themselves with a group. Typically, training is inherently easier for extraverted people, although some introverts can roleplay convincingly when a situation requires it. (Introverts will simply find that facilitating a group expends a great deal of energy and may shy away from it.) Fortunately, individuals with these qualities are likely to be drawn naturally to the role of training facilitator.

Relating Skills

Obviously, trainers must have well-cultivated communication skills. However, effective training involves more than the ability to deliver a coherent and interesting lecture. Training at its best involves managing lively discussion generated by knowledgeable participants with diverse opinions as well as processing experiential exercises designed to engage and enlighten. Successful facilitators *relate* well to individual trainees and to the group as a whole, and they can help trainees *relate* to each other and to the material being discussed.

Developing Facilitation Skills

Because prerequisite characteristics are relatively fixed, the remainder of this chapter will focus on cultivating requisite communication skills for effective group facilitation.

Perhaps the most frequently violated rule of training is to use the same delivery mode faculty are most often tempted to use in the classroom—the lecture.

Facilitating a Group: Steps to Success

Facilitating a group is a challenge. As opposed to merely delivering a lecture, the trainer never quite knows what to expect; in training situations, ambiguity is unavoidable. What questions will participants ask? How interested will they be in the topic or exercise? Exactly how much time will an activity take? Is there too much or too little material planned for the allotted training time? What if individuals become hostile or unruly? What if they act bored or disinterested? Questions such as these are legitimate ones, and they identify factors that are critical to the success of a training program.

What follows is a checklist of suggestions to help you successfully plan and execute your training experience.

Assess training needs. How does a training facilitator decide which topics to focus on? Training needs must be assessed, either by asking trainees themselves, by using previously gathered assessment data from the course, or, although less reliable, by basing conclusions on informal input from various campus constituencies. Are trainees new to the course or are they experienced freshman seminar instructors? What disciplines do they represent? (Some disciplines have preferred teaching models which may or may not fit the model used in the freshman seminar. The sciences, for example, traditionally use a lecture/laboratory approach, as opposed to a small seminar format.) After topic selections are made and the facilitator decides how much time will be allotted to training, she or he must prioritize these needs and arrive at training objectives.

Model the first-year course. Sometimes the best way to train people is to model a desired behavior. If the training program is structured as enjoyable, non-threatening, and engaging, the facilitator can use the training experience to demonstrate how the first-year seminar itself should be structured. Participants should be encouraged to reflect back on particular factors in the training experience when they plan and conduct their own courses.

Create a comfortable climate. Like new first-year students, trainees sometimes feel uncomfortable and apprehensive. "What will I be asked to do? Will I embarrass myself? What if everyone discovers I'm not the authority (witty person, intellectual, etc.) they think I am?" Typically, participants will mirror the affect of facilitators; if facilitators are relaxed and comfortable with their roles, participants will respond in like fashion. Using humor, encouraging movement, involving right-brain activities, and sending positive nonverbal messages are techniques that may do a great deal to generate intimacy and lower potential anxiety among participants.

Balance the speaking/listening ratio. Giving participants a voice early in a training program (without totally surrendering control) is a good rule of thumb. Generally speaking, participants are more willing to listen to facilitators who have already demonstrated their willingness to listen to participants. This can take place naturally during an icebreaker activity in which trainees introduce themselves or during an introductory, abbreviated needs assessment in which the facilitator elicits the group's expectations for the session.

Focus on involvement. Perhaps the most frequently violated rule of training is to use the same delivery mode faculty are most often tempted to use in the classroom—the lecture. But lecturing is often no more effective in the training room than it is in the classroom. In order to be most effective, training should be a dynamic, interactive activity—"The more the learners participate in the training, the greater will be its effectiveness and the more likely will the learners internalize the concepts under consideration" (Michalak & Yager, 1979, p. 97). According to research, four principles accurately characterize andragogy, as opposed to pedagogy (Arnold & McClure, 1996; Knowles, 1984). Adult learners:

- learn by doing
- have prior experience which operates as a learning base
- have clear motives for learning, i.e., are pragmatic
- have legitimate and pressing preoccupations which limit their willingness to invest in training and can interfere with learning
- prefer hands-on, experiential, and collaborative activities interspersed with occasional "lecturettes"

Present information professionally. When training goals are primarily informational, delivering a lecturette may, in fact, be the preferred method of delivery. However, even then, questions should be encouraged, and a two-way (rather than a simply one-way) exchange of information should be the goal (O'Connor, Bronner, & Delaney, 1996).

However, presenting information to a roomful of people who present information for a living is indeed a challenge. There are four keys to success: (a) organize information for effortless processing, (b) use professional quality materials, (c) invite colleagues to co-facilitate, and (d) develop a style that is credible but not condescending.

Faculty often expect students to take notes furiously during class and process information later. In a dynamic training situation (or class, for that matter), *later* is often too late. A savvy facilitator will want participants to act upon, comment on, and communicate about the content of the training as it occurs. For this to happen, ease of processing is a requirement. Sequence activities so that skill building can take place, and use visual aids in the form of handouts, overheads, computer-generated graphics, sticky-note flip charts, etc.

Materials used for faculty training must be polished (but not glitzy). The training sponsor or facilitator should develop a logo for the training program, assemble participant notebooks, and provide practical handouts for in-class use later. "Dirty purples" are obsolete, not only in the classroom, but in the training room as well, and skewed, faintly-printed copies erode trainers' credibility.

Finally, the best way to develop a credible, non-condescending presentation style is to ask for feedback from a "coach" (a colleague in the Speech Department, for example). Facilitators may also want to view critically a videotape of himself or herself facilitating a group.

Manage group discussion. One of the most difficult challenges of training is managing lively discussion. There are a number of reasons why this is true:

1. Facilitators must be keenly aware of where the discussion has been, where it currently is, and where she or he would like it to go—past, present, and future—all at the same time.

2. Facilitators must continually monitor the nonverbal feedback of a diverse group of participants. Are trainees understanding the main points? Are questions developing? Are participants engaged? Is it time for a break?

3. Facilitators must manage over- and under-communicators so that everyone feels a part of the discussion.

4. Facilitators must maintain their own energy while monitoring, summarizing, and linking—in short, while orchestrating the discussion.

Perhaps the most difficult challenge of facilitating a group is managing multiple communication styles. Some participants may sit back and wait for others to take the lead in discussion, often because they feel unprepared, intimidated, or shy. Other participants may monopolize the discussion, either because they are highly knowledgeable, have dominant personalities, or are truly enthusiastic about the material. As they say, "People have one thing in common: They are all different." Regardless of why, groups often have non-egalitarian participation levels; yet as facilitator, your goal is to ensure that everyone feels a part of the training experience and is benefitting from the discussion. Consider the following array of potential problematic training participants (Benne & Sheats, 1948; Engleberg & Wynn, 1997; Staley & Staley, 1992):

- *Blocker*: constantly objects to others' ideas and opinions; plays district attorney by cross-examining others in an attempt to impede the acceptance of an idea—("I've already tried the exercise Mary's describing in my class. I can tell you right now, it just won't work.")
- *Aggressor*: insults and criticizes other participants in order to promote him or herself—("What a ridiculous idea! Why not reconsider my earlier suggestion?")
- *Storyteller*: tells often interesting but irrelevant stories which lead the group astray—("You'll never believe what happened to me when I taught this course at another school!")
- *Recognition seeker*: calls attention to his or her own accomplishments—("When I won the Teaching Award last year, I . . . .")
- *Dominator*: monopolizes group interaction for selfish reasons or because of high interest and good preparation—("My earlier idea leads me to suggest another alternative . . . . I also suggest we consider . . . . Furthermore, I'd like to propose . . . .")
- *Confessor*: uses the group to share personal problems as a substitute for group therapy—("I've always felt inferior because I'm a much better researcher than I am a teacher. It's a wonder I was chosen to teach this course.")
- *Special interest pleader*: represents another group or a special cause and argues this point of view relentlessly—("The Student Support Division isn't going to like us insisting on doing the course our way. I worked in that office for three years, and I think we should look at things from their perspective.")
- *Clown*: distracts the group with jokes and "off-the-wall" comments, often well-liked and thus difficult to handle—("Hey, hey, what do you say we break for lunch, man? I feel like I haven't eaten in weeks!")
- *Mute*: participates little or not at all, possibly due to lack of preparation or nervousness—(Silence . . . .)
- *Deserter*: appears aloof and "above it all," withdraws from the group—("I have another meeting in ten minutes. Are you going to cover anything really important before I have to leave?")

Discussions can become emotional battlegrounds with participants promoting and defending their own egos (Brookfield, 1990). Extraverts naturally tend to "think out loud" or send up intellectual "trial balloons" to test others' reactions, while introverts prefer to process ideas and rehearse contributions internally.

Facilitators must learn to manage the challenges of group dynamics successfully. This may be done with subtle verbal comments (i.e., "Donna has many good ideas about how to engage first-year students in the classroom, but what positive experiences have others in the group had?") or with nonverbal signals (i.e., breaking eye contact with a dominating contributor and physically moving to the other side of the room). Patterns of participation can emerge early in a training session, such that eventually dominators are "expected" to overcontribute and mutes are "expected" to undercontribute. Such relatively fixed communication patterns may result in participants' frustration, dissatisfaction, and lowered self-esteem; facilitator intervention helps to redistribute opportunities to communicate and create group cohesion.

Pace group activities. Pacing the training activities is another challenge that facilitators face.

How much time should be devoted to any one activity? How often should a change of pace take place? How long can participants sit in one spot? How does the group's energy level rise and fall? How much time should be allowed for debriefing or processing after a group activity? Selecting, directing, and sequencing both content and activities are the responsibility of the facilitator. Planning appropriately with these questions in mind affects the success of any training program.

Invite training partners. Although successful co-facilitation (alternating between two concurrent trainers) is extremely challenging, facilitators should consider inviting several individual trainers to present portions of the training program. This practice has several benefits: (a) it lightens each facilitators's individual workload, (b) it generates buy-in for the training, and (c) the variety makes the training more interesting to participants. While the natural tendency of many trainers may be the desire to "do it all" themselves, this tendency should be squelched. Involving colleagues will help them feel like contributors whose expertise is also valued by the group. Further, occasionally inviting training facilitators from other institutions can provide additional perspectives, heightened credibility, and refreshing change.

Stress integration and transfer. The ultimate test of the worth of a training experience is whether participants actually use what they have learned during training. While it is true that participants will value information that is immediately transferable, trainers should never assume that transfer will be automatic. An important aspect of facilitating a group is discussing ways to transfer the content of the training program to the context of the classroom, not only in the freshman seminar, but within participants' disciplines as well.

Close memorably. If training has been successful, the program will end on a "high" note. Participants will feel energized and enthusiastic about implementing what they have learned. Generally, it is a good idea to refer back to goals outlined at the beginning of the training experience to summarize and provide closure. Celebrate the time together and the contributions of individuals who participated.

Evaluating Facilitation Efforts: The Goal of Continual Improvement

Critiquing Facilitation Skills

Evaluating the effectiveness of a group facilitator is important, not only to note areas for improvement but also to report the results of the training effort to decision makers. Facilitators who study the training process, know adult learning theories, and cultivate their communication skills will undoubtedly give participants a positive training experience. Tallied critiques and verbatim written comments are much more convincing to those making budgetary decisions than are stories from participants about the "great time" they had.

Designing Improvements for Future Training

Obviously the real value of evaluation to the facilitator him or herself is the information it provides about methods that "worked," additional topics for future training, and areas for change in the future. For those people who wish to improve their facilitation skills, I recommend a visit to the campus speech skills center or auditing a public speaking, group dynamics, teaching methods, or training course. Other recommendations include experimenting with alternative training activities, noting the results, and modifying the activities accordingly (Bourner, Martin, & Race, 1993).

Facilitating a group is a challenge, yet training is a powerful *evolutionary* and *revolutionary* tool—to pass on program traditions and perspectives, to bring together people with diverse backgrounds, and to initiate campus-wide positive cultural change.

References

Arnold, W. E., & McClure, L. (1996). *Communication, training and development* (2nd ed.). Prospect Heights, IL: Waveland.

Benne, K. D., & Sheats, P. (1948). Functional roles of group members. *Journal of Social Issues, 4,* 41-49.

Bourner, T., Martin, V., & Race, P. (1993). *Workshops that work.* London: McGraw-Hill.

Brookfield, S. D. (1990). *The skillful teacher*. San Francisco: Jossey-Bass.

Engleberg, I. N., & Wynn, D. R. (1997). *Working in groups*. Boston: Houghton Mifflin.

Knowles, M. (1984). *Andragogy in action*. San Francisco: Jossey-Bass.

Michalak, D. F., & Yager, E. G. (1979). *Making the training process work*. New York: Harper & Row.

O'Connor, B. N., Bronner, M., & Delaney, C. (1996). *South-western training for organizations*. Cincinnati, OH: South-Western Educational Publishing.

Staley, C. (1998). *Teaching college success*. Belmont, CA: Wadsworth.

Staley, C. C., & Staley, R. S. (1992). *Communicating in business and the professions: The inside word*. Belmont, CA: Wadsworth.

Ensuring the Success of Faculty Training Workshops

Mary Stuart Hunter and Joseph B. Cuseo

CHAPTER 7

While the primary goal of instructor training workshops is to improve the quality of the undergraduate learning experience, researchers and practitioners cite a number of collateral benefits. In addition to improving the quality of instruction and of student learning, training workshops may also lead to increased collegiality among faculty, to the forging of campus-wide partnerships, and to a greater sense of faculty vitality. This chapter highlights some of these potential benefits of an instructor training program. Additionally, it addresses the important issues of administration and logistics that affect the success of instructor training efforts.

Administrative Issues and Outcomes

Recruitment and Selection of Course Instructors

Probably the first issue in the administration of an instructor training program is deciding *who* should be recruited to serve as course instructors. As Gordon and Grites (1984) argue, "Freshman students deserve the best instructors the institution can provide in a course that will be critically important to their understanding of the college experience and to their success" (p. 316). Moreover, when an institution offers the new-student seminar for the very first time, selecting the best possible instructors becomes imperative because this will maximize the seminar's positive impact, ensure its initial acceptance, and increase the likelihood that it will receive long-term institutional support. As Gardner (1989) recommends,

> Those selected for the first offering must be "the cream"—those most likely to do the kind of teaching that will enhance the success of the seminar. Any innovation will develop a reputation very early in its life based on the success and quality of those who first participate in it. (p. 242)

National data indicate that those who teach the new-student seminar are most frequently college faculty, followed by student affairs personnel (Barefoot & Fidler, 1996). Academic support service-providers (e.g., learning center staff) and administrators (e.g., academic dean or college president) have also served as course instructors. At some colleges, such as Concordia College (Wisconsin) and the University of Maine, academic advisors are seminar instructors for class sections comprised of their own first-year advisees (Barefoot, 1993). In their analysis of national survey data gathered on the new-student seminar, Barefoot and Fidler (1992) offer the following observation: "It is noteworthy that a wide variety of personnel from faculty, to students, to alumni are used to teach the seminar. Perhaps no other college course utilizes as wide a variety of instructors as the freshman seminar" (p. 30).

One advantage of having faculty serve as course instructors is that their involvement may increase the seminar's perceived academic credibility and its centrality to the educational mission of the college. However, given the seminar's nontraditional content and its student-centered focus, not all faculty are equally qualified candidates for course instruction. Recruitment efforts should target faculty who possess the following characteristics:

1. course evaluations and campus reputations which suggest that the faculty are accessible to and relate well to students and are capable of creating a classroom climate characterized by a high degree of teacher-student rapport

2. a willingness to go beyond the traditional lecture method of instruction and experiment with student-centered instructional strategies (for example, pedagogical practices that promote active student involvement via small group work and experiential learning activities)

3. a history of student advocacy (as opposed to student bashing)—for example, faculty who have high expectations of students, including first-year students who may initially lack academic preparation or motivation, and who work diligently to ensure their success

4. are high-profile, respected by their peers as effective educators with high academic standards, and respected by administrators for their history of commitment and service to the college

If there is a faculty member on campus who serves as an instructional development or faculty development specialist, seminar coordinators may tap this person as a resource for identifying faculty who are open to experimentation with student-centered teaching techniques. Top-level administrators may also play a key role in the identification and recruitment of new-student seminar instructors who have the foregoing qualities by encouraging their personal involvement (e.g., via personal note, call, or lunch contact) and by enlisting the support of their department chairs. Such administrative involvement in recruiting the most student-centered and committed faculty and staff on campus to serve as new-student seminar instructors represents an institutional practice that is consistent with the principle of "front loading"—reallocating or redistributing the institution's best educational resources to serve the critical needs of first-year students (Study Group on the Conditions of Excellence in Higher Education, 1984).

While high-level administrators are valuable in identifying potential course instructors, they themselves may be excellent candidates for involvement in the new-student seminar. At Chicago State University and the State University of New York-Morrisville, upper-level administrators, including the president and academic vice president, have taught sections of the new-student seminar (Cross, 1993; "Freshman Experience Course Improves Retention," 1994). Seminar coordinators may want to target recruitment efforts at administrators who possess the following characteristics:

1. a working knowledge of student development theory

2. job responsibilities that provide a high level of student contact

3. accessibility to students and the ability to work with students effectively

4. a high profile on campus and a demonstrated commitment to students and the institution

Building Collegiality

Austin's (1993) findings from extensive interviews with faculty suggest the potential value of an instructor training program for building supportive communities within or among college faculty and staff. She comments that,

> Many faculty, both new and experienced, speak of a longing for a greater sense of community and collegiality within the academy.... (They) often speak of their early years as characterized by a sense of isolation from colleagues and a lack of connection or even acquaintance with colleagues outside their immediate departments. (p. 8)

The instructor training program has the potential to ameliorate faculty feelings of intradisciplinary isolation. Gardner (1980) observes, "The faculty develop a support group . . . [which] draws its faculty from across all disciplines and departmental lines" (1980, p. 6).

An additional strategy for meeting the need for greater collegiality expressed by both new and experienced faculty is to use teaching teams. Teaching teams consisting of new faculty paired with veteran faculty allow the instructor training program to function as a faculty mentoring program, whereby faculty veterans serve as mentors to their new faculty protegés.

Research on career development suggests that, in general, mentors can play key roles in an individual's professional development (Levinson, 1978). This is especially true for college and university faculty (Torrance, 1984). Benefits of the mentoring relationship are not limited to the protege; research reported by Busch (1985) and Gerstein (1985) suggests that the mentor also reaps significant professional and personal benefits from the mentoring process. Unfortunately, higher education research finds that mentoring does not seem to occur naturally or spontaneously among college faculty (Turner & Boice, 1987). Interviews with new faculty indicate that they expect frequent and informal interactions with senior colleagues, anticipating that experienced faculty will be a source of companionship and constructive advice. However, most new faculty report low levels of collegiality with senior faculty. They also report that frustration stemming from the failure to realize these collegial expectations is a major source of professional dissatisfaction (Fink, 1984; Sorcinelli, 1988; Turner & Boice, 1987). Hipps (1980) suggests that because effective mentoring does not take place spontaneously, it must be cultivated within the context of a deliberately structured or designed program. The new-student seminar instructor training program may provide a structure within which an effective faculty mentoring program can be designed and delivered.

One other type of mentoring relationship—between veteran faculty and graduate students—could be developed intentionally via the instructor training program. Research on graduate education points to the failure of graduate programs to prepare prospective college faculty adequately for their role as teachers of undergraduates (see discussion of this issue in Chapter 1). Including graduate students as participants in the instructor training program and pairing graduate students with veteran, teaching-oriented and student-centered faculty as part of a mentoring/team-teaching partnership may be the type of teaching "apprenticeship" cited as the key element missing in the preparation of future faculty (Edgerton, 1994).

Facilitating the Development of Campus-wide Partnerships

In the same way that instructor training programs serve to increase collegiality among faculty, they may also promote partnerships between faculty and many other members of the college community. In addition to the veteran/new faculty teaching team, a wide range of viable teaching teams exists for the new-student seminar, including the following:

- faculty from different academic disciplines, i.e., interdisciplinary teaching teams
- faculty and student affairs professionals (e.g., dean of students, director of student activities, residence life staff)
- faculty and academic support service professionals (e.g., library science and/or learning assistance professionals)
- faculty and academic administrators (e.g., academic dean or college president)
- faculty and students (e.g., graduate students, upper-division undergraduates, or sophomores)
- faculty and alumni

Bringing together such diverse members of the college community for an initial training workshop and, perhaps, for team-teaching partnerships serves to unite them in pursuit of a common educational cause. This common quest, in turn, (a) promotes collaboration across different units of the college, (b) builds a sense of campus community, (c) allows for campus-wide ownership of the new-student seminar, and (d) raises college-wide consciousness of the seminar's value. One of

Gardner's (1980) earliest reports on the University 101 program at South Carolina reinforces the community-building potential of the new-student seminar's instructor training program:

> The program integrates faculty and professional staff at the university in a joint undertaking [which] tends to reduce the barriers between the faculty and staff camps, reduces stereotyping . . . and has promoted better relationships between faculty and especially student affairs staff. (pp. 6-7)

The potential of the instructor training program for promoting partnerships between faculty and student development professionals is especially significant because historically there has been, and their continues to be, a "schism" between student life and academic life in higher education (Barr & Upcraft, 1990; Boyer, 1987; Carnegie Foundation, 1990).

Increasing Faculty Vitality

Research on "faculty vitality" indicates that veteran faculty who have remained "vital" (i.e., energetic and enthusiastic about their profession) are typically those who engage in innovative or nontraditional professional activities during their career. In particular, experimenting with new teaching strategies, engaging in interdisciplinary activities, and participating in team-teaching ventures are among the first steps that vital professors take to add variety and excitement to their work lives (Baldwin, 1990). Teaching the new-student seminar and participating in its instructor training program have the potential for providing veteran faculty with all these ingredients for faculty vitality—giving them an opportunity to practice new teaching strategies, to engage in cross-disciplinary interaction during the training experience, and to team teach the seminar with faculty from other academic disciplines.

Planning and Logistics of an Initial Instructor Training Effort

Seminar coordinators will need to make many decisions when planning the actual training program. Many of these decisions, along with recommendations, are addressed below.

Workshop Content Development

The content and process included in an instructor training workshop should, first and foremost, reflect and support the content of the new-student seminar itself. The purpose, after all, is to prepare faculty and administrators to teach a new-student seminar—a course new to most instructors. In this regard, the content for each institutionally based training program will be unique because the course and the institution are themselves unique. Workshop coordinators should design the training so that important course content is presented, especially that content which may be challenging or threatening for instructors to address, i.e., sexuality, diversity, and academic honesty. Further, workshop facilitators should model active learning strategies throughout the workshop and should use experiential activities whenever possible to introduce various content topics. Thus they will model a teaching method that goes beyond the traditional lecture method alone.

The development of both content and process for a workshop agenda can in itself be a powerful collaborative process that continuously improves the seminar program. An agenda developed by a small committee or task force of educators who are interested in and committed to the new-student seminar program has the potential to evolve into a better workshop than does an agenda created and planned by one person, no matter how able and talented the person may be. A planning team composed of individuals with various teaching and learning styles, representing different disciplines and administrative departments within the institution, will bring a variety of perspectives and creative ideas to the planning process. It may be a more time-consuming task, but the final outcome—the workshop agenda—has the potential to be a "better built mousetrap."

Choosing Facilitators

No less important than the content and process of the workshop is the ability of the workshop leaders to deliver the planned agenda. A team of several skilled facilitators can ensure the success of a well-planned training event. Chapter 6 of this monograph outlines in detail information on effective workshop facilitation and related skills.

Scheduling the Initial Instructor Training Program

For maximum participation in instructor training, workshop coordinators should schedule the sessions at times when potential conflicts are minimal. Optimal time periods during which instructor training programs may be offered are immediately prior to or immediately following the fall and spring terms. One advantage of offering the instructor training program prior to the start of the academic year is that it may then also be used as one component of a new faculty and staff orientation program for those who are about to begin their first year of service at the college. Topics typically covered in new-student seminar instructor training, such as "understanding the institution" and "understanding first-year students," would be valuable for all new faculty and staff, whether or not they will be teaching the seminar. The teaching assignments of new faculty typically include a heavy load of introductory courses, exposing them to many first-year students. These faculty members could profit immeasurably from discussions of effective college-teaching strategies—some of which they might be able to adopt immediately in their introductory, discipline-based courses.

> **The development of both content and process for a workshop agenda can in itself be a powerful collaborative process that continuously improves the seminar program.**

Research indicating that most new faculty settle into a stable, long-term pattern of instructional practices within the first one or two years of college teaching underscores the value of offering a proactive, intrusively-delivered instructional development program for new faculty prior to their very first semester of college teaching (Levinson-Rose & Menges, 1981). Further, new faculty are often very enthusiastic about acquiring effective instructional practices because they feel that their graduate school experience has not prepared them for college teaching (Austin, 1993).

In its landmark report, *Integrity in the Curriculum*, The Association of American Colleges (1985) concludes that "Institutions of higher education must demonstrate their commitment to teaching at the outset of every new appointment by offering a program which systematically helps the new recruits to improve their teaching styles and their intellectual reach" (p. 36). Given the institution-wide advantages of scheduling new student seminar instructor training workshops prior to the beginning of a term, there are also disadvantages that provide compelling reasons to consider scheduling training at other times. The optimal time for scheduling from the perspective of the seminar itself might be earlier in the annual academic cycle. Because most seminar instructors will be teaching this unique course for the first time, some extended time for reflection on the training experience and for planning is desirable. As is obvious in this discussion, there is no "right" time; rather, each institution must weigh the advantages and disadvantages of various times and make a decision that works best for their specific situation.

Elements of a Successful Workshop

Atmosphere counts—choose a place that provides an inviting ambience and conveys a warm welcome. First and foremost, the workshop site must be accessible. It should be easy to find and well-marked, have ample parking, and be wheelchair accessible. Nothing destroys the positive start of a training event more than participants who arrive disgruntled because of difficulty finding or accessing the workshop. The meeting room itself must be inviting. For example, a well-furnished lounge or conference room will be a more comfortable setting than a sterile classroom. Keene College (New Hampshire) conducts its instructor training program at an off-campus retreat site (Backes, 1994). This environment is ideal for eliminating on-campus distractions or interruptions, such as phone or mail messages and provides a more intimate atmosphere for team building among program participants.

In response to the question of where training should be conducted, Gardner (1992) offers the following recommendation:

> In my experience, the ideal location for training is an off-campus location, a retreat setting where the educators are removed from their normal work environment and hence are on

> turf that is more psychologically neutral and detached. A reasonable substitute is a campus location or property removed from the mainstream hub of campus activities. (p. 5)

The room itself should have adequate lighting (so as not to put participants to sleep!), comfortable and movable chairs, and a self-controlled heating and air system. The room should be large enough and have suitable acoustics to allow small group work wherein conversations from different groups do not interfere with one another.

Do it with class. Be generous with food, beverages, and personalized materials. This sends a message that the college values the new-student seminar, its instructor training program, and its course instructors. Since the workshop often represents the participants' initial experience with, and *first impression* of the program, it could have a powerful impact on their overall perception of the value of the new-student seminar. (As the aphorism goes, "You never get a second chance to make a first impression.")

If the culture on your campus makes it appropriate, try to provide a small honorarium for the participants—it doesn't have to be much—just enough to send the message that their presence is valued. Costs incurred for mailing, photocopying expenses, food, and honoraria might be funded through the establishment of an annual budget base, with a fixed sum added for each new participant.

Officially "kick off" the workshop with a personal welcome from a high-level administrator. This should send an early message to instructors that their participation is important and valued by the college. It is also useful to provide historical information describing the development of the new student seminar on your campus. Additional information on new student seminars across the nation can also help to put the campus's program into perspective.

Give participants input or control with respect to the program by allowing them some choice concerning topics to be discussed. For example, participants may complete a short "needs assessment" or "interest inventory" containing a list of possible topics or issues with extra space so that they can add their own topics to the list. This input could be solicited as part of a pre-workshop mailing packet, or it could be obtained from participants at the outset of the program.

Get participants actively involved. Trainers should develop exercises that require participants to act on the program content and that encourage participant interaction. The first step in the instructor training program at the University of South Carolina is to have participants engage in small-group interactions designed to build a sense of teamwork and community. For example, participants may share autobiographical information and personal recollections of what it was like for them when they were first-year students. Personal time that allows for individual participants to reflect actively on and to apply the ideas that are presented can also be built into the program. One possible activity is to give participants some time near the end of the workshop to sketch out a tentative syllabus.

Use the process of instructor training to simulate or model the actual process of course instruction. Trainers can simulate the teaching and learning process of the new-student seminar by having participants assume the roles of both student and instructor. This practice should serve to enhance instructor empathy for first-year students and promote positive transfer between the artificial context of instructor training to the real context of classroom teaching.

Vary the format, i.e., "mix it up" with different activities. Workshops that employ a variety of delivery formats such as (a) individual presentations, (b) panel discussions, (c) role plays of realistic, soon-to-be-encountered situations, (d) small-group discussions, (e) large-group brainstorming or open forums, and (f) short reflection exercises may be more effective. Such varied, participant-centered strategies promote active involvement, keeping participants awake and engaged and facilitating the retention of ideas presented during the program.

Include content in the workshop that will increase participants' knowledge of the institution. Increased knowledge of campus services and facilities will improve an instructor's ability to facilitate student utilization of them. Bringing workshop participants into contact with as many key campus offices and officers will help them associate the face with the place. A campus tour is one way to accomplish this, as long as it does not include too many successive stops, demanding that too much information be processed consecutively (resulting in "information overload"). Breaking the tour into two shorter sessions—one in the morning and one early in the afternoon—would reduce information overload.

Incorporate supportive, successful veteran instructors into the day's activities. Doing so can build enthusiasm and positive anticipation among instructors and provide them with potential mentors. To maximize the effectiveness of guest speakers or star panelists, workshop facilitators should provide them with very specific objectives as to their role in the training program, how long they should speak, and what process they should follow during their presentations. If one goal of training is increased participation, guest presenters should actively involve participants and leave ample time for questions or comments. Mentoring relationships between veteran and new seminar instructors can be either allowed to develop informally and spontaneously, or workshop coordinators can designate specific mentor-protege pairs in advance.

Incorporate "nearly new" instructors into workshop activities. Those who have recently completed their first new-student seminar teaching experience should have high credibility because, as "sophomores," they have just "been there," and their memories may be fresh and replete with timely experiential tips that can be shared with "rookies."

Build in some free time during the program. These breaks (e.g., 15 to 20 minute coffee breaks; a solid hour for lunch) allow participants the opportunity for periodic, informal interaction and further discussion on workshop activities.

End the program on a light and upbeat note. For example, a mini-reception with wine, cheese, and nonalcoholic alternatives might provide a nice finishing touch to the day's work (as well as a positive last impression of the training experience). Gardner (1992) recommends that the workshop conclude with,

> . . . some kind of formal recognition/graduation ceremony at which at least one campus VIP conveys institutional respect and appreciation for the sacrifice of time and energy made by participants. . . . Another nice touch is to have a group photo made and to provide copies of the photo to participants as a memento of the workshop experience. (p. 15)

Allow participants the opportunity to evaluate the program's activities, identifying its strengths and the areas needing improvement. Encourage participants to make specific suggestions for future programs and solicit their ideas about follow-up activities for new instructors during the remainder of the academic year.

Continuous Training and Development Programs

The well-conceptualized, well-developed, and flawlessly delivered initial training program is indeed essential to prepare instructors to teach the new-student seminar successfully. Yet the need for ongoing opportunities to learn and share effective teaching strategies continues. A comprehensive training program should also include follow-up experiences for instructors.

The instructor training program can be extended from a pre-semester, preparatory experience into an "extended" (semester-long) support and development program. The initial workshop could be followed with periodic activities to ensure program continuity and ongoing support for first-time and veteran seminar instructors. Research suggests that such follow-up activities play an important role in determining whether the workshop has any significant long-term benefits for participants (Joyce & Showers, 1983). As two veteran scholars in the area of faculty development note, "A workshop should be used primarily to whet the appetite of a faculty member. More intensive one-on-one consultation usually is needed to effect significant change" (Bergquist & Phillips, 1981, p. 156). Many of the following formats have proven useful.

Follow-up Contacts

This follow-up could take the form of (a) a simple phone call to touch base with participants and to ask how things are going, (b) a short interview with participants to assess whether program activities effectively prepared them for their instructional role, or (c) a user-friendly "needs assessment" or "reaction questionnaire" to be completed by participants to obtain their retrospective perspective on the program's effectiveness. In some ways, these assessments may be more useful than initial workshop evaluations. Seminar instructors may be in a better position to identify their real needs and reactions to the training program's effectiveness after they have had actual teaching experience with the course. A final follow-up contact could be a formal or semiformal "reunion" of participants at the end of the semester to celebrate the completion of their inaugural experience as seminar instructors.

Follow-up Activities

Offer a weekly "instructor development hour" throughout the semester. These sessions can provide seminar instructors with a regular forum in which to share their course experiences. The sessions could be conducted either as informal get-togethers, at which attendance would be entirely optional (e.g., informal "brown bag lunches"), or formal meetings held at times when seminar instructors are expected to attend. For instance, at Keene College (New Hampshire), monthly dinner meetings are held throughout the term for seminar instructors. At Champlain College (Vermont), the seminar is offered as a two-unit course that meets for two, hour-long sessions per week. However, the course counts as three units of teaching load because seminar instructors are expected to meet for an additional (third) hour per week to discuss their instructional experiences and strategies (Goldsweig, 1993).

Research suggests that such follow-up activities play an important role in determining whether the workshop has any significant long-term benefits for participants (Joyce & Showers, 1983).

Link instructor training with a semester-long instructional development program for new faculty. Instructional development seminars could be offered under the aegis of instructor training for the new-student seminar, and newly-hired faculty could be allowed to participate in them during their first semester of college employment, perhaps in lieu of some other institutional responsibility (for example, expectations for committee work or research may be waived during their first semester at the college). This practice would not only provide an incentive for new faculty to participate, but it would also send a clear message that the institution values the program and their participation in it. Some institutions such as Miami Dade Community College, offer an ongoing instructional development seminar for all newly hired faculty during their first semester on campus (Quinlan, 1991). If all newly-hired faculty experience the seminar training workshop as part of this type of faculty development program, then institutions can be assured that both first-time seminar instructors and faculty new to the college have the opportunity for regular contact with colleagues. The program would be a regular forum for timely discussion and resolution of instructional adjustment issues—as these issues actually arise during the oft-stressful first semester of teaching. Such ongoing instructional support could serve as a proactive mechanism for short-circuiting some of the professional difficulties and anxieties often experienced by first-year instructors that can sometimes contribute to their eventual attrition.

A semester-long instructional development program can also provide multiple opportunities for new instructors to explore, in greater depth, issues and practices related to effective college teaching. Time would be available for practicing a variety of pedagogical strategies during the semester. The University of Rhode Island offers a semester-long seminar on teaching first-year students that meets biweekly. Each meeting focuses on one particular teaching method, which faculty read about in advance. Discussion at the scheduled sessions focuses on ways to implement the method. In other meetings, faculty are invited to discuss how they use a particular method of instruction (e.g., small-group work), and the participants agree to try a variation of the method in one of their classes before the next meeting—at which time they report the results of their instructional experiment (Erikson & Strommer, 1991).

Such highly visible institutional programs designed to promote effective teaching may help stimulate the development of a culture on campus where faculty are open to discussing teaching and willing to engage in instructional improvement activities. Expansion of the instructor training program into a semester-long experience that also includes newly hired faculty may have the potential for producing pervasive change in the overall quality of instruction of first-year students at the institution. The importance of promoting such systemic improvement in the quality of instruction for first-year students is well articulated by Barefoot and Fidler (1992): "The academic fate of freshmen is often dependent upon the quality of teaching they receive. . . . The finest freshman seminar or the most elaborate system of co-curricular programming cannot compensate for inadequate instruction in a student's traditional first-year courses" (pp. 62-63).

Moreover, the quality of teaching to which first-year students are exposed in introductory courses may shape their overall attitude about the college experience and establish an anticipatory "mental set" that can influence their approach to learning in subsequent courses. As Spear (1984) claims in *Rejuvenating Introductory Courses*: "In these formative experiences, [first-year students] learn what it is to be a student, what is required to get by, what it means to acquire an education, and whether college is nothing more than acquiring job certification" (p. 6).

Distribute a monthly newsletter to new-student seminar faculty. The program director or coordinator could be responsible for this publication. It could contain practical, professionally relevant news that seminar faculty could use immediately in their courses (for example, research-based "tips" on teaching and advising first-year students, or information on recent trends and innovations related to new-student seminars in higher education). Functioning in this fashion, the newsletter could serve as a conduit for delivery of timely information to seminar faculty who may not have the time to peruse the professional literature relating to the first-year experience. Appended to the newsletter could be a response form that individual instructors could use to request additional information, express an opinion or reaction, or provide practical suggestions of their own. For instance, the newsletter could contain a "what works for me" section to accommodate instructors' suggested practices drawn from their personal teaching experiences in the seminar.

Establish an instructional development resource center. Housed in a section of the library, the first-year experience office, or faculty lounge, such a center could be stocked with continually updated literature on issues relating to the first year and the teaching of first-year students. The resource center could also keep audiovisual resources on hand (for example, videotapes of successful new-student seminar instructors practicing their craft or illustrating specific instructional techniques, or videotapes of successful first-year students sharing their strategies for success).

Conduct periodic teaching seminars or workshops. These could be offered at various times during the academic year by the program director or by outside speakers, perhaps in response to specific issues identified by seminar instructors in personal interviews or on needs-assessment surveys.

Follow-up events could also be offered as part of an off-campus weekend conference or retreat, or as part of a post-semester reunion and celebration for seminar instructors, during which time their contributions to the program might be recognized. Administrators could demonstrate their commitment to the seminar program by the provision of fiscal resources to support an instructor recognition event and also by their attendance at the event. Such celebratory, recognition activities both ensure that contributions of participants to the program are not forgotten and encourage future participation.

The need for administrative commitment to such faculty recognition and development experiences is underscored by a report issued by The Carnegie Foundation for The Advancement of College Teaching (Boyer, 1987) which was based on three years of site visits and extensive national survey research:

> The undergraduate college, which depends so much on vitality in the classroom, must be served by faculty members who can be renewed throughout their careers. And yet, we found that such an obvious and important

practice as setting aside a portion of the budget for faculty development is rare. We strongly recommend that every college commit itself to the professional growth of all faculty. (p. 134)

Conclusion

Faculty development opportunities yoked to the new-student seminar instructor training program can provide a student-centered form of professional growth that can contribute simultaneously to both student development and faculty development. Viewed from this perspective, administrative support for, and investment in, a faculty development program that is structurally linked with instructor training for the new-student seminar represents an investment in the institution's most important constituents—its teachers and its learners.

References

Association of American Colleges. (1985). *Integrity in the curriculum: A report to the academic community. Project on redefining the meaning and purpose of baccalaureate degrees.* Washington, DC: Author.

Austin, A. (1993). Developing college faculty as teachers. In *The development of faculty as teachers* (Compendium of discussion papers prepared for the NJICTL-NCTLA Invitational Conference, February 1993), pp. 6-8. South Orange, NJ: Seton Hall University.

Backes, P. S. (1994, July). *Infusing FYE concepts into traditional first-year courses: An innovative program's effect on retention and student success.* Paper presented at The Seventh International Conference on The First-Year Experience, Dublin, Ireland.

Baldwin, R. G. (1990). Faculty vitality beyond the research university: Extending a contextual concept. *Journal of Higher Education, 61*(2), 160-180.

Baldwin, R. G., & Blackburn, R. T. (1981, November/December). The academic career as a developmental process: Implications for higher education. *Journal of Higher Education, 52*, 598-614.

Barefoot. B. O. (1993). *Exploring the evidence: Reporting outcomes of freshman seminars.* (Monograph No. 11). Columbia, SC: National Resource Center for The Freshman Year Experience, University of South Carolina.

Barefoot, B. O., & Fidler, P. P. (1992). *Helping students climb the ladder: 1991 national survey of freshman seminar programs.* (Monograph No. 10). Columbia, SC: University of South Carolina, National Resource Center for The Freshman Year Experience.

Barefoot, B. O., & Fidler, P. P. (1996). *The 1994 survey of freshman seminar programs: Continuing innovations in the collegiate curriculum.* (Monograph No. 20). Columbia, SC: University of South Carolina, National Resource Center for The Freshman Year Experience and Students in Transition.

Barr, M. J., & Upcraft, M. L. (Eds.) (1990). *New futures for student affairs: Building a vision for professional leadership and practice.* San Francisco: Jossey-Bass.

Bergquist, W., & Phillips, S. (1981). *A handbook for faculty development, Vol. III.* Washington, DC: Council of Independent Colleges.

Boyer, E. L. (1987). *College: The undergraduate experience in America.* New York: Harper & Row.

Busch, J. W. (1985). Mentoring in graduate schools of education: Mentors' perceptions. *American Educational Research Journal, 22*(2), 257-265.

Carnegie Foundation for the Advancement of Teaching. (1975, 1984). National surveys of faculty. (Reprinted in *College: The undergraduate experience in America.* by E. L. Boyer, 1987, New York: Harper & Row)

Carnegie Foundation for the Advancement of Teaching. (1990). *Campus life: In search of community.* Princeton, NJ: Author.

Cross, D. E. (1993, February). *CSU Freshman Seminar 090: An initial step toward ultimate success at an urban university.* Plenary address delivered at the National Conference for The Freshman Year Experience, Columbia, SC.

Erickson, B. L., & Strommer, D. W. (1991). *Teaching college freshmen.* San Francisco: Jossey-Bass.

Fink, L. D. (1984). First year on the faculty: Being there. *Journal of Geography in Higher Education, 8*, 11-25.

Freshman Experience Course Improves Retention. (1994). *The Freshman Year Experience Newsletter, 7*(1), p. 10.

Gardner, J. N. (1980). *University 101: A concept for improving university teaching and learning*. Columbia, SC: University of South Carolina. (Eric Reproduction No. 192 706)

Gardner, J. N. (1989). Starting a freshman seminar program. In M. L. Upcraft, J. N. Gardner, & Associates, *The freshman year experience* (pp. 238-249). San Francisco: Jossey-Bass.

Gardner, J. N. (1992). *Freshman seminar instructor training: Guidelines for design and implementation*. Columbia, SC: University of South Carolina, National Resource Center for The Freshman Year Experience.

Gerstein, M. (1985). Mentoring: An age old practice in a knowledge-based society. *Journal of Counseling and Development, 64*, 156-157.

Goldsweig, S. (1993, October). *Coming full circle: From at-risk to empowerment*. Paper presented at The Freshman Year Experience Small College Conference. Philadelphia, PA.

Gordon, V. N., & Grites, T. J. (1984). The freshman seminar course: Helping students succeed. *Journal of College Student Personnel, 25*(4), 315-320.

Hipps, G. M. (1980). Talking about teaching: The contributions of senior faculty to junior faculty. In W. C. Nelsen & M. E. Siegel (Eds.), *Effective approaches to faculty development* (pp. 43-48). Washington, DC: Association of American Colleges.

Joyce, B., & Showers, B. (1983). *Power in staff development through research on training*. Alexandria, VA: Association for Supervision of Curriculum Development.

Levinson, D. J. (1978). *The seasons of a man's life*. New York: Knopf.

Levinson-Rose, J., & Menges, R. J. (1981). Improving college teaching: A critical review of research. *Review of Educational Research, 51*, 403-434.

Quinlan, K. M. (1991). About teaching and learning centers. *AAHE Bulletin, 44*(2), pp. 12-14

Sorcinelli, M.D. (1988). Satisfactions and concerns of new university teachers. In J. Kurfiss (Ed.), *To improve the academy: Resources for student, faculty, and institutional development, Vol. 7* (pp. 121-133). Stillwater, OK: New Forums Press, The Professional and Organizational Development Network in Higher Education.

Spear, K. I. (1984). Editor's notes. In Spear, K. I. (Ed.) *Rejuvenating introductory courses* (pp. 1-9). San Francisco: Jossey-Bass.

Study Group on the Conditions of Excellence in Higher Education.(1984). *Involvement in learning*. Washington, DC: National Institute of Education.

Torrance, E. P. (1984). *Mentor relationships: How they aid creative achievement, endure, change, and die*. Buffalo, NY: Baerly.

Turner, J. L., & Boice, R. (1987). Starting at the beginning: The concerns and needs of new faculty. In J. Kurfiss (Ed.), *To improve the academy: Resources for student, faculty, and institutional development, Vol. 6* (pp. 41-47). Stillwater, OK: New Forums Press, The Professional and Organizational Development Network in Higher Education.

CHAPTER

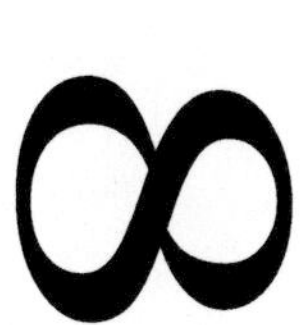

The Teaching Experience: A Faculty Development Workshop Series at the University of South Carolina

Dan Berman and Mary Stuart Hunter

Colleagues from other colleges and universities often ask what is the most unique feature of the University of South Carolina's University 101 first-year seminar course. Many factors could be highlighted, but invariably we identify "The Teaching Experience," a faculty development and instructor training workshop series, as the central and most critical component.

It is not coincidental that this feature of the program is also the most fundamental element—the foundation of the entire first-year seminar program. Although new students are the beneficiaries and focus of the seminar, the origins of the University 101 program at the University of South Carolina have as much to do with faculty development as with student development. Student unrest during the Vietnam era and an actual riot on campus in May 1970 led then University President Thomas F. Jones to conclude that a number of wide-ranging issues on campus resulted in students feeling ignored. Graham (1999) notes, "Many of the student grievances were legitimate, [but] the students did not have a substantial voice in the governance of the University." Under Jones's leadership, a number of new programs and services were implemented to address this less than desirable situation, one of which was University 101. The freshman seminar was the vehicle through which a creative and comprehensive faculty/staff development experience was implemented.

During the early years of University 101, a workshop was created with the support of a Ford Foundation Venture Fund Grant to prepare faculty and professional staff to teach the course. The 45-hour workshop included in its content communication skills, student needs and characteristics, and campus resource information. Heavily experiential in approach, the workshop provided the setting for a substantial human growth experience for the participants. Although the instructor development workshop has evolved with the changing times since its creation in the early 1970s, it has remained a centerpiece of the University 101 program.

At the heart of any successful programmatic institutional endeavor is the quality of the preparation and support for those who must transform pedagogical theory into action. For the first-year seminar, intensive preparation should be provided for all course instructors and, if applicable, graduate student leaders and undergraduate peer leaders. In short, anyone who represents our instructional programs and/or teaches in the classroom should be provided with access to the knowledge, strategies, and skills essential to producing successful student outcomes.

Workshops designed to enhance the teaching experience are a direct and efficient means of supporting an effective first-year seminar or college orientation program. Several strategies and approaches that have been employed at the University of South Carolina will be discussed. These are not intended to be all-inclusive; rather, the overriding purpose is to present a model for designing a preparatory experience that can then be adapted to a variety of higher education institutions and first-year student programs.

Where to Start

The most productive starting point in designing an instructor training program necessitates the identification and delineation of the central purposes of your course or program. This involves answering several key questions:

1. For whom is the course or program designed?

2. What type of course or program will be implemented or is currently in place?

3. What resources and/or delivery systems are available?

4. Who will teach the course and/or administer the program?

5. Who can be recruited as facilitators for instructor training and what individual strengths does each facilitator possess?

6. What skills and/or knowledge should instructors be prepared to convey to the students?

7. What teaching methods will prove most effective?

8. What are the desired outcomes and/or goals of both the workshop and the course and/or program?

Workshop Goals and Participants

At the University of South Carolina, an initial training workshop is required of all instructors. Currently, this three-day workshop, entitled "The Teaching Experience," is offered twice a year and is open to all employees of the institution. Workshop participants may be faculty, administrators, support staff, or student development professionals. Prior to the workshop, most participants are strangers and often have at best a casual acquaintance with each other. However, the workshops bring together participants with the common goals of learning more about students, the first-year seminar, and the guidelines for teaching the course. Not all workshop participants will teach the seminar; however, all instructors who teach the course must have participated in "The Teaching Experience."

The workshop is designed to achieve the following goals:

1. to increase sensitivity to the needs and characteristics of first-year students

2. to foster understanding of course content and objectives

3. to provide opportunities for small group, collaborative work designed to generate information and resources to be used in teaching

4. to demonstrate diverse and innovative teaching strategies

5. to give participants the opportunity to practice what they have learned in the workshop by engaging in teaching activities

In short, to prepare participants to teach the course, workshop facilitators—often a team of faculty and student affairs professionals—must provide participants with the knowledge and skills necessary to be effective first-year seminar instructors. Through experiential learning and creative activities, the participants become fully involved in the planning and implementation of the course.

The University 101 Four-Phase Workshop Model

In recent years, the University 101 workshops have placed more emphasis on teaching strategies and techniques than during the program's formative years. Nevertheless, workshop content and process continue to reflect the four-phase model delineated in John N. Gardner's (1981) seminal article, "Developing Faculty as Facilitators and Mentors." Gardner identifies the four phases of faculty development as follows:

Phase 1. Developing a sense of community and building group trust

Phase 2. Identifying the needs of learners

Phase 3. Identifying and developing resources to address these needs

Phase 4. Developing strategies to utilize and incorporate workshop content and outcomes in other settings

It is not accidental or coincidental that the students who take our course will move through the same four phases. Essentially, the workshop is a microcosm of the first-year seminar course. The format allows workshop participants to experience growth and changes that parallel those of the students enrolled in a one-semester, first-year seminar experience. Many colleges may find providing an extensive workshop difficult, but we recommend a minimum of a two-day workshop to accomplish the goals outlined above.

The selection and ordering of activities will vary in particular workshops; however, each workshop addresses the objectives of the four-phase model. Examples of strategies and activities presented in each of the four phases follow.

Phase 1: Developing a Sense of Community and Building Group Trust

At the beginning of the workshop, facilitators ask participants to complete the following statement on an index card: "My hopes and expectations for this workshop are . . . ." The facilitators collect the cards and post them in a prominent location in the workshop facility. This enables facilitators and participants to obtain an overview of why participants are attending the workshop and what they want to learn or experience.

What occurs next may, at first, seem antithetical to building group solidarity and creating an inviting, comfortable atmosphere, but this activity is designed to present a traditional, formally structured college classroom model that soon will be contrasted with a more experiential, informally-structured model. With participants seated in a traditional classroom arrangement, the facilitators first introduce themselves to the participants in a quasi-formal manner. Then one of the facilitators makes a more formal presentation in lecture mode to the group. Topics covered may include the history of the course or program and a structured explanation of the workshop agenda and goals. At the conclusion of this session, the facilitators ask participants to form a mental snapshot of what they have heard and how they experienced it.

A 10-minute refreshment break follows as the facilitators rearrange the chairs to form a circle. The formal, quasi-adversarial seating structure has been replaced by an informal, personal configuration. Now everyone can see the faces of all the participants, and no one sits or stands in a position of leadership or authority. The shape of a circle encourages openness, inclusion, and group cohesiveness.

Once the participants are seated, the facilitators initiate an icebreaker activity—usually, a name-chain in which participants state their name and share with the group two of their favorite hobbies or interests. The central goal is for the participants to see each other as accessible human beings rather than as professors, administrators, or other educators. The activity also allows participants to learn each other's names and to explore commonalities and shared interests. At the end of this activity, facilitators ask participants to form a second mental snapshot and then compare this to the earlier one configured in the more formal setting. Invariably the group responds more favorably to the second, more personal model and begins to bond as informal sharing breaks down interpersonal barriers.

Facilitators encourage participants to process the experience and discuss other icebreakers and methods of encouraging group building. Then, both facilitators and participants share ideas for beginning a class that previously have worked for them. Usually, this phase concludes with participants composing "lifelines," drawings on poster-size pieces of paper featuring the key events in their lives, and sharing these drawings in groups of five or six participants. By the time this activity concludes, participants tend to feel comfortable and close to each other while enthusiastically looking forward to the upcoming activities.

Phase 2: Identifying the Needs of Learners

The central goal in this phase is to increase the sensitivity toward and understanding of the needs of students in the first-year seminar course. The exercises used at this point should encourage participants to recall empathetically what they were like when they were first-year college students.

Often, a second stage is added in which participants create two lists comparing the needs and characteristics of today's students to those of students when the participants entered college. Participants share their discoveries of what has changed over the years and what has remained constant. The goal of this exercise is to enhance understanding of and empathy for today's students through introspective awareness of the participants' commonalities and differences.

Ideally, first-year students can be invited to participate in this phase of the workshop. These students would be asked to form their own lists of student needs and characteristics that can be compared with the lists created by the workshop participants. This also is an appropriate juncture to begin exploring the central components of the first-year seminar course. Participants begin to formulate ideas about how the course can be designed to address those student needs identified in the previous exercises.

> . . . the content of the teaching experience workshop is "process-oriented," dealing more with teaching strategies and approaches than with specific course content.

The format for these and most other workshop activities is as follows. The workshop facilitators provide background information and direction in preparation for a group exercise. Workshop facilitators ask participants to form small groups of five to seven. Each group selects a spokesperson who later will present the small group's findings to the workshop participants as a whole. The small group presentations will present alternate and innovative approaches to common tasks and challenges, expanding the knowledge-base of not only the participants but also of the workshop facilitators.

Phase 3: Identifying and Developing Resources to Address These Needs

During this phase, workshop participants are led to identify resources within the workshop group, at the institution, and in the local community. A major portion of this activity involves introducing the workshop participants to university or college personnel who head key campus resource areas with which students need to become familiar. This knowledge becomes increasingly important as course requirements become more demanding and diverse.

Course instructors must become familiar with such key student success areas as the campus library, the career center, computer and other technological resources, academic support services, student health services, student affairs offices, campus groups and organizations, college advisement procedures, and cultural growth opportunities. The workshop facilitators identify essential university or college programs and suggest effective ways to integrate this information into the course.

Frequently, as first-year seminars develop more traditional academic content, greater emphasis must be placed on preparing instructors to teach and present course content through effective and stimulating methodologies. However, the increased academic content emphases should not be seen as antithetical to the more affective teaching methodologies that have been promoted since the creation of the program. Rather, the affective and cognitive areas now must be seen as connected and interrelated. Essentially the affective teaching approaches often are the most effective means of achieving cognitive goals. Consequently, both values clarification and critical thinking are emphasized as essential goals of the course and as integral components of the workshop. Again, these are *not* mutually exclusive or opposite areas. Students are encouraged to develop a personal, ethical system of values. However, critical thinking skills often prove invaluable in helping students clarify their values and communicate those values clearly and effectively. Furthermore, this dual area of emphasis also encourages respect for diverse viewpoints and willingness to learn from and about others who can bring new ideas and viewpoints into the classroom or workshop setting.

No teaching preparation workshop would be complete without providing opportunities for the participants to practice teaching within the workshop. One effective means of preparing participants to teach is by bringing experienced seminar teachers into the workshop to share their most successful teaching strategies and experiences. A question and answer follow-up session is essential in building relationships between novice and experienced course instructors and in identifying additional instructional resources.

Next, several key topic areas, covered in chapters of the designated first-year seminar textbook, are chosen. Workshop participants might be asked to read each of the chapters dealing with such topics as diversity, developing a personal system of values, academic integrity, selecting an academic major, or the value of a liberal arts education. The facilitators then create groups and assign each a chapter to prepare to teach. The group members identify the key ideas in the chapter that they most want to convey to their students. Then they devise a creative teaching strategy to enliven that chapter for their students. Finally each group then must teach their chapter creatively to the remaining workshop participants.

Everyone in the workshop has the opportunity to interact in the role of both teacher and student. Of course many "students" will make additional suggestions to the "teachers." By so doing, the teacher-student continuum and the ideal of lifelong learning will be delineated and emphasized.

Phase 4: Developing Strategies to Utilize and Incorporate Workshop Content and Outcomes in Other Settings

In Phase 3, the generation of effective teaching strategies and the sharing of successful strategies by experienced University 101 instructors represent important experiential components of the workshop. Another very effective experiential link is to do something all instructors must do—namely, prepare a course syllabus.

By this stage in the workshop, participants should be thoroughly familiar with the goals of the course and should have learned and demonstrated effective teaching strategies. As a trigger or stimulus for syllabus planning in small groups, visualization strategies often are presented.

Participants visualize how they expect their students to act on the first day of class and then how they would like them to act on the final day of the course. Prior to creating a detailed syllabus with content schedule, they create, in two columns, "Before" and "After" lists describing student characteristics in the two stages identified above.

This exercise also provides an excellent opportunity to present the concept of teaching for epiphany. The instructor is encouraged to create "learning moment" opportunities when students will be challenged to experience compelling insights into their academic and co-curricular lives. As an example, sequences from a stimulating film, such as Barry Levinson's *Rain Man* (1988), can be interpreted as illustrating a significant epiphany as well as demonstrating characteristics of poor and excellent teaching. A corollary benefit is the demonstration of how a wide range of media can be incorporated into classroom instruction.

At the conclusion of the workshop a "strengths bombardment" exercise is used as a final bonding and celebrating activity. Again, using large sheets of paper, the participants list approximately five of their perceived strengths related to teaching college students. Once the lists have been posted, participants move around the room and add to each other's list of strengths while validating those previously cited. This is a powerful positive reinforcement activity, and participants usually leave the workshop with positive feelings, confident in their ability to teach a first-year seminar.

To summarize, some variation of "The Teaching Experience" is essential to the success of a first-year seminar course. At the University of South Carolina, initial workshops are provided for future instructors and shorter versions of the workshops are provided for graduate student leaders and undergraduate peer leaders. The bottom line is that everyone who has an instructional role in the University 101 course must complete the appropriate training workshop for their group.

These teaching experience workshops are the cornerstones of the training efforts at the University of South Carolina. The workshops, as described, are the foundation upon which instructors build their teaching approaches. It can be noted that the content of the teaching experience workshop is "process-oriented," dealing more with teaching strategies and approaches than with specific course content. Detailed information on course content is provided in follow-up training workshops for the teaching faculty each academic year. Recall, that those who participate in "The Teaching Experience" do not necessarily teach the first-year seminar. "The Teaching Experience" workshops are the foundational training experience in that they introduce participants to program background, philosophy, active learning strategies, and provide a limited introduction to actual course content. When the instructional staff is selected for the upcoming academic year, additional half-day workshops are arranged to cover current content emphasis areas, changes in program administration, and specific information that instructors need in order to teach the course successfully. Additionally, team-building workshops are arranged and held for instructors who are team teaching with peer leaders and/or graduate leaders. Through didactic and experiential means, the teams work together in these required training events to explore the potential roles and responsibilities of team members, effective elements of partnerships, and course content requirements.

A successful training program will provide participants with an understanding of the following:

1. the purposes/goals of the course

2. the needs and characteristics of students

3. major campus support resources

4. innovative teaching methodologies

5. several models for successful syllabi

All of the above can be incorporated to meet a variety of goals and be adapted to courses with different areas of emphasis.

The first-year seminar course is constantly changing and adapting to the increasingly diverse needs of our students. This constant flux emphasizes the need to prepare instructors to adapt to these changes while still fulfilling the common, shared characteristics of the course. In conclusion, the primary workshop design should stress what is enduring and consistent in the seminar, yet it should also have the flexibility to adapt to change by establishing successful variations of the basic course model.

References

Gardner, J. N. (1981). Developing faculty as facilitators and mentors. In V. A. Harren (Ed.), Facilitating student's career development (pp. 67-79). *New Directions for Student Services, 14.* San Francisco: Jossey-Bass.

Graham, M. R. (1999). *University 101: Education's Aladdin's lamp at the University of South Carolina, 1972-1999.* Unpublished paper. Columbia, SC: University of South Carolina.

Assessment and Evaluation of Instructor Training Programs

Joseph B. Cuseo

CHAPTER 9

Program evaluation is an important component of any effective educational program or intervention. Its importance is magnified if the program is associated with the new-student seminar because this nontraditional course is likely to be the target of skeptics and critics (Gardner, 1989). One way to combat such skepticism effectively is by careful evaluation and documentation of the program's total benefits, including evaluation of its instructor training component. Thus, one major purpose of assessment is to obtain evaluative information on the overall effectiveness or impact of instructor training for use in bottom-line decisions about maintaining, funding, or expanding this program. A second major purpose of instructor training assessment is to obtain evaluative information on the program for the purpose of improving or fine-tuning its quality. In assessment terminology, the first purpose is referred to as "summative evaluation"—assessment designed to "sum up" a program's overall value, and the second purpose is referred to as "formative evaluation"—assessment intended to help form, shape, or further develop a program's effectiveness (Scriven, 1967).

Identifying intended outcomes of the instructor training program must be addressed first if meaningful program evaluation is to take place. The pivotal role of outcomes in the assessment process is underscored by Trudy Banta, a nationally-recognized assessment scholar, and her colleagues (1996):

> Assessment is most effective when it is based on clear and focused goals and objectives. It is from these goals that educators fashion the coherent frameworks around which they can carry out inquiry. When such frameworks are not constructed, assessment outcomes fall short of providing the direction necessary to improve programs. (p. 22)

In this chapter, intended outcomes common to many instructor training efforts will be identified, along with potential measures of these outcomes. This general discussion of program outcomes and related outcome measures will be followed by a more detailed examination of quantitative and qualitative program evaluation methods, including methodological issues relating to design and administration of program evaluation instruments. Lastly, strategies for construction and dissemination of an evaluation report will be suggested as an important final step in the program assessment process.

Potential Outcomes of Instructor Training and Related Outcome Measures

Participants' Immediate Satisfaction with the Instructor Training Program

The most basic outcome of an instructor training program is participant satisfaction with the program's usefulness in preparing them to teach the new-student seminar.

This outcome may be most conveniently measured by assessing participants' perceptions of the program effectiveness immediately after the training experience. For example, paper and pencil ratings of participants' level of satisfaction with the program, or individual interviews with participants to assess their perceptions of program effectiveness could be used as measures of this outcome. These assessments should include questions about the program's overall quality, as well as its specific components.

To assess the impact of program components most effectively, end-of-program evaluations should be supplemented with more frequent and focused assessments administered immediately after the participants experience individual presentations, particular pedagogical models, or specific learning activities. One way to obtain feedback on specific program experiences is the "minute paper," a strategy developed by an engineering professor at the University of California-Berkeley (Davis, Wood, & Wilson, 1983) and popularized by Cross and Angelo (1988). Minute papers require participants to provide a short (one-minute) answer in response to a question posed at the end of a particular learning experience (e.g., "What was the most memorable or useful thing you learned in this session?"). The nature of the question can vary depending on the nature and objective of the learning experience, but the one constant among all types of minute papers is that they serve to provide facilitator(s) with frequent and immediate feedback on how participants respond to specific learning experiences. Three by five index cards distributed by workshop leaders can facilitate the use of this simple assessment technique. Such focused forms of learning assessment could be adopted in the instructor training program to provide instructors with direct feedback on individual program components which otherwise may be masked or "averaged out" when respondents report their perceptions after the entire program has been experienced.

> This cyclical process of (a) evaluation, (b) feedback, (c) program revision in response to feedback, and (d) reevaluation . . . has great potential for isolating and "teasing out"... components or processes that have the most dramatic impact on program effectiveness.

Frequent assessments of specific program components, conducted immediately after participants experience them during the training program, may also provide assessment data of greater validity because the evaluations are more sharply focused and the experience is more readily recalled by the evaluators. In contrast, typical end-of-program instruments tend to ask more global questions about general program characteristics. Even if questions are included that ask about particular program components, they typically require the respondents to recall specific experiences that are usually preceded and followed by a number of other specific experiences. These successive experiences can cause memory "interference," resulting in forgetting or inaccurate recall of the particular component being evaluated.

Participants' Retrospective Perceptions after Teaching the New-Student Seminar

Very little published information exists on how course instructors view the new-student seminar (e.g., their sources of instructional satisfaction and frustration or their opinions of course strengths and weaknesses). Since most instructors who teach the new-student seminar are stepping out of their own area of disciplinary or professional specialization and stepping into a role that may involve the learning of new content and new teaching techniques, it would be useful to assess the degree to which they feel the instructor training program prepared them for this new teaching role.

First-time seminar instructors' written responses to open-ended surveys, or their verbal responses during personal interviews or structured group discussions, could be used to assess their course experiences. Another possible source of information on instructors' course experiences might be the teaching portfolio, an instructor self-assessment procedure whereby teachers collect their ideas and materials relating to course instruction (e.g., responses to student evaluations and/or peer assessments, course handouts and assignments, teaching goal statements, or "teaching journal" entries). The portfolio may be useful not only to individual instructors for self-reflection and instructional improvement but also for assessment purposes. For instance, portfolios of different instructors could be reviewed and their content analyzed to assess whether teaching the new-student seminar impacts instructors in predictable ways and whether or not the instructor training program prepared them for this teaching experience.

Another strategy for obtaining specific, frequent feedback from new instructors is to ask small groups of instructors to provide verbal feedback on specific course components as they experience them for the first time. This could be accomplished by adopting a modified version of a feedback procedure called the "student advisory committee" (Haug, 1992). This type of student-centered assessment strategy is designed to provide specific and continuous feedback on course effectiveness by vesting the responsibility with a group of students, typically referred to as a "student advisory committee," whose role is to solicit evaluative comments from their classmates periodically and to meet regularly with their instructor throughout the term. These meetings between the instructor and student advisory committee members are designed to discuss students' general satisfaction with the course and the effectiveness of specific instructional practices—while the course is still in progress. This practice could be modified to assess the effectiveness of instructor training by having a few first-time seminar instructors serve as the advisory committee members whose role is to solicit feedback from other first-time instructors and to meet periodically throughout the term to share this feedback with the director of the new-student seminar program.

Information gleaned from these experiences could be valuable for fine-tuning the instructor training program, perhaps leading to important modifications in its duration, content, or delivery. After these program modifications are made in response to feedback, it might be possible to assess whether the modified program has beneficial effects on the teaching experiences of subsequent cohorts of new instructors. This cyclical process of (a) evaluation, (b) feedback, (c) program revision in response to feedback, and (d) reevaluation of the revised program has great potential for isolating and "teasing out" instructor training components or processes that have the most dramatic impact on program effectiveness.

Systemic Outcomes of Instructor Training

While preparation for course instruction clearly is the most important intended outcome of the instructor training program, other outcomes might be realized by the program that are more pervasive or systemic in nature. Drawing on their many years of instructor training at the University of South Carolina, Gardner and Hunter (1994) suggest that there are six potential positive outcomes associated with a comprehensive instructor training program for teaching the new-student seminar:

1. faculty growth and development
2. development of professional support groups
3. bridging of "gaps" between faculty and staff
4. increased institutional awareness
5. increased sensitivity of faculty and staff to the needs of first-year students
6. adoption of student-centered teaching techniques

Related research and program evaluation strategies for assessing these comprehensive and potentially pervasive outcomes of instructor training are discussed below.

Impact on participants' teaching effectiveness in courses other than the new-student seminar. While there is emerging evidence suggesting that faculty who teach the seminar self-report becoming more student-centered (University of Wyoming, in Barefoot, 1993) and more willing to try new instructional methods in other courses (Montana State University-Bozeman, in Barefoot, Warnock, Dickinson, Richardson, & Roberts, 1998), the question of whether such faculty are actually perceived as providing more effective instruction by students in other courses still remains.

It is reasonable to hypothesize that faculty involvement in instructor training will have a positive impact on student evaluations received by faculty in their discipline-based courses because of two common elements that characterize instructor training and new-student seminar instruction: (a) focus on instructional strategies that promote teacher-student interaction, and (b) emphasis on instructional methods that promote student-student interaction in small groups. Both of these instructional characteristics have been found to correlate positively with student evaluations of college teaching effectiveness (Bligh, 1972; Kulik & Kulik, 1979; Lowman, 1984). If faculty use of these instructional methods in the new-student seminar is transferred to their regular classes—as research at one university already suggests (Central Missouri State University, cited in Barefoot, 1993), then it may be reasonable to expect that this transfer of interactive teaching techniques may result in improved student evaluations in the usual courses taught by faculty in their academic discipline.

Given that student evaluations are among the most commonly used methods for assessing college teaching and that the frequency of their use is increasing (Seldin, 1993), it would be valuable to assess whether participation in the instructor training program and subsequent teaching of the new-student seminar can contribute to improved student evaluations for courses taught by instructors in their own academic disciplines. This might be accomplished by comparing instructors' student ratings for courses taught after their participation in the instructor training program with ratings they received for the same courses taught before participating in the training program. Course enrollment patterns of students could also be compared in this fashion, such as the number of student withdrawals from classes taught by instructors before versus after participating in the instructor training program.

Promotion of campus community and the development of professional partnerships across different divisions or units of the college. One oft-cited benefit of instructor training programs and subsequent teaching of the new-student seminar is the heightened sense of community that is generated on campus, particularly if members from different divisions of the college community are involved in instructor training and seminar instruction (e.g., faculty from different academic disciplines, academic support and student development staff, and college administrators). This is a potentially powerful perquisite of instructor training because the lack of campus community and of a sense of common purpose have been identified as significant problems at many higher education institutions (The Carnegie Foundation, 1990). In particular, a perennial schism or "persistent gap" between the divisions of academic and student affairs appears to exist (Brown, 1988; Smith, 1988).

Unfortunately, evidence for the community building impact of instructor training programs appears only in the form of personal observations or anecdotal reports. If these informal observations and anecdotes could be transformed into "hard data," or at least well-organized qualitative data, an important institutional outcome of instructor training programs could be assessed systematically.

Increased sensitivity to the needs of first-year students. This subjective outcome may be measured by the amount of reported change in participants' knowledge and attitudes between the onset and completion of the instructor training program. Participant responses given at the end of the training program can be compared to those given before the training begins. This can be accomplished by means of a pre-/post-evaluation procedure in which the evaluation instrument, or selected items from it, are answered before the training begins. These responses can then be used as a baseline (pre-training) against which participants' post-training responses can be compared.

Another strategy for assessing program impact on promoting positive change in knowledge of or attitudes toward first-year students is to simply include items on the questionnaire which ask participants if their attitudes toward different student issues were changed as a result of their program experience. For example, at the University of South Carolina, participants are asked to rate whether their attitudes about students become "more positive," "less positive," or remain unchanged by the instructor training experience (M. S. Hunter, personal communication, November 7, 1996).

To measure whether instructor training promotes sensitivity to the needs of first-year students, pre- versus post-training "change scores" could be tallied for participants' attitudes toward, or knowledge of first-year students' (a) academic and personal characteristics at college entry, (b) high school-to-college transitional adjustments, and (c) common anxieties or fears about succeeding in college.

Increased institutional awareness and appreciation. This potential positive outcome of instructor training could also be measured via a pre-/post-procedure, or by reported change scores in participants' knowledge or appreciation of services provided by the institution (e.g., academic support services, such as the learning resource center and library, and student development services, such as the counseling center and office of student life).

Program participants' self-reported changes in institutional knowledge or appreciation could be supplemented by behavioral measures, such as the number of student referrals to these services made by program participants following their instructor training experience, relative to the number made prior to the training experience.

Research Methods for Evaluating Instructor Training Programs

Which research method(s) will be used to assess whether intended outcomes of instructor training have been realized is an important decision that should be made before data are collected and analyzed (Halpern, 1987). Thus, decisions about the research design or method for evaluating the program should be made early in the process of program research and evaluation. In this section, two major types of research methods will be examined—quantitative and qualitative. Descriptions of specific versions of these methods will be provided, accompanied by a discussion of their relative advantages and disadvantages.

Quantitative Methods

Astin (1991) suggests a taxonomy for classifying types of quantitative data that fall into two broad categories: (a) behavioral data reflecting actions or activities; and (b) psychological data reflecting internal states, such as perceptions, opinions, or attitudes. The former may be gathered via frequency counts and the latter by numerical ratings reported on surveys or questionnaires. Each of these strategies will be discussed in turn.

Frequency counts. One quantitative method for evaluating the effectiveness of an instructor training program is the frequency count. For instance, an examination of participant behavior can reveal: (a) number and variety of participants who attend the program, (b) number of instructional strategies presented in the program that are actually implemented during course instruction, (c) number of participants who make follow-up inquiries about effective teaching strategies after participating in the program, and (d) number of participants reporting ongoing contact or collaboration with other faculty and staff members who were met initially during the training experience.

Numerical ratings. Probably the most common and convenient quantitative measure of participant opinions or perceptions of program effectiveness is a numerical rating, typically gathered by means of such instruments as surveys or questionnaires. The following recommendations are offered for improving the content and form of surveys or questionnaires, thereby increasing the validity and interpretability of evaluative ratings reported by program participants on these instruments.

- Clustering individual items into logical categories that represent important program components is one way to improve survey design. For instance, items could be grouped in terms of their relevance to each of the following key components of the program experience: (a) course planning and design (e.g., questions pertaining to overall course organization and clarity of course objectives), (b) classroom instruction (e.g., items pertaining to classroom teaching, such as clarity and organization of program presentations), and (c) evaluation of student performance (e.g., items pertaining to tests, assignments, and grading practices). Also, a healthy balance of questions pertaining to both course content (topics and subtopics) and instructional processes (in-class and out-of-class learning activities) should be included on the evaluation form.

  One major advantage of this clustering or categorizing strategy is that the categories can function as signposts or retrieval cues for the designers of the survey, ensuring that the items selected for inclusion in the instrument reflect a well-balanced sample of the major course dimensions that should be addressed in a comprehensive instructor training program.

Another advantage of grouping items under section headings is its potential for functioning as a cue or signal to the evaluators completing the instrument, reminding them of the different dimensions of the program and that these dimensions may have differed in terms of their relative degree of effectiveness. This may help respondents to discriminate among separate components nested within the instructor training program, increasing the likelihood that these independent components will be assessed independently.

Lastly, partitioning the instrument into separate sections, reflecting separate program components, should also help to reduce the risk of a general "halo effect," i.e., the tendency for some respondents to complete the evaluation instrument by going right down the same column (e.g., filling in all "1s" or "5s" for all items), depending on whether they generally liked or disliked the training experience.

- Rating scales should allow five to seven choice points or response options. Research suggests that fewer than five choices reduces an instrument's ability to discriminate between satisfied and dissatisfied respondents, and more than seven rating scale options adds nothing to the instrument's discriminability (Cashin, 1990).

- A neutral option (e.g., "don't know" or "not sure") should *not* be included as a response alternative if at all possible. This option could generate misleading results because it may be used as an "escape route" by respondents who do have strong opinions but are reluctant to offer them (Arreola, 1983).

- The word "comments" should be printed beneath each item on the instrument with a small space for any written remarks that participants would like to make with respect to that particular item. Written comments often serve to clarify or elucidate numerical ratings, and research suggests that written comments are most useful for instructional improvement purposes, especially if such comments are specific (Seldin, 1992). At the University of South Carolina, assessment of its instructor training program involves numerical ratings of each workshop activity and presentation; after each item, space is provided for written comments with respect to that particular activity or presentation (M. S. Hunter, personal communication, November 7, 1996).

  Allowing participants to write comments with respect to each individual item, rather than restricting them to the usual "general comments" section at the very end of the evaluation form, should also serve to increase the specificity of participants' written remarks and, consequently, their utility for program improvement.

- The inclusion on the evaluation instrument of at least two global items pertaining to overall program effectiveness or impact can be effective for summative evaluation purposes. The following statements illustrate global items that are useful for summative evaluation:

  1. I would rate the overall quality of this program as: (poor <- - -> excellent).
  2. I would rate the general usefulness of this program as: (very low <- - -> very high).
  3. I would recommend this program to other faculty and staff: (strongly agree <- - -> strongly disagree).

Comprehensive evaluation of an instructor training program should include assessment of its individual components as well the program's overall quality. Participants' responses to global items can provide an effective and convenient snapshot of their overall evaluation of the program which can be readily used in program assessment reports. Research on college students has repeatedly shown that global ratings are more predictive of learning than ratings given to individual survey items pertaining to specific aspects or dimensions of instruction

(Braskamp & Ory, 1994; Centra, 1993; Cohen, 1986). As Cashin (1990) puts it, global items function "like a final course grade" (p. 2).

While ratings on global items may be used to make summative (overall) assessments of the program, it is *not* advisable to add up the ratings for all individual items on the instrument and then average them to obtain an overall program evaluation score. This procedure is not only inefficient, but it is also an ineffective index of overall program satisfaction because it gratuitously assumes that each individual item on the instrument carries equal weight in shaping respondents' overall evaluation of the program.

An advantage of including global items on the evaluation instrument is that it allows for the examination of possible relationships between participants' overall program rating and their ratings of individual items that pertain to specific program dimensions or components. Examining these relationships could help answer the following question: Among those participants who give the program high global ratings, versus those who give the program low overall ratings, on which particular items in the evaluation instrument do these two groups display the largest discrepancy in ratings? These particular items could reveal those specific aspects or dimensions of the program which carry the most weight in determining participants' overall perception and general level of satisfaction with the instructor training program. These specific program dimensions may represent key target areas for program improvement which, if made, could significantly enhance the quality of future instructor training experiences.

- A few open-ended questions that ask participants for their written comments about the program's strengths and weaknesses and how the latter may be improved should be included on the evaluation form. Such questions can often provide useful information about participants' general reaction to the program as well as specific suggestions for program improvement. As Schilling and Schilling (1998) point out, "Although surveys that use numerical rating scales may be easier to summarize, those that are open-ended may invite more thoughtful reflection and yield the kinds of detailed understanding that are often difficult to extract from a mean score on a rating scale" (p. 254).

  For example, at the end of the program evaluation form, questions could be included which ask participants to "describe a major change (if any) in their approach to teaching that resulted from their participation in the training program." Or, participants could be asked, "What would have been useful for you to learn that was not addressed in the training program?" Written responses given to these questions could be aggregated and analyzed to identify recurrent themes.

- Participants can also be asked to suggest questions which they think should be included on the evaluation. This opportunity could be cued by the following prompt placed at the end of the evaluation form: "Suggested Questions for Future Evaluations." This practice has three major advantages: (a) It may identify participant perspectives and concerns that the evaluation form fails to address; (b) it shows respect for participant input; and (c) it gives participants some sense of control or ownership of the evaluation process.

- The wording of evaluation items should avoid vague or ambiguous descriptors which may be difficult to interpret, or whose meaning may be interpreted by different participants in different ways (for example, "Pacing of program presentations was *appropriate*.").

- Items should be worded using the singular, first-person pronoun ("I" or "me") rather than the third-person plural ("participants"). For instance, "The program gave *me* effective information on how *I* could improve my instructional performance" should be used rather than, "The program gave *participants* effective feedback on how *they* could improve their instructional performance." The rationale underlying this recommendation is that an individual participant can make a valid personal judgment with respect to his or her own program experience, but he or she is not in a position to judge and report how other participants, or participants in general, perceive the program.

- Items should be structured so that respondents are not asked to rate two different aspects of the program simultaneously (e.g., "The program's *presentations* and *activities* were useful."). This practice forces respondents to give the same rating to both aspects, even if they are more satisfied with one aspect than the other. For example, a participant may feel that the presentations were more useful than the activities.

- One or two negatively-worded items should be included in the evaluation. Negatively worded items (e.g., "I did *not* receive effective feedback on how I could improve my performance.") require respondents to reverse the rating scale and serve two purposes. First, they encourage participants to read and rate each item carefully, serving to reduce the probability of "positive response set" mistakes (Arreola & Aleamoni, 1990) in which respondents go straight down a rating column and fill in uniformly high ratings for all items. Second, they can help identify evaluation forms which have not been completed carefully and may need to be deleted from the data analysis. For example, participants who have responded hastily by filling in all positive or all negative ratings may be identified by their failure to reverse their responses on the negatively worded item(s).

- Instructions read prior to distribution of evaluation forms should prepare or prime participants for the important role that participants play in evaluating the program and should provide them with a positive "anticipatory set." To increase participants' motivation for program evaluation and the effort they expend in the evaluation process (thereby improving the validity and usefulness of the results obtained), the assessment team should consider including the following information in the instructions read to participants prior to the program evaluation.

  1. Facilitators should articulate the reasons why evaluations are being conducted. If items relating to specific program activities are to be used for program improvement purposes and global items for overall program evaluation purposes, then this distinction should be mentioned in the instructions.

  2. Participants should be reminded that evaluating the program is an opportunity for them to provide meaningful input that could improve the quality of instructor training for future cohorts of seminar instructors.

  3. Facilitators will want to assure participants that their evaluations will be read carefully and taken seriously by the program presenters and director.

  4. Participants should be encouraged to provide written comments in order to clarify or justify their numerical ratings, and facilitators should emphasize that specific comments are especially welcome because they provide specific feedback on program strengths and suggest ideas for overcoming program weaknesses.

- A pilot study should be conducted before using the instrument for program evaluation purposes. The pilot study can be given to a sample of faculty and staff who assess whether (a) the instrument's instructions are clear, (b) the wording of individual items is unambiguous, and (c) the total time needed to complete the instrument is manageable. As Fidler (1992) notes, "Seasoned researchers recommend pilot studies before every research project in order to identify and quickly alter procedures, thereby alleviating problems before they can invalidate an entire study" (p. 16).

Qualitative Research Methods

Quantitative data, such as survey ratings and behavioral measures, provide evaluative information that can be readily summarized and manipulated numerically. Such data can be scored efficiently by machine or computer and are amenable to statistical analysis (e.g., correlation coefficients or chi-square analysis). In contrast, qualitative data take the form of human actions and words (e.g., respondents' written or verbal comments), and they are analyzed by means of "human instruments" (Kuh, Schuh, & Whitt, 1991, p. 273). Also, in contrast to the hypothesis testing and scientific methodology that characterizes quantitative research, qualitative research is "exploratory [and] inductive, . . . one does not manipulate variables or administer a treatment. What one does is observe, intuit, [and] sense what is occurring in natural settings" (Merriam, 1988, p. 17).

Increasing emphasis is being placed on qualitative research in higher education (Fidler, 1992). Some of its more radical proponents argue that it should displace or replace the dominant quantitative paradigm which, they feel, has exerted an almost hegemonic hold on the research methodology used in education and the social sciences (Duffy & Jonassen, 1992). On the other hand, those in the quantitative camp argue that qualitative research often lacks reliability or objectivity, yielding data dangerously subject to biased interpretation (Reigeluth, 1992).

As is usually the case with such thesis-antithesis dichotomies, an effective synthesis lies somewhere between these two polar positions. While acknowledging that quantitative and qualitative research emerge from contrasting philosophical traditions and rest on very different epistemological assumptions (Smith & Heshusius, 1986), the position taken here is that the data generated by these two styles of inquiry can provide complementary sources of evidence, with the disadvantages of one method being offset or counterbalanced by the advantages of the other. For instance, participants' written comments on surveys can be used to help interpret averaged numerical rating scores, while averaged numerical rating scores can be used to counterbalance the tendency to draw overgeneralized conclusions from several written comments that happen to be particularly poignant and powerful, but which are not representative of participants as a whole.

". . . partitioning the instrument into separate sections, reflecting separate program components, should also help to reduce the risk of a general "halo effect,"

Among program evaluation scholars, it is almost axiomatic that the use of "multiple measures" in the assessment process provides more reliable and valid information than exclusive reliance on a single research method or data source (Wergin, 1988). Including multiple measures in the assessment plan for an instructor training program increases the likelihood that subtle differences in the effects of the program will be detected. Multiple methods also can be useful in demonstrating a consistent pattern of results across different methods—a cross-validation procedure known in the assessment literature as "triangulation" (Fetterman, 1991) or "convergent validity" (Campbell & Fiske, 1959). Such cross-validation serves to minimize the likelihood that the results obtained are merely an artifact of any one single method used to obtain them, and cross-validation also magnifies the persuasive power of the results obtained so that they be used more effectively to silence critics and convert skeptics.

As Fidler (1992) notes in her primer for research on the first-year experience,

> All research designs have strengths and weaknesses; therefore, no single piece of research can fully answer a research question. Researchers can select between qualitative or quantitative designs, and ideally a body of literature contains both types of designs in order to balance the strengths and weaknesses of each. (p. 11)

Consequently, a comprehensive and well-balanced evaluation of instructor training programs should include not only quantitative methods, but also qualitative methods, such as those described below.

Analysis of participants' written comments. Written comments made on surveys of participants can provide a good source of qualitative data. These comments may be difficult to summarize and manipulate statistically, but they have the potential for providing poignant, in-depth information on the program's strengths and weaknesses, as well as providing an index of participants' subjective feelings about the program. As Davis and Murrell (1993) note, "These descriptions provide much texture and offer rich, often powerful images of the [learning] experience" (p. 50).

Historically, surveys and questionnaires have not been considered to be qualitative research tools because they generate quantitative data (numerical ratings). However, any written comments made by respondents beneath their ratings do represent legitimate qualitative data, the content of which can be analyzed and classified systematically. Even the sheer number of positive or negative written responses made beneath a specific item on a rating survey may itself serve as a measure of the importance or intensity of respondent feelings about the issue addressed by that item. The following recommendation made by the National Orientation Directors Association (NODA) for surveys of orientation programs is also relevant to instructor training evaluation surveys,

> Request individual written comments and provide space on the evaluation for these remarks. Participants with strong opinions about certain activities will state them if adequate space is provided. Summarize written comments in detail; consider indicating the number of times the same negative or positive comments were made. (Mullendore & Abraham, 1992, pp. 39- 40)

Another potential source of written comments for instructor training assessment is personal documents, which qualitative researchers describe broadly as "any first-person narrative that describes an individual's actions, experiences, and beliefs" (Bogdan & Biklen, 1992, p. 132). For example, teaching journals used in the new-student seminar qualify as personal documents that could be reviewed to gain insight into feelings of instructors about the program and how the instructor training program prepared them for teaching it. Also, after completing their first teaching experience with the new-student seminar, instructors could be asked to write a short letter to new instructors, advising these prospective teachers on what to do, and what not to do, in order to be successful during their first teaching experience with the seminar. These letters could be sent first to the director of the instructor training program for qualitative analysis of recurrent themes before being relayed to new instructors.

One particular qualitative research method that can be used to enhance the representativeness and meaningfulness of participants' written comments is "category analysis." With this procedure, the reader engages in inductive data analysis, identifying common themes that emerge among the comments as they are read and then organizes these comments into categories (Lincoln & Guba, 1985). A succinct procedural summary of the major steps involved in categorical analysis is provided by Bogdan and Biklen (1992):

> You search through your data for regularities and patterns as well as for topics your data cover, and then you write down words and phrases to represent these topics and patterns. These words and phrases are *coding categories*. They are a means of sorting the descriptive data you have collected so that the material bearing on a given topic can be physically separated from other data. Some coding categories will come to you while you are collecting data. These should be jotted down for future use. Developing a list of coding categories after the data have been collected . . . is a crucial step in data analysis. (p. 166)

A tally of the number of written comments per category may also be kept and reported along with the identified categories. These category-specific frequency counts can then be used as quantitative data to help summarize and interpret the representativeness of written comments (qualitative data). Such a fusion of quantitative and qualitative methods in the evaluation of narrative comments is referred to as "content analysis" (Holsti, 1969).

Interviews. Qualitative data and useful feedback on program effectiveness can be gleaned from personal interviews with program participants. A program director, who openly seeks honest feedback and responds to it in a non-defensive manner, is likely to gain access to a subtle yet rich source of assessment information which would be missed if he or she relied exclusively on formal, structured measures. As veteran faculty development specialists, Bergquist and Phillips (1981) suggest: "Questionnaires and environmental scales rarely tap the rich insights, telling biases, and deep-felt convictions that often surface during an intensive interview" (pp. 316-317).

These interviews could be conducted with individual participants immediately after the instructor training experience or during the semester when instructors are first teaching the course. An advantage of conducting interviews during the latter time frame is that instructors will have had some teaching experience with the seminar, perhaps better positioning them to provide useful feedback regarding the training program's preparatory effectiveness.

Focus groups. Succinctly defined, a focus group is a small (6- to 12-person) group that meets with a trained moderator in a relaxed environment to discuss a selected topic or issue, with the goal of eliciting participants' perceptions, attitudes, and ideas (Bers, 1989). In contrast to surveys or questionnaires which solicit respondents' written comments, focus group interviews solicit their verbal responses in a discussion-group setting. Verbal responses to questions often turn out to be more elaborate and extensive than written comments, and they may reveal underlying beliefs or assumptions that are not amenable to behavioral observation (Reinharz, 1993).

The following strategies are recommended for improving the validity and representativeness of qualitative data gathered from focus groups.

- *When forming focus groups, be sure that all key participant subpopulations are represented (e.g., faculty, staff, students, and administrators).* This representation can be achieved in either of two ways. The first is heterogeneous group formation whereby members of different subpopulations are represented in each focus group. The advantage of this procedure is that a cross-section of members from different subgroups are present at the same time, serving to enrich the diversity of focus-group dialogue. Homogeneous group formation in which members of the same subpopulations comprise separate focus groups (e.g., separate focus groups comprised entirely of student development staff, college faculty, or administrators) is a second alternative. The primary advantage of this grouping procedure is that it allows participants to share their perceptions and concerns with others who have similar professional experiences and with whom they may feel more comfortable expressing their views.
- *The same questions should be posed to all focus groups.* One essential attribute of qualitative research is its flexibility: It allows the researcher to respond to the flow of data as they are collected and to change directions of the research as it proceeds (Delamont, 1992). This also is a cardinal feature of the focus-group interview, and it is the one which serves to define it as a qualitative research method (Morgan, 1988). However, some initial standardization of questions across focus groups can serve to increase the reliability of the data obtained and their amenability to comparisons across different groups.
- *Interviewers should provide the same instructions to all focus groups.* In particular, this recommendation should be followed with respect to (a) ensuring the participants' confidentiality, (b) encouraging equal participation by all group members, and (c) describing the moderator's role as an unobtrusive, non-judgmental facilitator—not as an evaluative "expert" or authority figure (Tierney,1991).

The Evaluation Report: Summarizing, Interpreting, and Disseminating the Results

An important final step in the assessment process is the construction and distribution of an evaluation report. As Fidler (1992) states emphatically, "Publishing the results is a serious responsibility to those whose findings may suggest changes in educational policy and/or practice. . . [it] is the final step for an ethical researcher" (p. 17).

A well written report of the results of assessment may mean the difference between continued support or elimination of an educational program. As Banta (1988) notes, "Assessment information is often particularly useful in selling a decision once it has been taken. Because it is concrete, such information can be extremely effective in communicating needs and priorities to those responsible for making resource allocation decisions" (p. 24). This recommendation is particularly pertinent to programs associated with the new-student seminar because of the course's perennial struggle to gain institutional credibility and credit-earning status (Gardner, 1989). Furthermore, publication and dissemination of assessment results can have a positive impact on the morale of those involved with the program by enabling them to "see" tangible results for their efforts and to be recognized publicly for their contributions. This can serve to maintain their interest in and commitment to the instructor training program. It is for these reasons that a well-written and strategically distributed program assessment report is strongly recommended. The following suggestions are offered as strategies for enhancing the report's quality and impact.

Relate the assessment results to the college mission statement and to specific institutional goals.

As Ewell (1988) argues, "A critical task for institutional researchers is the transformation of data into useful information [and] the usefulness of information will be determined by its reasonable and demonstrable linkage to particular institutional goals" (p. 24). The viability of this recommendation for assessment of instructor training programs is promising because the program pursues student-centered objectives and holistic development goals which are often strikingly consistent with the majority of college mission statements. Mission statements tend to embrace institutional goals that are much broader than discipline-specific academic knowledge and include educational outcomes that are more often psychosocial, experiential, and student-centered (Kuh, Schuh, & Whitt, 1987; Lenning, 1988). Consequently, the student-centered outcomes typically pursued by instructor training programs are likely to be compatible with most institutional goals. Capitalizing on this fortuitous compatibility should serve to increase the persuasive scope and power of the instructor training assessment report.

Report results for different subpopulations of participants.

The outcomes of an instructor training program may vary for different participant subpopulations (subgroups) who experience it. For example, the training program may have different effects on different participants—veteran faculty, new (or nearly new) faculty, student development staff, academic support staff, and college administrators. To allow for such comparative analyses across participant subpopulations, a demographics section should be included on all assessment instruments so that the respondents' subgroup can be identified. Interesting interactions can emerge from analysis of subgroup differences that otherwise might be missed if results are reported only in the form of aggregate data that have been gathered on all participants and collapsed into one "average" profile. Important differences among respondent populations may be masked or canceled out in this averaging process, concealing the unique effects of the training program on particular participant subgroups.

Include discussion of how the assessment results can be used.

Analyzing and summarizing the results are two important elements of an assessment report, but the report is not complete until it includes at least some discussion of practical implications and intended action strategies. The distinction between these components of an assessment report is clearly articulated by Astin (1991):

> Analysis refers primarily to the statistical or analytical procedures that are applied to the raw assessment data and to the manner in which the results of these analyses are displayed visually; utilization has to do with how the results of assessment analyses are actually used by educators and policy makers to improve the talent development process. (p. 94)

A common complaint about assessment initiatives in higher education is that they frequently fail to "close the loop" (Johnson, 1993, p. 7), i.e., the results often sit in some office without any meaningful follow-up action. To ensure that instructor training evaluation efforts do not culminate in the same state of "permanent storage," a well-defined plan for follow-up action should be incorporated into the assessment report. This plan should include answers to the following implementation questions: (a) What needs to be done? (b) Who will do it? (c) When can action be initiated and completed? and (d) What anticipated obstacles or roadblocks need to be overcome in order to initiate, execute, and complete the action plan?

The ultimate power of an assessment report rests neither in the sheer compilation of data nor in the knowledge gained from its analysis; instead, it rests in the conversion of acquired data and knowledge into informed practice. As the influential empirical philosopher, Francis Bacon, once stated: "Knowledge is power; but mere knowledge is not power; it is only possibility. Action is power; and its highest manifestation is when it is directed by knowledge" (quoted in Nemko, 1988, p. 6).

Conclusion

When accompanied by substantive instructor training and development, the new-student seminar becomes much more than just an introductory course for first-semester students. Viewed from this broader perspective, the new-student seminar—in conjunction with its instructor training experience—functions as a professional and institutional development program with the potential for producing systemic salutary effects on students, faculty, staff, and administration.

As suggested by the breadth of potentially positive outcomes cited in this chapter, a comprehensive instructor development program that is yoked with the new-student seminar can have multiple benefits for the institution and its constituents. Carefully conducted evaluation of the instructor training experience can serve to document the breadth and depth of its impact, ensuring that the program continues to receive the institutional support and recognition it deserves.

References

Arreola, R. A. (1983). Establishing successful faculty evaluation and development programs. In A. Smith (Ed.), Evaluating faculty and staff. *New Directions for Community Colleges, 41*. San Francisco: Jossey-Bass.

Arreola, R. A., & Aleamoni, L. M. (1990). Practical decisions in developing and operating a faculty evaluation system. In M. Theall & J. Franklin (Eds.), Student ratings of instruction: Issues for improving practice (pp. 37-56). *New Directions for Teaching and Learning, 43*. San Francisco: Jossey-Bass.

Astin, A. W. (1991). *Assessment for excellence: The philosophy and practice of assessment and evaluation in higher education*. New York: Macmillan.

Banta, T. W. (1988). Promise and perils. In T. W. Banta (Ed.), Implementing outcomes assessment: Promise and perils (pp. 95-98). *New Directions for Institutional Research, 59*. San Francisco: Jossey-Bass.

Banta, T. W., Lund, J. P., Black, K. E., & Oblander, F. W. (1996). *Assessment in practice: Putting principles to work on college campuses*. San Francisco: Jossey-Bass.

Barefoot, B. O. (Ed.). (1993). *Exploring the evidence: Reporting outcomes of freshman seminars*. (Monograph No. 11). Columbia, SC: University of South Carolina, National Resource Center for The Freshman Year Experience.

Barefoot, B. O., Warnock, C. L., Dickinson, M. P., Richardson, S. E., & Roberts, M. R. (Eds.). (1998). *Exploring the evidence: Reporting outcomes of first-year seminars, Vol. II*. Columbia, SC: University of South Carolina, National Resource Center for The First-Year Experience and Students in Transition.

Bergquist, W., & Phillips, S. (1981). *A handbook for faculty development, Vol. III*. Washington, D.C.: Council of Independent Colleges.

Bers, T. H. (1989). The popularity and problems of focus-group research. *College & University, 64*(3), 260-268.

Bligh, D. A. (1972). *What's the use of lectures*. Harmondsworth, England: Penguin.

Bogdan, R. C., & Biklen, S. K. (1992). *Qualitative research for education* (2nd ed.). Boston: Allyn & Bacon.

Braskamp, L. A., & Ory, J. C. (1994). *Assessing faculty work: Enhancing individual and institutional performance*. San Francisco: Jossey-Bass.

Campbell, D. T., & Fiske, D. W. (1959). Convergent and discriminant validation by the multitrait-multimethod matrix. *Psychological Bulletin, 56*, 81-105.

Carnegie Foundation for the Advancement of Teaching. (1990). *Campus life: In search of community*. Princeton, NJ: Author.

Cashin, W. E. (1990). Students do rate different

academic fields differently. In M. Theall & J. Franklin (Eds.), Student ratings of instruction: Issues for improving practice (pp. 113-121). *New Directions for Teaching and Learning, 43*. San Francisco: Jossey Bass.

Centra, J. A. (1993). *Reflective faculty evaluation: Enhancing teaching and determining faculty effectiveness*. San Francisco: Jossey-Bass.

Cohen, P. A. (1986). *An updated and expanded meta-analysis of multisection student rating validity studies*. Paper presented at the annual meeting of the American Educational Research Association, San Francisco.

Cross, K. P., & Angelo, T. A. (1988). *Classroom assessment techniques: A handbook for faculty*. Ann Arbor, MI: University of Michigan, National Center for Research to Improve Postsecondary Teaching and Learning.

Davis, T. M., & Murrell, P. H. (1993). *Turning teaching into learning: The role of student responsibility in the collegiate experience*. ASHE-ERIC Higher Education Report No. 8. Washington, DC: The George Washington University, School of Education and Human Development.

Davis, B. G., Wood, L., & Wilson, R. C. (1983). *ABCs of teaching with excellence*. Berkeley, CA: University of California.

Delamont, S. (1992). *Fieldwork in educational settings: Methods, pitfalls, and perspectives*. Bristol, PA: The Falmer Press.

Duffy, T. M., & Jonassen, D. H. (1992). Constructivism: New implications for instructional technology. In T. M. Duffy & D. H. Jonassen (Eds.), *Constructivism and the technology of instruction: A conversation* (pp. 1-16). Hillsdale, NJ: Laurence Erblaum & Associates.

Ewell, P. T. (1988). Implementing assessment: Some organizational issues. In T. W. Banta (Ed.), Implementing outcomes assessment: Promise and perils (pp. 15-28). *New Directions for Institutional Research, 50*. San Francisco: Jossey-Bass.

Fetterman, D. M. (1991). Auditing as institutional research: A qualitative focus. In D. M. Fetterman (Ed.), Using qualitative methods in institutional research (pp. 23-34). *New Directions for Institutional Research, 72*. San Francisco: Jossey-Bass.

Fidler, D. S. (1992). *Primer for research on the freshman year experience*. Columbia, SC: University of South Carolina, National Resource Center for The Freshman Year Experience.

Gardner, J. N. (1989), Starting a freshman seminar program. In M. L. Upcraft, J. N. Gardner, & Associates, *The freshman year experience* (pp. 238-249). San Francisco: Jossey-Bass.

Gardner, J. N, & Hunter, M. S. (1994, July). *First-year seminar instructor training*. Preconference workshop presented at the Seventh International Conference on The First-Year Experience, Dublin, Ireland.

Halpern. D. F. (1987). Recommendations and caveats. In D. F. Halpern (Ed.), Student outcomes assessment: What institutions stand to gain (pp. 109-111). *New Directions for Higher Education, 59*. San Francisco: Jossey-Bass.

Haug, P. (1992). Guidelines for student advisory committees. *The Teaching Professor, 6*(10), 7.

Holsti, O. R. (1969). *Content analysis for the social sciences and humanities*. Reading, MA: Addison-Wesley.

Johnson, R. (1993). Assessment and institutional quality. *TQM in Higher Education, 2*(9), 7.

Kuh, G., Schuh, J., Whitt, E., & Associates (1991). *Involving colleges*. San Francisco: Jossey-Bass.

Kulik, J. A., & Kulik, C. L. C. (1979). College teaching. In P. L. Peterson & H. J. Walberg (Eds.), *Research on teaching: Concepts, findings, and implications*. Berkeley, CA: McCutcheon.

Lenning, O. T. (1988). Use of noncognitive measures in assessment. In T. W. Banta (Ed.), Implementing outcomes assessment: Promise and perils (pp. 41-52). *New Directions for Institutional Research, 50*. San Francisco: Jossey-Bass.

Lincoln, Y. S., & Guba, E. (1985). *Naturalistic inquiry*. Beverly Hills, CA: Sage.

Lowman, J. (1984). *Mastering the techniques of teaching*. San Francisco: Jossey-Bass.

Merriam, S. B. (1988). *Case study research in education: A qualitative approach*. San Francisco: Jossey-Bass.

Morgan, D. L. (1988). *Focus groups as qualitative research*. Newbury Park, CA : Sage.

Mullendore, R., & Abraham, J. (1992). *Orientation director's manual*. Statesboro, GA: National Orientation Director's Association.

Nemko, M. (1988). *How to get an ivy league education at a state university*. New York: Avon Books.

Reigeluth, C. M. (1992). Reflections on the implications of constructivism for educational technology. In T. M. Duffy & D. H. Jonassen (Eds.), *Constructivism and the technology of instruction: A conversation* (pp. 147-156). Hillsdale, NJ: Laurence Erblaum & Associates.

Reinharz, S. (1993). *On becoming a social scientist*. New Brunswick, NJ: Transaction Publishers.

Schilling, K. L., & Schilling, K. M. (1998). Looking back, moving ahead: Assessment in the senior year. In J. N. Gardner, G. Van der Veer, & Associates, *The senior year experience: Facilitating integration, reflection, closure, and transition* (pp. 245-255). San Francisco: Jossey-Bass.

Scriven, M. (1967). The methodology of evaluation. In Perspectives of curriculum evaluation, *AERA Monograph Series on Curriculum Evaluation, 1*. Chicago: Rand McNally & Co.

Seldin, P. (1992). *Evaluating teaching: New lessons learned*. Keynote address presented at "Evaluating Teaching: More Than a Grade" conference held at the University of Wisconsin-Madison. Sponsored by the University of Wisconsin System, Undergraduate Teaching Improvement Council.

Seldin, P. (1993). How colleges evaluate professors, 1983 vs. 1993. *AAHE Bulletin, 42*(6), 6-8.

Smith, D. G. (1988). A window of opportunity for intra-institutional collaboration. *NASPA Journal, 26*(1), 8-13.

Smith, J. K., & Heshusius, L. (1986). Closing down the conversation: The end of the quantitative-qualitative debate among educational inquirers. *Educational Researcher, 15*(1), 4-12.

Tierney, W. G. (1991). Utilizing ethnographic interviews to enhance academic decision making. In D. M. Fetterman (Ed.), Using qualitative methods in institutional research (pp. 7-22). *New Directions for Institutional Research, 72*. San Francisco: Jossey-Bass.

Wergin, J. F. (1988). Basic issues and principles in classroom assessment. In J. H. McMillan (Ed.), Assessing students' learning (pp. 5-17). *New Directions for Teaching and Learning, 34*. San Francisco: Jossey-Bass.

Outcomes and Future Directions of Instructor Training Programs

Mary Stuart Hunter and John N. Gardner

CHAPTER 10

The title of this monograph, "Solid Foundations: Building Success for First-Year Seminars through Instructor Training and Development" reflects our strong belief that a quality program of instructor preparation for first-year seminar faculty can provide a very sound basis for a successful and effective seminar. As a result of our work with colleges and universities across this country and around the world, we realize that first-year seminar programs may be very powerful vehicles for facilitating many outcomes that enhance campus life for the entire campus community—students, faculty, and staff. We submit that these efforts and outcomes are both desirable and necessary for institutions striving to keep pace with the dynamic society in which we teach and learn.

Potential Outcomes

Campus-wide Faculty Development

Colleges and universities vary in their commitment to and support for overall faculty development. Some institutions have no faculty development program; others have well-developed programs, including teaching and learning centers. The interdisciplinary first-year seminar provides an outstanding vehicle for the provision of campus-wide faculty development opportunities. Faculty and staff who participate in a carefully designed training seminar will learn a great deal about a variety of topics including information about their institution, its services and resources, first-year student needs and characteristics, theories of student development and learning styles, and new teaching methods. A workshop modeled on experiential learning techniques can be a powerful tool to help faculty remember what it was like to be a student and to engender empathy for students who themselves will experience learning in a new setting—the collegiate environment. An experiential learning model also enables participants to learn from one another and provides an approach that can be replicated in the classroom. Educators in the training workshop and students in the classroom experience feelings of empowerment as they become both learner and teacher/expert in the training and seminar setting. Finally, if we ask instructors to employ an experiential approach in the first-year seminar, we need to provide a training experience that models this approach for them.

Professional and Personal Development

Perhaps the outcome most difficult to quantify is the long-term effect that participation in a first-year seminar has on students and instructors. An instructor development program that incorporates reflection and self-assessment in addition to the content of the first-year seminar can provide a unique opportunity for personal and professional development, allowing participants to experience growth that affects them in ways far beyond their work in the first-year seminar.

Development of Community

Participation in first-year seminar training and development workshops has the potential to bring together individuals from all academic disciplines and from many administrative support units of an institution. This coming together with a singular focus on preparing to teach first-year students provides exciting opportunities for the development of camaraderie. Workshop activities facilitate learning experiences in which institutional/departmental politics are set aside; internal, institutional barriers disappear or become easily traversed. The removal of obstacles allows participants to share common concerns and to establish intra-institutional networks. Without the interference of departmental barriers and politics, participants begin to see themselves as members of a larger community encompassing the entire campus.

Academic Affairs/Student Affairs Partnerships

The first-year seminar has the potential to be an effective instrument in faculty/student affairs staff collaboration. The institutionalization of a comprehensive and successful first-year seminar program results in participation of and commitment by key individuals from many different institutional constituencies and/or units. The resulting creation of effective partnerships across traditional campus boundaries is a frequent outcome of first-year seminar programs. When a team of facilitators representing both academic and student affairs creates, develops, and implements instructor training programs and when the participants (the seminar instructors) reflect a similarly broad spectrum of campus departments, boundary-crossing partnerships are especially likely to result.

Improvements in Teaching and Learning

For most college and university educators, academic preparation includes little or no attention to the principles of college teaching. Preparation for an academic career in the disciplines typically consists of intense study and research in a narrowly focused field. Although faculty are experts in their fields, often they have not studied teaching and learning theory, college student development, adult development, or college teaching pedagogies. Because seminar instructor development has the potential to enhance skills in teaching college courses, especially those at the introductory level, college teaching and learning improves across the curriculum at all levels. Further, because all seminar instructors are teaching "out of field," they often need the support of the training workshop to handle the unique content and instructional demands of this course. In other words, no graduate degree in "first-year seminars" exists!

A well-constructed, comprehensive training and development program will address the differing needs of new and veteran instructors, perhaps requiring several different training levels.

Placing individuals who are accustomed to occupying the powerful role of teacher into the opposite role of student learner can set the stage for a potent learning experience. For some participants, the attention given to teaching methods maybe the first time such topics have been addressed in a serious and sustained manner. Training and development programs which model a variety of teaching and learning methods provide participants with new ideas and techniques that can then be incorporated in both the first-year seminar and other courses. The focus on new and varied teaching techniques can contribute to the improvement of teaching and learning across campus for faculty who choose to employ these new methods in the courses they teach in their disciplines.

Quality and Consistency Across Seminar Sections

Instructor training also provides a forum for the program administrator to communicate a commonality and consistency in course goals, process, and content. The basic philosophical underpinnings, the goals, and desired outcomes are shared and demonstrated through instructor training and development events. For institutions in which seminars have common content across sections, workshops highlight the purposes and rationale for including the selected content. Program administrators also have the opportunity to observe potential instructors during workshop activities as they learn, interact with others, and demonstrate leadership qualities. A participant who is not comfortable with the culture, philosophy, and approach of the workshop itself may also be uncomfortable or ineffective in the first-year seminar classroom.

Employee Orientation, Assimilation, and Education

Instructor training and development efforts can assist institutions in their orientation and assimilation of new faculty and staff into the institutional culture. Workshop facilitators can formally share information about campus resources, services, and facilities intended to meet student needs, and workshop participants can share information on the campus community through their informal interactions. Networking with other participants develops naturally through small group work and other workshop activities. New employees of an institution may benefit especially from the outcomes of such workshops. In addition, anecdotal comments from longtime employees indicate that even they have learned much about their institution that they did not know before participating in the training workshop.

Future Directions and Recommendations

First-year seminars have been in existence since 1882; however, systematically preparing instructors to teach first-year seminars is a relatively new undertaking and dates to efforts begun by the University of South Carolina in 1972. Very little is found in the literature about the instructor training component of seminar programs. Yet in the short time since 1972, new developments in first-year seminars have emerged, and the future holds great potential for much more development and change in the programs and related faculty development activities. The following are considerations and recommendations for those responsible for instructor training and development.

Changes, Changes, Changes

We believe that successful first-year programs are those which effectively meet the changing needs of students, institutions, and society. As these constituencies inevitably change over time, so must the preparation provided for instructors of first-year seminars. Because new issues arise, first-year seminar training and development, like the seminar itself, must be dynamic. Who would have guessed 15 or even 10 years ago that many first-year seminars would include content on the pervasiveness of date rape drugs or the dangers of credit card debt and sexually transmitted diseases? Who would have guessed 10 years ago that the first-year seminar would be used to introduce students to the potentially transformational experience of service learning or that first-year seminars would become a major curriculum vehicle for introducing students to computer technology and for teaching information literacy and library research skills? Modes of learning and working have changed dramatically over the last decade with advances in and availability of computer technology. Teaching methods must change to incorporate these new ways that students learn. As the demand for a computer-literate work force increases, college faculty are often called upon to meet this new technological imperative by incorporating electronic media sources and instruction into their discipline. Instructors must keep pace with these changes and frequently require training in this important area. Thus, changes in first-year seminar training programs are not only desirable but sometimes necessary.

Training Formats

In the years following the implementation of a first-year seminar, program coordinators should not be surprised when instructors ask for more training. The attraction of the learning process is lifelong, especially for academics who first chose their careers because they were comfortable and fulfilled in collegiate learning environments. Additional workshop opportunities will need to be developed to satisfy the desire for ongoing training and development. A decision on the format of additional training is a complex one. Do all instructors need the same preparation each year? Is a basic introductory workshop a prerequisite for teaching for the first time? Should refresher workshops be offered or required for instructors each time they teach the seminar? How are new content areas incorporated into the seminar, and how are instructors prepared to teach this new content? A well-constructed, comprehensive training and development program will address the differing needs of new and veteran instructors, perhaps requiring several different training levels.

Peer Teachers

An increasing number of institutions are involving students as peer teachers in their first-year seminar programs. These peer teachers may be undergraduate or graduate students who are involved to varying degrees in the instruction. Some have extensive individual responsibility for the instruction, others assist or team teach with a faculty or staff member. Whatever their level of responsibility in the classroom may be, peer leaders also need proper preparation for their instructional role, and decisions must be made as to how their training will be delivered. Institutional approaches to the training of student peer teachers vary from brief preparatory workshops to required enrollment in pre-requisite or co-requisite teaching and/or leadership courses offered for credit.

An Ethical Mandate

Nearly half (47%) of the institutions offering a first-year seminar require it of all their new students (National Resource Center for The First-Year Experience & Students in Transition, 1998). Meeting the demand for a new mandatory course may necessitate the non-voluntary assignment of faculty and staff as instructors. Does this not, then, create an ethical obligation on the part of institutions to the faculty and staff assigned to teach a course "out of field" for which they are largely unprepared and in regard to the students enrolled in those sections? Instructors assigned to this course are more likely to be graduate students or new faculty—those members of the institution who may have the least knowledge of and experience with classroom pedagogy. For them, an instructor training program is essential. Pity the unsuspecting new students who may take such courses in which training has not been provided.

Learning from Mistakes

The perfect instructor training program does not exist. Each time a workshop is delivered, lessons will be learned and adjustments must be made for future offerings. Serious and ongoing assessment of instructor training and development workshops can assist in further refinement and improvement. Unfortunately, there is very little research on the impact of such training experiences on the long-term attitudes, values, behaviors, and pedagogies adopted by the participating educators. We especially need to know more about whether the training carries over beyond its application to the teaching of the first-year seminar. Are first-year seminar instructors using these newly acquired pedagogies in their primary discipline-based teaching? If so, what is the relative impact of this on students?

Conclusion

The first and most important aspect of building is laying the foundation. Without a solid foundation, the structures dependent on it for support cannot be built. Additionally, the strength of that original foundation determines the life of the building and whether or not it will survive the passing of years. Likewise, the first-year seminar cannot grow and survive without a solid foundation. Quality training and development of seminar instructors form the cornerstone of this foundation. The first-year seminar can have a transforming effect on institutional cultures, providing opportunities for growth and development in the students and in the corps of instructors, helping the institution adapt to the demands of a changing society.

References

National Resource Center for The First-Year Experience and Students in Transition. (1998). *1997 national survey of first-year seminar programming*. Columbia, SC: University of South Carolina, Author.

Bibliography of Suggested Readings and Resources

Mary Stuart Hunter

APPENDIX A

Alewynse, J. (1992). *Core-course faculty development series on methodology.* Hampton, VA: Hampton University. (ERIC Document Reproduction Service No. ED 414 856)

Barefoot, B.O., & Fidler, P. P. (1996). *The 1994 national survey of freshman seminar programs: Continuing innovations in the collegiate curriculum* (Monograph No. 20). Columbia, SC: University of South Carolina, National Resource Center for The First-Year Experience and Students in Transition.

Berman, D. (1990). Faculty development workshops train freshman seminar instructors. *The Freshman Year Experience Newsletter, 3*(1), p. 4

Bouton, C., & Garth, R. Y. (Eds.). (1983). *Learning in groups.* San Francisco: Jossey-Bass.

Brown, N. W. (1992). *Teaching group dynamics: Process and practice.* Westport, CT: Praeger.

Chickering, A. W., & Gamson, Z. F. (Eds.). (1991). *Applying the seven principles for good practice in undergraduate eduction.* San Francisco: Jossey-Bass.

Cuseo, J. B. (1991). *The freshman orientation seminar: A research-based rationale for its value, delivery, and content.* (Monograph No. 4). Columbia, SC: University of South Carolina, National Resource Center for The Freshman Year Experience.

Davis, J. R. (1993). *Better teaching, more learning: Strategies for success in postsecondary settings.* Washington, DC: American Council on Education, Oryx Press.

Dutton, M. D., Seaman, D. F., & Ulmer, C. (1972). *Understanding group dynamics in adult education.* Englewood Cliffs, NJ: Prentice-Hall.

Eble, K. E. (Ed.). (1980). *Improving teaching styles.* San Francisco: Jossey-Bass.

Erickson, B., & Strommer, D. W. (1993). *Teaching college freshmen.* San Francisco: Jossey-Bass.

Fidler, P. P., Neurerer-Rotholz, J., & Richardson, S. (1999). Teaching the freshman seminar: Its effectiveness in promoting faculty development. *Journal of The First-Year Experience, 11*(2), 7-22.

Finkelstein, M. J., & LaCelle-Peterson, M. W. (Eds.). (1993). *Developing senior faculty as teachers.* San Francisco: Jossey-Bass.

The Freshman Year Experience Newsletter. (1988-present). Columbia, SC: University of South Carolina, National Resource Center for The First-Year Experience and Students in Transition.

Friday, R. A. (1989). Training freshman seminar faculty. *Journal of The Freshman Year Experience, 1*(2), 57-80.

Friday, R. A. (1990). Faculty training: From group process to collaborative learning. *Journal of The Freshman Year Experience, 2*(1), 49-67.

Gardner, J. N. (1981). Developing faculty as facilitators and mentors. *New Directions for Student Services, 14* (pp. 67-80). San Francisco: Jossey-Bass.

Gardner, J. N. (1981). A guide for orientation course instructors. In W. Walter & A. Siebert (Eds.). *Student success: How to succeed in college and still have time for your friends.* New York: Holt, Rinehart, and Winston.

Gardner, J. N. (1986). The freshman year experience. *The Journal of the American Association of Collegiate Registrars and Admissions Officers, 61*(4), 261-274.

Gardner, J. N. (1992). *Freshman seminar instructor training: Guidelines for design and implementation.* Columbia, SC: University of South Carolina, National Resource Center for The Freshman Year Experience.

Guskin, A. E. (Ed.). (1981). *The administrator's role in effective teaching.* San Francisco: Jossey-Bass.

Hutchings, P., & Wutzdorff, A. (Eds.). (1988). *Knowing and doing: Learning through experience.* San Francisco: Jossey-Bass.

Jewler, J. (1989). Faculty vitality: The essence of campus revitalization. *The Freshman Year Experience Newsletter, 2*(2), p. 4.

Journal of The Freshman Year Experience & Students in Transition. (1989-present). Columbia, SC: University of South Carolina, National Resource Center for The First-Year Experience and Students in Transition.

Knowles, M., & Knowles, H. (1972). *Introduction to group dynamics.* New York: Association Press.

Menges, R. J., & Svinicki, M. D. (Eds.). (1991). *College teaching: From theory to practice.* San Francisco: Jossey-Bass.

Nix-Early, V. (1990). Training freshman seminar faculty to address issues of cultural diversity in the classroom. *The Freshman Year Experience Newsletter, 3*(2), p. 8.

Penland, P. R., & Fine, S. F. (1974). *Group dynamics and individual development.* New York: Marcel Dekker.

Pike, R., & Arch, D. (1997). *Dealing with difficult participants: 127 practical strategies for minimizing resistance and maximizing results in your presentations.* (Illus. by C. Hiatt). San Francisco: Jossey-Bass/Pfeiffer.

Powers, R. (1992). *Instructor excellence: Mastering the delivery of training.* San Francisco: Jossey-Bass.

Proceedings. (1982-present). The Freshman Year Experience Conference. Columbia, SC: University of South Carolina.

Showalter, E. (1999, July 9). The risks of good teaching: How 1 professor and 9 T.A.'s plunged into pedagogy. *The Chronicle of Higher Education,* pp. B5-B6.

Silberman, M., & Auerbach, C. (1998). *Active training: A handbook of techniques, designs, case examples, and tips.* (2nd ed.) San Francisco: Jossey-Bass/Pfeiffer.

Silberman, M., & Lawson, K. (1995). *101 ways to make training active.* San Francisco: Jossey-Bass/Pfeiffer.

Smith, P. B. (Ed.). (1970). *Group processes.* Middlesex, England: Penguin Books.

Sugar, S. (1998). *Games that teach: Experiential activities for reinforcing training*. San Francisco: Jossey-Bass/Pfeiffer.

Sutherland, T. E., & Bonwell, C. C. (1996). *Using active learning in college classes: A range of options for faculty*. San Francisco: Jossey-Bass.

To improve the academy: Resources for faculty, instructional, and organizational development. (1982-present). Stillwater, OK: Professional and Organizational Development Network in Higher Education, New Forum Press.

Ukens. L. L. (1997). *Getting together: Icebreakers and group energizers*. San Francisco: Jossey-Bass/Pfeiffer.

Upcraft, M. L., Gardner, J. N., & Associates. (1989). *The freshman year experience: Helping students survive and succeed in college*. San Francisco: Jossey-Bass.

Institutions Offering First-Year Seminar Instructor Training

Appendix B

In the fall of 1997, the National Resource Center for The First-Year Experience and Students in Transition conducted the fourth National Survey of First-Year Seminar Programs. The survey, which was mailed to 2,527 regionally-accredited, two- and four-year institutions, was designed to investigate the characteristics of new-student seminars that are currently being offered on American college and university campuses. The Center received 1,336 responses on the survey (52.9%). Of that number, 939 (70.3%) indicated that a new-student seminar is offered; in addition, 692 reported that some form of training is offered (or required) for seminar instructors. Following is a list of the 692 institutions offering instructor training; those marked with an asterisk require participation as a prerequisite for teaching the seminar.

Abilene Christian University*	Abilene, TX
Abraham Baldwin Agricultural College	Tifton, GA
Adirondack Community College	Queensbury, NY
Adrian College*	Adrian, MI
Alamance Community College	Graham, NC
Albertus Magnus College*	New Haven, CT
Allegany College of Maryland*	Cumberland, MD
Allen University	Columbia, SC
Alma College	Alma, MI
Andover College*	Portland, ME
Angelo State University*	San Angelo, TX
Appalachian State University*	Boone, NC
Aquinas College*	Grand Rapids, MI
Arizona State University*	Tempe, AZ
Armstrong Atlantic State University	Savannah, GA
Asbury College*	Wilmore, KY
Ashland Community College	Ashland, KY
Ashland University*	Ashland, OH
Atlanta Metropolitan College	Atlanta, GA
Auburn University*	Auburn, AL
Augusta State University	Augusta, GA
Aurora University*	Aurora, IL
Austin College*	Sherman, TX
Avila College*	Kansas City, MO
Babson College*	Babson Park, MA
Baker University*	Baldwin City, KS
Ball State University*	Muncie, IN
Baltimore City Community College*	Baltimore, MD
Bard College	Annandale-On-Hudson, NY
Barnard College	New York City, NY

Barry University*	Miami Shores, FL
Barton College*	Wilson, NC
Barton County Community College*	Great Bend, KS
Bates College	Lewiston, ME
Bayamon Central University*	Bayamon, PR
Beaver College*	Glenside, PA
Beloit College*	Beloit, WI
Benedictine University*	Lisle, IL
Berea College	Berea, KY
Berry College*	Mt. Berry, GA
Bethany College*	Bethany, WV
Bethany Lutheran College*	Mankato, MN
Bethel College*	McKenzie, TN
Bethel College*	North Newton, KS
Blackburn College*	Carlinville, IL
Black Hills State University*	Spearfish, SD
Bloomsburg University of Pennsylvania	Bloomsburg, PA
Bluefield College*	Bluefield, VA
Bluffton College	Bluffton, OH
Boise State University	Boise, ID
Bowling Green State University*	Bowling Green, OH
Bowling Green University - Firelands College	Huron, OH
Bradford College*	Bradford, MA
Bradley University*	Peoria, IL
Brandeis University	Waltham, MA
Brenau University*	Gainesville, GA
Brevard College	Hendersonville, NC
Brewton-Parker College	Mt. Vernon, GA
Bridgewater State College*	Bridgewater, MA
Bristol Community College*	Fall River, MA
Broome Community College*	Binghamton, NY
Bryant College*	Smithfield, RI
Bryn Mawr College	Bryn Mawr, PA
Buena Vista University	Storm Lake, IA
Bunker Hill Community College*	Boston, MA
Cabrini College	Radnor, PA
California Polytechnic State University	San Luis Obispo, CA
California State University - Bakersfield	Bakersfield, CA
California State University - Chico	Chico, CA
California State University - Fresno	Fresno, CA
California State University - Fullerton*	Fullerton, CA
California State University - Hayward*	Hayward, CA
California State University - Los Angeles	Los Angeles, CA
California State University - Long Beach*	Long Beach, CA
California State University - Northridge*	Northridge, CA
California State University - San Marcos	San Marcos, CA
California University of Pennsylvania*	California, PA
Cambria County Area Community College	Johnstown, PA
Cardinal Stritch University*	Milwaukee, WI
Carlow College*	Pittsburgh, PA
Carroll College*	Waukesha, WI
Carson-Newman College*	Jefferson City, TN

Carteret Community College*	Morehead City, NC
Carthage College*	Kenosha, WI
Castleton State College	Castleton, VT
Catawba Valley Community College*	Hickory, NC
Cedar Crest College*	Allentown, PA
Central Alabama Community College*	Alexander City, AL
Central Community College	Grand Island, NE
Central Connecticut State University*	New Britain, CT
Central Maine Technical College	Auburn, ME
Central Methodist College*	Fayette, MO
Central Missouri State University*	Warrensburg, MO
Central Piedmont Community College*	Charlotte, NC
Central State University*	Wilberforce, OH
Central Washington University*	Ellensburg, WA
Central Wyoming College*	Riverton, WY
Cerro Coso Community College	Ridgecrest, CA
Champlain College*	Burlington, VT
Chapman University*	Orange, CA
Charleston Southern University	Charleston, SC
Chicago State University*	Chicago, IL
Citrus College*	Glendora, CA
CUNY Hunter College*	New York, NY
CUNY Kingsborough Community College*	Brooklyn, NY
CUNY Medgar Evers College*	Brooklyn, NY
Clackamas Community College*	Oregon City, OR
Claremont McKenna College	Claremont, CA
Clarkson College*	Omaha, NE
Clemson University	Clemson, SC
Cleveland State Community College	Cleveland, TN
Clinch Valley College of the Univ. of Virginia*	Wise, VA
Clovis Community College	Clovis, NM
Coastal Georgia Community College*	Brunswick, GA
Coker College	Hartsville, SC
Colegio Universitario del Este*	Carolina, PR
Colgate University*	Hamilton, NY
College of Charleston*	Charleston, SC
College of New Jersey*	Trenton, NJ
College of St. Catherine*	St. Paul, MN
College of Santa Fe*	Santa Fe, NM
College of Wooster*	Wooster, OH
Colorado Northwestern Community College*	Rangely, CO
Colorado School of Mines	Golden, CO
Columbia College*	Chicago, IL
Columbia College	Columbia, MO
Columbia College	Columbia, SC
Columbus State University	Columbus, GA
Columbus State University*	Columbus, OH
Community College of Southern Nevada*	Las Vegas, NV
Concordia College*	Seward, NE
Concordia University*	St. Paul, MN
Concordia University at Austin*	Austin, TX
Concordia University, Wisconsin*	Mequon, WI

Connecticut College	New London, CT
Cornell University*	Ithaca, NY
Cottey College*	Nevada, MO
Curry College	Milton, MA
Cuyahoga Community College	Cleveland, OH
D'Youville College	Buffalo, NY
Dakota State University*	Madison, SD
Dalton College	Dalton, GA
Daniel Webster College	Nashua, NH
Dartmouth College	Hanover, NH
Darton College*	Albany, GA
Davidson County Community College*	Lexington, NC
Davis & Elkins College*	Elkins, WV
Del Mar College*	Corpus Christi, TX
Delaware Technical and Community College	Wilmington, DE
Delaware Valley College	Doylestown, PA
Delta College*	University Center, MI
Denison University	Granville, OH
Dickinson College*	Carlisle, PA
Dominican University*	River Forest, IL
Drexel University	Philadelphia, PA
Drury College*	Springfield, MO
Dyersburg State Community College*	Dyersburg, TN
East Carolina University	Greenville, NC
East Tennessee State University	Johnson City, TN
Eastern Illinois University*	Charleston, IL
Eastern Nazarene College	Quincy, MA
Eastern New Mexico University*	Portales, NM
Eastern New Mexico University-Roswell	Roswell, NM
Eckerd College*	St. Petersburg, FL
Edgewood College*	Madison, WI
Elgin Community College	Elgin, IL
Elizabethtown College*	Elizabethtown, PA
Elon College*	Elon College, NC
Emory & Henry College*	Emory, VA
Emory University*	Atlanta, GA
Emporia State University*	Emporia, KS
Eureka College	Eureka, IL
Evangel College*	Springfield, MO
Fairfield University*	Fairfield, CT
Fairleigh Dickinson University*	Teaneck, NJ
Fayetteville State University*	Fayetteville, NC
Felician College*	Lodi, NJ
Ferrum College*	Ferrum, VA
Finger Lakes Community College*	Canandaiqua, NY
Fisher College*	Boston, MA
Florida Atlantic University*	Boca Raton, FL
Florida Institute of Technology	Melbourne, FL
Florida International University*	Miami, FL
Floyd College*	Rome, GA
Fordham University*	Bronx, NY

Franklin College*	Franklin, IN
Franklin Pierce College*	Rindge, NH
Fresno Pacific University*	Fresno, CA
Gallaudet University*	Washington, DC
Garden City Community College*	Garden City, KS
Gardner-Webb University	Boiling Springs, NC
Garrett Community College	McHenry, MD
Genesee Community College*	Batavia, NY
Geneva College	Beaver Falls, PA
George Mason University*	Fairfax, VA
George Washington University	Washington, DC
Georgetown College*	Georgetown, KY
Georgia College and State University*	Milledgeville, GA
Georgia Institute of Technology	Atlanta, GA
Georgia Southern University*	Statesboro, GA
Georgia Southwestern State University	Americus, GA
Georgian Court College*	Lakewood, NJ
Glendale Community College	Glendale, CA
Gordon College	Wenham, MA
Goshen College	Goshen, IN
Goucher College*	Baltimore, MD
Graceland College*	Lamoni, IA
Grand Valley State University*	Allendale, MI
Green Mountain College*	Poultney, VT
Greensboro College*	Greensboro, NC
Grinnell College	Grinnell, IA
Guilford College*	Greensboro, NC
Gustavus Adolphus College*	St. Peter, MN
Gwinnett Technical Institute*	Lawrenceville, GA
Hagerstown Junior College*	Hagerstown, MD
Halifax Community College*	Weldon, NC
Hampden-Sydney College*	Hampden-Sydney, VA
Hannibal-La Grange College	Hannibal, MO
Harcum College	Bryn Mawr, PA
Hartwick College*	Oneonta, NY
Harvard University	Cambridge, MA
Haskell Indian Nations University	Lawrence, KS
Hastings College	Hastings, NE
Haywood Community College	Clyde, NC
Heartland Community College*	Bloomington, IL
Heidelberg College*	Tiffin, OH
Henderson State University*	Arkadelphia, AR
Herkimer County Community College*	Herkimer, NY
Highland Community College*	Freeport, IL
Highland Community College*	Highland, KS
Holy Cross College	Notre Dame, IN
Hope College*	Holland, MI
Hopkinsville Community College	Hopkinsville, KY
Howard Payne University*	Brownwood, TX
Howard University*	Washington, DC
Huntingdon College	Montgomery, AL

Institution	Location
Huntington College*	Huntington, IN
Hutchinson Community College and Area Vocational School*	Hutchinson, KS
Idaho State University	Pocatello, ID
Illinois College	Jacksonville, IL
Illinois Wesleyan University	Bloomington, IL
Indiana State University*	Terre Haute, IN
Indiana University-Purdue University Fort Wayne	Fort Wayne, IN
Indiana University-Purdue University Indianapolis	Indianapolis, IN
Indiana University East*	Richmond, IN
Inter American University of Puerto Rico San German Campus*	San German, PR
Iona College	New Rochelle, NY
Iowa Wesleyan College*	Mt. Pleasant, IA
Isothermal Community College*	Spindale, NC
Itasca Community College	Grand Rapids, MN
Ithaca College*	Ithaca, NY
Ivy Tech State College - East Central	Muncie, IN
Ivy Tech State College - Northcentral	South Bend, IN
Ivy Tech State College - Wabash Valley	Terre Haute, IN
Jackson State University*	Jackson, MS
Jacksonville University*	Jacksonville, FL
Jamestown Community College*	Jamestown, NY
Jarvis Christian College*	Hawkins, TX
Jefferson Community College	Steubenville, OH
Jefferson Community College	Watertown, NY
John Brown University	Siloam Springs, AR
John Carroll University*	Cleveland, OH
Johns Hopkins University*	Baltimore, MD
Joliet Junior College*	Joliet, IL
Judson College*	Marion, AL
Juilliard School*	New York, NY
Kalamazoo College	Kalamazoo, MI
Kean University*	Union, NJ
Kennesaw State University*	Kennesaw, GA
Kent State University - Stark Campus	Canton, OH
Kent State University - Trumbull Campus*	Warren, OH
Kentucky Wesleyan College*	Owensboro, KY
Keuka College*	Keuka Park, NY
Keystone College*	La Plume, PA
King's College*	Wilkes-Barre, PA
Knox College*	Galesburg, IL
Lackawanna Junior College	Scranton, PA
Lafayette College	Easton, PA
Lake Washington Technical College*	Kirkland, WA
Lancaster Bible College*	Lancaster, PA
Lander University*	Greenwood, SC
Langston University*	Langston, OK
Lawrence University	Appleton, WI
Lawson State Community College*	Birmingham, AL
Le Moyne College	Syracuse, NY
LeTourneau University*	Longview, TX

Lee College*	Baytown, TX
Lee University*	Cleveland, TN
Lenoir Community College	Kinston, NC
Lewis University*	Romeoville, IL
Liberty University	Lynchburg, VA
Limestone College*	Gaffney, SC
Lincoln University*	Jefferson City, MO
Lindsey Wilson College*	Columbia, KY
Linfield College*	McMinnville, OR
Lipscomb University	Nashville, TN
Longwood College*	Farmville, VA
Lord Fairfax Community College*	Middletown, VA
Los Angeles Southwest College	Los Angeles, CA
Louisiana College*	Pineville, LA
Louisiana State University	Baton Rouge, LA
Loyola College in Maryland*	Baltimore, MD
Loyola University of Chicago	Chicago, IL
Lubbock Christian University*	Lubbock, TX
Lyndon State College*	Lyndonville, VT
Lynn University*	Boca Raton, FL
Lyon College*	Batesville, AR
MacMurray College*	Jacksonville, IL
Madonna University	Livonia, MI
Malone College*	Canton, OH
Manchester College*	North Manchester, IN
Mankato State University*	Mankato, MN
Marietta College	Marietta, OH
Marist College*	Poughkeepsie, NY
Marquette University*	Milwaukee, WI
Mars Hill College*	Mars Hill, NC
Marshall University	Huntington, WV
Mary Baldwin College*	Staunton, VA
Marygrove College*	Detroit, MI
Marymount College*	Rancho Palos Verdes, CA
Marymount Manhattan College*	New York, NY
Maryville College*	Maryville, TN
Maryville University of St. Louis	St. Louis, MO
Massachusetts Institute of Technology	Cambridge, MA
McKendree College*	Lebanon, IL
McMurry University*	Abilene, TX
McNeese State University	Lake Charles, LA
McPherson College*	McPherson, KS
Medaille College*	Buffalo, NY
Mercer County Community College	Trenton, NJ
Mercy College*	Dobbs Ferry, NY
Meredith College*	Raleigh, NC
Merrimack College*	North Andover, MA
Methodist College*	Fayetteville, NC
Metropolitan State University*	St. Paul, MN
Michigan Technological University*	Houghton, MI
Mid-South Community College	West Memphis, AR
Middle Georgia College	Cochran, GA

Middle Tennessee State University*	Murfreesboro, TN
Middlebury College	Middlebury, VT
Middlesex Community College*	Bedford, MA
Middlesex Community-Technical College	Middletown, CT
Middlesex County College*	Edison, NJ
Midlands Technical College*	Columbia, SC
Midway College*	Midway, KY
Millsaps College*	Jackson, MS
Milwaukee Area Technical College	Milwaukee, WI
Milwaukee Institute of Art & Design*	Milwaukee, WI
Minnesota West Community & Technical College	Granite Falls, MN
Minot State University	Minot, ND
Missouri Valley College*	Marshall, MO
Missouri Western State College*	St. Joseph, MO
Mitchell College*	New London, CT
Monmouth College	Monmouth, IL
Monmouth University*	West Long Branch, NJ
Montana State University - Billings	Billings, MT
Montana State University - Bozeman*	Bozeman, MT
Montgomery County Community College*	Blue Bell, PA
Moorhead State University*	Moorhead, MN
Moraine Valley Community College*	Palos Hills, IL
Morehead State University*	Morehead, KY
Morningside College*	Sioux City, IA
Mount Carmel College of Nursing	Columbus, OH
Mount Ida College	Newton Centre, MA
Mount Mary College*	Milwaukee, WI
Mount Mercy College	Cedar Rapids, IA
Mount Olive College*	Mount Olive, NC
Mount Saint Mary's College and Seminary*	Emmitsburg, MD
Mount Union College*	Alliance, OH
Mountain Empire Community College*	Big Stone Gap, VA
Murray State University	Murray, KY
Muscatine Community College	Muscatine, IA
Nassau Community College*	Garden City, NY
Navarro College	Corsicana, TX
Nazareth College of Rochester	Rochester, NY
Nebraska Wesleyan University	Lincoln, NE
Neosho County Community College*	Chanute, KS
New Hampshire College*	Manchester, NH
New Hampshire Community Technical College	Manchester, NH
New Hampshire Community Technical College	Nashua, NH
Niagara County Community College	Sanborn, NY
Niagara University*	Niagara University, NY
North Carolina Central University*	Durham, NC
North Carolina State University*	Raleigh, NC
North Carolina Wesleyan College	Rocky Mount, NC
North Central College*	Naperville, IL
North Central Missouri College	Trenton, MO
North Dakota State University	Fargo, ND
North Georgia College & State University*	Dahlonega, GA
North Lake College*	Irving, TX

Institution	Location
North Shore Community College*	Danvers, MA
Northeast Mississippi Community College*	Booneville, MS
Northeastern Illinois University*	Chicago, IL
Northeastern Junior College*	Sterling, CO
Northeastern University	Boston, MA
Northern Illinois University*	De Kalb, IL
Northern Kentucky University*	Highland Heights, KY
Northern Michigan University	Marquette, MI
Northern State University	Aberdeen, SD
Northland College*	Ashland, WI
NorthWest Arkansas Community College	Bentonville, AR
Northwestern Michigan College	Traverse City, MI
Northwestern University	Evanston, IL
Norwich University*	Northfield, VT
Oakton Community College*	Des Plaines, IL
Ohio Northern University	Ada, OH
Ohio State University*	Columbus, OH
Ohio State University Agricultural Technical Institute	Wooster, OH
Ohio State University - Mansfield	Mansfield, OH
Ohio State University - Newark	Newark, OH
Ohio University*	Athens, OH
Ohio University Chillicothe*	Chillicothe, OH
Oklahoma City University*	Oklahoma City, OK
Oklahoma State University - Main Campus	Stillwater, OK
Oklahoma State University - Oklahoma City	Oklahoma City, OK
Oklahoma State University - Okmulgee*	Okmulgee, OK
Olivet Nazarene University*	Kankakee, IL
Oral Roberts University*	Tulsa, OK
Orangeburg-Calhoun Technical College*	Orangeburg, SC
Oregon Institute of Technology*	Klamath Falls, OR
Oregon State University	Corvallis, OR
Ouachita Technical College*	Malvern, AR
Our Lady of the Lake College	Baton Rouge, LA
Our Lady of the Lake University*	San Antonio, TX
Ozarka Technical College*	Melbourne, AR
Pace University New York Campus*	New York, NY
Pacific Lutheran University	Tacoma, WA
Pacific University*	Forest Grove, OR
Passaic County Community College	Paterson, NJ
Pennsylvania State University Delaware County	Media, PA
Petit Jean College	Morrilton, AR
Piedmont College*	Demorest, GA
Pierce College*	Tacoma, WA
Pittsburg State University*	Pittsburg, KS
Pitzer College*	Claremont, CA
Plymouth State College*	Plymouth, NH
Point Loma Nazarene University	San Diego, CA
Pomona College	Claremont, CA
Pontifical Catholic University of Puerto Rico*	Ponce, PR
Portland State University*	Portland, OR
Prairie State College	Chicago Heights, IL

Pratt Institute*	Brooklyn, NY
Prince George's Community College*	Largo, MD
Purdue University Calumet*	Hammond, IN
Quincy University	Quincy, IL
Radford University*	Radford, VA
Ramapo College of New Jersey	Mahwah, NJ
Redlands Community College*	El Reno, OK
Regis College*	Weston, MA
Regis University*	Denver, CO
Rhode Island College	Providence, RI
Richard Stockton College of New Jersey	Pomona, NJ
Rider University*	Lawrenceville, NJ
Rio Salado College*	Tempe, AZ
Riverside Community College	Riverside, CA
Roane State Community College	Harriman, TN
Roberts Wesleyan College	Rochester, NY
Rockford College*	Rockford, IL
Russell Sage College*	Troy, NY
SUNY College at Brockport*	Brockport, NY
SUNY College at Buffalo	Buffalo, NY
SUNY College at Cortland*	Cortland, NY
SUNY College at Geneseo*	Geneseo, NY
SUNY College at Plattsburgh	Plattsburgh, NY
SUNY College at Potsdam	Potsdam, NY
SUNY College of Technology at Delhi*	Delhi, NY
Sacred Heart University	Fairfield, CT
Saginaw Valley State University*	University Center, MI
Saint Anselm College*	Manchester, NH
Saint Cloud State University*	St. Cloud, MN
Saint Francis College	Loretto, PA
Saint Joseph's College	Rensselaer, IN
Saint Louis University*	St. Louis, MO
Saint Mary College*	Leavenworth, KS
Saint Mary's College of California*	Moraga, CA
Saint Mary-of-the-Woods College	St. Mary-of-the-Woods, IN
Saint Olaf College	Northfield, MN
Saint Xavier University	Chicago, IL
Salem State College*	Salem, MA
Salve Regina University*	Newport, RI
San Diego State University*	San Diego, CA
San Francisco State University	San Francisco, CA
Santa Fe Community College*	Gainesville, FL
Schreiner College*	Kerrville, TX
Seminole Community College*	Sanford, FL
Seton Hall University	South Orange, NJ
Shasta College*	Redding, CA
Shimer College	Waukegan, IL
Shippensburg University of Pennsylvania*	Shippensburg, PA
Shorter College*	Rome, GA
Siena College*	Loudonville, NY
Sierra College*	Rocklin, CA
Simon's Rock College of Bard	Great Barrington, MA

Simpson College*	Indianola, IA
Slippery Rock University of Pennsylvania	Slippery Rock, PA
Sonoma State University*	Rohnert Park, CA
South Central Technical College	North Mankato, MN
South Dakota State University*	Brookings, SD
South Puget Sound Community College*	Olympia, WA
Southeast Missouri State University*	Cape Girardeau, MO
Southeastern Community College*	Whiteville, NC
Southeastern Louisiana University	Hammond, LA
Southeastern Oklahoma State University*	Durant, OK
Southern Arkansas University	Magnolia, AR
Southern Illinois University*	Carbondale, IL
Southern Nazarene University	Bethany, OK
Southern Oregon University*	Ashland, OR
Southern Wesleyan University	Central, SC
Southwest Baptist University*	Bolivar, MO
Southwest Missouri State University*	Springfield, MO
Southwestern University*	Georgetown, TX
Spartanburg Methodist College*	Spartanburg, SC
Spartanburg Technical College*	Spartanburg, SC
Springfield College*	Springfield, IL
St. Ambrose College*	Davenport, IA
St. Bonaventure University*	St. Bonaventure, NY
St. Charles County Community College	St. Peters, MO
St. Edward's University*	Austin, TX
St. Petersburg Junior College*	St. Petersburg, FL
Stephen F. Austin State University*	Nacogdoches, TX
Sterling College*	Sterling, KS
Stillman College*	Tuscaloosa, AL
Stonehill College*	Easton, MA
Suffolk County Community College Eastern Campus*	Riverhead, NY
Sullivan County Community College*	Loch Sheldrake, NY
Syracuse University Main Campus*	Syracuse, NY
Tabor College*	Hillsboro, KS
Tacoma Community College*	Tacoma, WA
Tallahassee Community College*	Tallahassee, FL
Taylor University*	Upland, IN
Teikyo Post University*	Waterbury, CT
Temple University*	Philadelphia, PA
Tennessee Technological University*	Cookeville, TN
Texas A & M University	College Station, TX
Texas A & M University at Commerce*	Commerce, TX
Texas State Technical College - Waco/Marshall*	Waco, TX
Texas Tech University*	Lubbock, TX
Texas Woman's University*	Denton, TX
Thomas College*	Waterville, ME
Thomas More College	Crestview Hills, KY
Three Rivers Community-Technical College*	Norwich, CT
Tidewater Community College	Norfolk, VA
Tiffin University*	Tiffin, OH
Treasure Valley Community College*	Ontario, OR

Trinity College*	Washington, DC
Trinity University*	San Antonio, TX
Triton College*	River Grove, IL
Trocaire College*	Buffalo, NY
Troy State University*	Troy, AL
Truman State University*	Kirksville, MO
Tuskegee University	Tuskegee Institute, AL
Umpqua Community College*	Roseburg, OR
Union College*	Barbourville, KY
Union University*	Jackson, TN
United States Air Force Academy*	USAF Academy, CO
United States Coast Guard Academy	New London, CT
University of Alabama	Tuscaloosa, AL
University of Arkansas at Monticello	Monticello, AR
University of California - Santa Cruz*	Santa Cruz, CA
University of Central Arkansas*	Conway, AR
University of Charleston*	Charleston, WV
University of Colorado at Colorado Springs*	Colorado Springs, CO
University of Connecticut	Storrs, CT
University of Evansville*	Evansville, IN
University of Houston*	Houston, TX
University of Idaho*	Moscow, ID
University of Illinois at Chicago	Chicago, IL
University of Iowa	Iowa City, IA
University of Kansas Main Campus	Lawrence, KS
University of Kentucky*	Lexington, KY
University of LaVerne*	LaVerne, CA
University of Maine*	Orono, ME
University of Maine at Presque Isle*	Presque Isle, ME
University of Mary	Bismarck, ND
University of Maryland College Park*	College Park, MD
University of Memphis*	Memphis, TN
University of Michigan	Ann Arbor, MI
University of Minnesota - Duluth*	Duluth, MN
University of Mississippi*	Oxford, MS
University of Montana*	Missoula, MT
University of Nebraska at Omaha*	Omaha, NE
University of Nevada, Las Vegas*	Las Vegas, NV
University of North Alabama	Florence, AL
University of North Carolina at Asheville	Asheville, NC
University of North Carolina at Charlotte	Charlotte, NC
University of North Carolina at Pembroke*	Pembroke, NC
University of North Carolina at Greensboro	Greensboro, NC
University of North Carolina at Wilmington*	Wilmington, NC
University of Notre Dame	Notre Dame, IN
University of Oklahoma Norman Campus*	Norman, OK
University of Oregon	Eugene, OR
University of Phoenix*	Phoenix, AZ
University of Pittsburgh	Pittsburgh, PA
University of Pittsburgh at Bradford*	Bradford, PA
University of Pittsburgh Johnstown Campus*	Johnstown, PA
University of Pittsburgh Titusville Campus	Titusville, PA

University of Portland*	Portland, OR
University of Puerto Rico Humacao University College*	Humacao, PR
University of Puerto Rico La Montana Regional College*	Utuado, PR
University of Rhode Island	Kingston, RI
University of Richmond*	Richmond, VA
University of Rio Grande	Rio Grande, OH
University of Saint Thomas	Houston, TX
University of South Carolina - Beaufort*	Beaufort, SC
University of South Carolina - Columbia*	Columbia, SC
University of South Carolina - Salkehatchie*	Allendale, SC
University of South Carolina - Spartanburg	Spartanburg, SC
University of South Carolina - Sumter*	Sumter, SC
University of South Florida*	Tampa, FL
University of Southern Colorado*	Pueblo, CO
University of Southern Indiana*	Evansville, IN
University of Southwestern Louisiana	Lafayette, LA
University of Tennessee at Chattanooga*	Chattanooga, TN
University of Tennessee at Knoxville	Knoxville, TN
University of Tennessee at Martin*	Martin, TN
University of Texas at Arlington*	Arlington, TX
University of Texas at Austin	Austin, TX
University of Toledo	Toledo, OH
University of Tulsa	Tulsa, OK
University of Virginia	Charlottesville, VA
University of Washington*	Seattle, WA
University of West Florida	Pensacola, FL
University of Wisconsin - Milwaukee*	Milwaukee, WI
University of Wisconsin - Parkside	Kenosha, WI
University of Wisconsin - Whitewater*	Whitewater, WI
University of Wyoming*	Laramie, WY
University of the District of Columbia	Washington, DC
University of the Incarnate Word*	San Antonio, TX
University of the Virgin Islands	St. Thomas, VI
Upper Iowa University*	Fayette, IA
Ursinus College*	Collegeville, PA
Utah State University*	Logan, UT
Utah Valley State College	Orem, UT
Valdosta State University*	Valdosta, GA
Valencia Community College*	Orlando, FL
Valley City State University*	Valley City, ND
Valley Forge Military College*	Wayne, PA
Vassar College	Poughkeepsie, NY
Vermont Technical College	Randolph Center, VT
Villa Julie College	Stevenson, MD
Villanova University*	Villanova, PA
Virginia College	Birmingham, AL
Virginia Intermont College	Bristol, VA
Virginia Polytechnic Institute and State University	Blacksburg, VA
Viterbo College	La Crosse, WI
Voorhees College*	Denmark, SC

Wabash Valley College*	Mt. Carmel, IL
Wake Forest University	Winston-Salem, NC
Waldorf College*	Forest City, IA
Walsh University*	Canton, OH
Walters State Community College*	Morristown, TN
Washington and Jefferson College	Washington, PA
Washington State University*	Pullman, WA
Waycross College	Waycross, GA
Wayne Community College*	Goldsboro, NC
Wayne State College*	Wayne, NE
Wayne State University*	Detroit, MI
Waynesburg College	Waynesburg, PA
Weber State University*	Ogden, UT
Wesleyan College*	Macon, GA
West Texas A & M University*	Canyon, TX
West Virginia State College	Institute, WV
Western Baptist College*	Salem, OR
Western Illinois University*	Macomb, IL
Western Kentucky University	Bowling Green, KY
Western Maryland College	Westminster, MD
Western Michigan University*	Kalamazoo, MI
Western Montana College*	Dillon, MT
Western State College*	Gunnison, CO
Westfield State College*	Westfield, MA
Westminster College*	Fulton, MO
Westminster College*	New Wilmington, PA
Whitman College	Walla Walla, WA
Whitworth College*	Spokane, WA
Wichita State University*	Wichita, KS
Widener University*	Chester, PA
Willamette University*	Salem, OR
William Paterson University of New Jersey*	Wayne, NJ
William Penn College	Oskaloosa, IA
William Woods University	Fulton, MO
Wilson Technical Community College	Wilson, NC
Winona State University	Winona, MN
Wittenberg University	Springfield, OH
Woodbury University	Burbank, CA
Worcester State College*	Worcester, MA
Wright State University	Dayton, OH
Wytheville Community College*	Wytheville, VA
Xavier University of Louisiana*	New Orleans, LA
Yakima Valley Community College*	Yakima, WA
York County Technical College	Wells, ME
Young Harris College*	Young Harris, GA

National Resource Center for The First-Year Experience and Students in Transition. (1998). *1997 national survey of first-year seminar programming*. Columbia, SC: University of South Carolina, Author.

About the Contributors

Dan Berman has served as the University of South Carolina's University 101 Co-Director for Instruction and Faculty Development for over a decade. His responsibilities include oversight for course content, faculty instruction, and instructor training for the first-year seminar course. Berman has conducted more than 80 national and international faculty development/instructor training workshops for over 2,200 higher education professionals at institutions of all types across the United States, in Canada, and in the United Kingdom. He continues to teach in the Division of Media Arts, specializing in film criticism and visual imagery. Visual thinking techniques and the uses of film in the classroom are incorporated frequently into his first-year seminar instructor training workshops.

Jennifer L. Crissman is an assistant professor of counseling education in the College of Education at The Pennsylvania State University. She received her B.S. in elementary education from Millersville University, her M.S. in counseling/student personnel administration from Shippenburg University, and her Ed.D. in higher education from Penn State. She has served as Director of New Students at Mount Saint Mary College in New York, responsible for administering orientation programs, teaching a freshman seminar, and advising undeclared new students. Her primary research interests include first-year programs, student affairs administration, and integrating academic and students affairs.

Joseph B. Cuseo holds an M.S. in experimental psychology and a Ph.D. in educational psychology and assessment from the University of Iowa. Currently, he is a professor of psychology at Marymount College (CA) where he has coordinated the college's faculty development program and directs the freshman seminar, including its instructor training and development activities. He is a member of the advisory board for the National Resource Center for The First-Year Experience and Students in Transition and has presented and written on topics related to the first-year experience, the transfer year experience, and the senior year experience. His other research interests included cooperative learning, student retention, and effective college teaching.

John N. Gardner is Senior Fellow of the National Resource Center for The First-Year Experience and Students in Transition and Distinguished Professor Emeritus of Library and Information Science. Gardner previously served as Executive Director of University 101 and the National Resource Center for The First-Year Experience and Students in Transition. Gardner administered the University 101 program at the University of South Carolina for 23 years and founded the National Resource Center in 1986. In his capacity as Senior Fellow, he will continue to be actively involved in hosting and presenting at Center conferences, seminars, workshops, and teleconferences. He will also continue his involvement in the Center's scholarship and research activities, including a new national survey on the status of senior capstone courses.

Mary Stuart Hunter is Co-Director of the National Resource Center for The First-Year Experience and Students in Transition and has a broad background in student development administration, academic advising, instructor training, and teaching. Since 1978, she has taught University 101 at the University of South Carolina and since 1996 has taught EDLP 520, the course for University 101 peer leaders. In addition to her teaching responsibilities, she serves as co-host and conference administrator for the series of annual national and international Conferences on The First-Year Experience hosted by the University of South Carolina. She also co-facilitates the faculty development workshops for University 101 instructors and peer leaders at the University. Hunter has published chapters on academic advising and related topics in a number of publications.

Tracy L. Skipper is currently pursuing an M.A. in American literature at the University of South Carolina and works as an assistant editor at the National Resource Center for The First-Year Experience and Students in Transition. She earned a B.S. in psychology from the University of South Carolina and an M.S. in higher education from Florida State University. She served as Director of Residence Life and Judicial Affairs at Shorter College (Rome, Georgia) where her duties included teaching in the College's first-year seminar program and serving as an academic advisor for first-year students.

Constance Staley is a Professor of Communication at the University of Colorado, Colorado Springs. She teaches undergraduate courses in business communication, conflict management, and leadership and a graduate seminar in training and development. Dr. Staley holds a B.S. in education, an M.A. in linguistics, and a Ph.D. in communication. In addition to teaching, she conducts organizational training on personality profiling and team building, conflict management, group dynamics, and effective speaking and writing. She trains first-year seminar faculty across the county and works with institutions to develop and refine their college success programs. Her recent work, *Teaching College Success*, is a multimedia training package designed to prepare first-year seminar instructors. Dr. Staley was recently presented the "Outstanding Teacher Award."

Pamela S. Stephens is a doctoral candidate in the higher education program at The Pennsylvania State University. She received her B.A. degree in English from Penn State and her M.S. in educational leadership from Troy State University. She served as Regional Coordinator for Central Texas College in Okinawa, Japan and as an advisor for the Freshman Testing, Counseling, and Advising Program at Penn State. Her primary research interests include student affairs administration, freshman orientation, and academic advising.

Diane W. Strommer is the co-author of *Teaching College Freshmen* (1991) and the author of three other books and numerous articles. Strommer consults widely on teaching, academic advising, service learning, general education, and other issues pertaining to undergraduate education. Dr. Strommer earned her baccalaureate in English literature from the Ohio State University. She has held faculty positions at Boston University and Texas A & M where she was also the Associate Dean of the College of Liberal Arts. Prior to her current position as Dean of Zayed University in the United Arab Emirates, Dr. Strommer served as the Dean of University College and Special Academic Programs and Interim Director of the Office of International Education at the University of Rhode Island.

M. Lee Upcraft is Assistant Vice President Emeritus for Student Affairs, Affiliate Professor Emeritus of Higher Education, and a Research Associate in the Center for the Study of Higher Education at The Pennsylvania State University. His publications include *The Freshman Year Experience* (with J. N. Gardner), *First-Year Academic Advising: Patterns in the Present, Pathways to the Future* (with G. Kramer), *Designing Successful Transitions: A Guide for Orienting Students to College* (with R. H. Mullendore, B. O. Barefoot, and D. S. Fidler), and *Assessment in Student Affairs: A Guide for Practitioners* (with J. H. Schuh). Upcraft is Senior Scholar of the American College Personnel Association and a recipient of the Outstanding Contribution to the Orientation Profession Award from the National Orientation Directors Association.